Social Detective Academy

How to Become a Social Detective
and Solve Social Mysteries Like a Pro

Jeffrey E. Jessum, Ph.D.

Illustrations by Anya Jessum

© 2022 Jeffrey E. Jessum

All rights reserved. No part of the material protected by this copyright notice may be reproduced or used in any form or by any means, electronic or mechanical, including photocopying, recording, or by any information storage and retrieval system, without the prior written permission of the copyright owner.

Publisher's Cataloging-In-Publication

Names: Jessum, Jeffrey E., author. | Jessum, Anya, illustrator.

Title: Social Detective Academy : how to become a social detective and solve social mysteries like a pro / Jeffrey E. Jessum ; [Anya Jessum, illustrator].

Identifiers: ISBN: 9781957984520

Subjects: LCSH: Autistic children--Life skills guides--Juvenile literature. | Children with autism spectrum disorders--Life skills guides--Juvenile literature. | Social skills--Study and teaching--Juvenile literature. | Children with social disabilities--Life skills guides-- Juvenile literature. | Interpersonal relations in children--Juvenile literature. | Social interaction in children--Juvenile literature. | Autistic children--Behavior modification--Juvenile literature. | Children with autism spectrum disorders--Behavior modification--Juvenile literature. | Autism spectrum disorders--Patients--Behavior modification--Juvenile literature. | Parents of autistic children--Handbooks, manuals, etc. | CYAC: Autism--Life skills guides. | Social skills. | Interpersonal relations. | Social isolation--Prevention.

Classification: LCC: RJ506.A9 J472 2022 | DDC: 618.92/85882--dc23

To my children and all the children of the world. May your hearts be happy, healthy and whole and your lives full with deep, nourishing, meaningful relationships.

Special thanks to Anya Jessum for her wonderful artistic contribution. Kaia Jessum for her in-depth review and feedback. Vera Ginzburg for all her support and encouragement with Social Detective Academy and this book. Michael Khachanov for his performance, and Mehrnaz Mohammadi for her editing in the bonus video.

As well as Jason Lange for his post video polishing and William Hooper for his eagle eye review of the book formatting. I could not have done it without them.

CONTENTS

Introduction 9
    The Calling to Be a Social Detective 10
    The Birth of the First-Ever Social Detective Academy 11
    Welcome to Social Detective Academy! 11

PART ONE
The Fundamentals of Social Detection or What Every Social Detective Needs to Know

Chapter 1: The Basics of Solving Mysteries 13
    Six Keys for Gathering Facts 13
    Five Steps for Making Sense of the Facts 14
    Creating Social Remedies 14
    The Usual Suspects 15

Chapter 2: Attention 17
    So, What is Attention? 17
    The Importance of Attention 17
    Difficulty with Attention 18
    How We Show Attention 18
    Things That Get in the Way of Attention 20
    Tools for Paying Attention 21

PART TWO
Verbal Communication: Listening and Responding

Chapter 3: Verbal Listening 31
    How to Figure Out What the Main Topic Is 32
    How to Identify Mood or Feeling in What Someone is Saying. 34

Chapter 4: Verbal Responding 39
    Social Remedies for Resisting the Itch to Talk Off-Topic 40
    Befriending our Bodies 43
    Fear of Forgetting 43
    Things That Might Get in the Way of Responding to Mood 45
    Techniques for Effectively Responding to Mood 46

    Under-responding.. 52
    Remedies for Under-responding.. 53
    Over-responding.. 54
    Remedies for Over-responding... 56

Chapter 5: Verbal Dancing 63
    Remedies for Fast Talking and Crowding... 65
    What makes silences awkward?... 69
    What might make an awkward silence a problem?... 70
    Things That Can Make it Hard to Have a Nice Verbal Dance 71
    Remedies for Managing the Awkward Silence... 72
    How to Make Silences Less Awkward... 73
    Sharing Responsibility For the Conversation... 73
    Remembering That Silence is Not Forever and Comfort Grows Over Time 73
    Sharing Activities.. 74
    Do Things in Groups... 75
    How to Decrease Negative Effects of Awkward Silences. 76
    Take Advantage of the Power of the Pause... 76
    Ask Open Questions... 76
    Share Some of Your Own Experience... 77
    Stay Aware of Our Responses to Awkward Silences.. 77
    Starting a Good Verbal Dance and Keeping It Going 78
    Keeping a Good Mental Attitude and Staying Relaxed.. 78
    Detective Work... 78
    Being Creative.. 79
    Taking Positive Action.. 82
    How to Tell if Topic Lingering is an Issue... 87
    How to Shift Topics Smoothly.. 87
    Example of Bridging from Minecraft to Other Topics 91

PART THREE
NONVERBAL COMMUNICATION: LISTENING AND RESPONDING

Chapter 6: Nonverbal Communication 97
    Nonverbal Listening... 98
    Nonverbal Listening Suspects.. 99

Chapter 7: Listening to the Face 101
    Face Mapping... 101
    Putting the Pieces Together... 124
    Facial Combos.. 124
    Crazy Combos 135
    The Importance of Clear Facial Communication 137
    A Note on RGF.. 138
    Combining Clues to Test Our Hunches.. 140

Chapter 8: Listening to the Body 141
    Body Posture.. 141

Neck Posture 141
Shoulders and Back Posture 153
Arm Posture 155
Abdomen and Leg Posture 171
Abdomen 171
Legs 173
Sitting 176
Body Placement 180
Personal, Intrapersonal, and Impersonal space 180
The Effects of Being Too Close for Comfort or Too Far for Friendship 184
Space in Group Settings 184
Body Direction 185
The Basics of Body Movement: Speed, Smoothness and Flow 186
Some Specific Body Movements 188
How Walking Does the Talking 188
Statue Versus Sway 189
Hand and Arm Dancing 189
Laser Gazing and Attentional Personal Space 190
Shifty Eye Syndrome 191
Nose Gazing 192
Soft Focus 193
Using the Eyebrows to Create Eye Contact Comfort 193
Conversation and Eye Contact Comfort 196
Gaze Avoiders 197
The Power of Eyes in Hellos and Goodbyes 197

Chapter 9: Listening to the Voice 199
Decibel Deafness 199
Melody Missing 200
Rhythm Missing 201
Phrase Missing 201
Tempo Missing 203
Timbre Deafness 203
Robot Talkers 204

PART FOUR
Getting to Know the Senses

Chapter 10: The Eight Senses 207
Getting to Know Our Eight Senses 207
How the First Five Senses Help Us Gather the Facts 208
The 6th, 7th, and 8th Senses 208
The 6th Sense 209
Building Awareness of the 6th Sense 210
The 7th Sense 211
Observing the Observer 216
The 8th Sense 217

Sensing Relationships in the Body 218
Sensing Relationships in the Mind 219

PART FIVE
CONTEXT AND PERSPECTIVE TAKING

Chapter 11: Context 225
Context and Making Sense of the Facts 225
How Context Helps Us Organize and Remember Things 226
Context Helps Us Understand Others Better 226
Types of Context 228
Personal Information 228
Example: Personality Traits of Humor vs. Sensitivity to Criticism 229
Example 1: Personal History of Criticism and Rejection 230
Example 2: Personal History – Culture 230
Mental Styles and Abilities 232
Example: Mental Styles and Abilities 233
Interpersonal Information 234
Types of Interpersonal Information 235
Example: Interpersonal Information and First Impressions 236
Situational Information 237
Example: The Mood of the Situation 239
Gathering and Making Sense of Contextual Information 240
Contextual Story Worksheet 242
"Tell me about your day" – the importance of contextual current events 242
Context and Social Media 244

Chapter 12: Perspective Taking 251
What is a Perspective? 251
Perspective Taking 252
Perspective Maps 252
Benefits of Perspective Taking 253
How to Take Perspectives 255
Tools for Perspective Taking 256
Buddy Scan 257
Fully Taking Perspective 261
Perspective Assuming and Perspective Denying 263
Checking Things Out 265
I Get It – The Art of Perspective Responding 269

Introduction

Johnny sat in his regular spot, third bench on the right, just past the vending machines. His eyes were closed as he savored the last few morsels of the freshly baked chocolate chip cookie his mom had packed in his lunch. As usual, his mom's homemade cookies made Johnny feel glad to be alive. As the last of the cookie said its final goodbye to Johnny's taste buds, he leaned back in his chair and let his eyes dance over the crowd of kids hustling and bustling through the cafeteria. He had helped so many of those kids over the years, some on many occasions. Through his work as a social detective, he had helped them to be happier, more socially successful humans. The feeling he had when thinking about this was even more satisfying than the chocolatey goodness that still lingered in his mouth. Helping people to be happy and more socially successful had a special meaning for Johnny.

You see, for a long time, Johnny had trouble fitting in. It seemed that wherever he went and whoever he was with, things seemed to go wrong. On good days, the other kids ignored him. But more often than not, his social world consisted of a daily dose of teasing, insults, rejection, and bullying. He even had a nickname –"John-ny Strange"– which he could not shake, no matter how hard he tried.

Johnny had always been a smart kid and knew a lot about a lot of things. But when it came to friends and fitting in, he was lost. The social world he lived in was a complete mystery to him, so Johnny ended up spending most of his time safely alone, reading and playing his favorite video games. In fact, Johnny was a superhero in the world of video games. He loved playing games where he could become a character and solve puzzles and uncover clues. And he loved reading detective books. Most of the time, when he was reading a good detective book, Johnny could solve the mystery way before the detective in the book could.

The harder things got with the kids at school and in the neighborhood, the deeper Johnny went into his computer and books. But the books and computer games did not fill him up the way he wanted. What he really wanted was to fit in, to not be Johnny Strange anymore. He tried to tell himself that he didn't care, but he was too smart to believe that. He was too smart to forget that all he ever really wanted was to be a regular kid, just like everyone else.

The truth was that Johnny was lonely. While he had solved countless mysteries and puzzles in his day, the most important mystery stumped him. "Why is it so easy for me to solve the mysteries and puzzles in my books and computer games, and so hard for me to solve the mystery of kids?" he would ask himself over and over.

As the kids got older, they all seemed to expect more from each other, and the social puzzles became increasingly challenging for Johnny. He became more and more hopeless about ever fitting in. Life seemed bleak for Johnny until one day he realized something that would change his life.

"Maybe I've been going about things all wrong," he thought to himself. "Every time I have problems with other kids, I put more energy into my games and books, and every time I put more energy into my games and books, I get better at solving puzzles and mysteries. Maybe what I need to do is think about this social mystery the same way I think about the mysteries in my books and games."

When Johnny thought this thought, a light went on inside of him. Once on, the light would never go off again. This light would guide him out of the loneliness he had been feeling for so long. Johnny vowed to himself then and there that he would not stop until he had solved the most important mystery of all. "All the other mysteries and puzzles have been training me for this," he told himself. "Just as Sherlock Holmes solved the mysteries of the crime world, I, Johnny Multony, will solve the mysteries of the social world."

The first thing Johnny did after having this realization was to devise a game plan. He created a list of procedures for solving social mysteries, and he began devising remedies and testing them out. Sometimes his remedies didn't work, but he would always try again. He had never given up on a video game or a detective story, and he was not going to give up now. Little by little, he developed a whole encyclopedia of social remedies that were effective in dealing with the social problems he had been having in school.

Slowly but surely, things started becoming clearer to Johnny. He started understanding things differently than he ever had before. He started understanding how other people were seeing him and his actions, and how other people might be feeling about things. Being able to see things from another person's point of view changed Johnny in an amazing way. He began to realize that he had a tremendous amount of power over his social world. The power came from understanding how things worked and realizing how much his actions had an impact on how people saw him.

Johnny was finally getting what he had always wanted, which was to fit in and be like all the other kids. Johnny Strange had transformed into Johnny Smooth. He flowed through social situations and navigated social rough spots with a smoothness that other kids admired. Johnny was incredibly happy with how things had changed for him.

The Calling to Be a Social Detective

As fitting in became a more normal part of his life, Johnny started to realize something else. He began to realize that there was a reason he had been different all those years. There was a reason why things had happened the way they did.

You see, most kids go through their lives never really thinking about social mysteries. They never really think about why certain things work socially and why other things don't. They just do what comes naturally. But for Johnny, these things did not come naturally. Because of that, he had to work hard to understand what was going on socially.

You could say the kids who never had to think about these things had it good because they naturally fit in. They didn't have to worry about social problems all the time. But when those kids had problems, they often didn't know how to deal with them. They didn't have the deeper understanding of social mysteries that comes from really thinking about your social world.

Johnny became an expert at solving social mysteries. And he knew that he could not let this new gift go unused. He felt an obligation to those who were unable to solve their own social mysteries. In the beginning, all Johnny had wanted was to fit in and not be Johnny Strange. But in time he realized that his destiny involved something much bigger. His destiny was bigger than earning the title of Johnny Smooth. His destiny involved helping others by starting the first-ever detective agency dedicated to solving social mysteries.

Johnny started small, offering his services to a select number of kids who desperately needed his help. But before long, the news of what he was doing had spread, and he became legendary in schools and neighborhoods far and wide. Kids from all over, and sometimes even adults, would come to Johnny to ask if he would help them with their social mysteries. It was never-ending, and there seemed to be more kids all the time.

The Birth of the First-Ever Social Detective Academy

Johnny watched as the kids moved around the cafeteria, thinking about how he had helped so many of them and about how far he had come to be the boy he was today. Just as he was finishing up the last tasty bits of his cookie, a group of students started circling his table. He knew from the looks on their faces what they wanted. They wanted his help. Kids would often come to Johnny in the cafeteria to seek his services in solving their social mysteries. The cafeteria was his official office, and most kids knew not to approach him until he was done with his lunch. A good detective can't work on an empty stomach, right?

On this particular day, the sight of all the kids sparked something in Johnny. He began thinking of all the schools all around the country, all around the world, that had kids who needed help solving their social mysteries. He realized that for every mystery he solved, there were probably thousands of mysteries occurring all over the world that were going unsolved every day because there were no qualified social detectives around to crack the cases.

"What if there were other social detectives like me?" he asked himself. "If I could train other kids to be social detectives, they could learn to solve their own mysteries. They might even be able to start their own social detective agencies and help other kids." Johnny decided right then and there that he had no choice. He had to train others to do what he did so well. He decided to start the first-ever school for social detectives.

This book is a firsthand account of the birth of Johnny Multony's Social Detective Academy. These are the exact teachings that Johnny shared with his very first group of social detective students. By following closely and practicing the lessons in your own life, you will be able to become a social detective just like Johnny. And who knows, maybe someday you will have packs of kids lining up at your cafeteria office for help in becoming happier, more socially successful people.

Welcome to Social Detective Academy!

In the chapters that follow, we are going to be talking about some of the most important things a social detective needs to be aware of. Learning these things will help you to become a skilled social detective capable of helping others solve their social mysteries. But even more than that, you will learn the tools for becoming a social ninja, capable of navigating some of the most complicated social mysteries that you might face in your own life.

The truth is that some of the best social detective training involves learning how to be more socially skilled yourself. If you can effectively navigate your own social world, you will be much more capable of helping others become successful in their own social journeys. This is how Johnny's first students learned to become excellent social detectives themselves—by practicing solving their own mysteries.

Throughout this book, you will have the opportunity to test your skills by trying to solve social mysteries alongside some of Johnny's first students. These mysteries came directly from these students' personal lives and show how they used their social detective skills to make their own social lives better. As you read through the chapters, see if you can use the tools you are learning to identify social mysteries you might have in your own life.

Some of the ideas in this book are going to be pretty easy and straightforward. You will probably understand them with very little effort. But some of the things we will be talking about might seem a little more complicated at first. If there is something that you don't quite get right away, don't worry about it. That is to be expected. Just keep going and don't let it hold you back. You can always come back to it later on.

If you don't fully understand something, you will still be able to understand later things in the book. In fact, some of the things in this book will probably make even more sense as you read later parts of the book, so if something is not completely clear, keep reading on and come back. Johnny actually encourages his social detective students to come back and reread things even if they understood them the first time because rereading about important ideas can help you to have a deeper understanding.

Each chapter will also have a social detective concept summary at the end. These summaries are there to help you organize the most important concepts in each chapter. They serve as a good reference guide to come back to if you need to refresh your memory later on.

PART ONE

The Fundamentals of Social Detection or What Every Social Detective Needs to Know

Chapter 1: The Basics of Solving Mysteries

What exactly is a social mystery? I get this question all the time. Most of us know what a mystery is. A mystery is something puzzling and difficult to understand--something unknown. There are all kinds of mysteries. There are crime mystery whodunnits, where you try to find out who the bad guy is. There are lost and found mysteries about finding a person or a puppy or a missing sock. (The missing sock mystery is one I have to deal with a lot.) There are bigger mysteries, mysteries of the universe, like if there was a big bang, or why we are here, or what is the meaning of life. And then there are social mysteries. These are mysteries about other people–friends, parents, brothers, and sisters–that are puzzling and sometimes difficult for us to understand.

A good detective has strategies he or she uses to solve their mysteries. Let's start with some of the basic strategies a good social detective can use.

Six Keys for Gathering Facts

To get started solving a mystery you need to have as many of the facts as possible. All good detectives–whether they are crime detectives, missing person detectives, detectives who are trying to solve the mysteries of the universe, or social detectives–all start with gathering the facts. Even missing sock detectives need to start with the facts.

As a social detective, there are six keys to help you gather the facts:

1. Collect all the facts and write them down. All good detectives collect the facts and write them down so they can go over them later. You can use a special detective notebook to help you organize and keep track of the facts.

2. Always have your eyes and ears open for clues. A good detective realizes that you never know where a really important clue might be hiding.

3. Pay good attention and always listen carefully, not only to what people are saying but also to how they say it. A good detective knows that actions, as well as words, give you information. You want to make sure to pay attention to things people say nonverbally, as well as what they say with words.

4. Always try to look at things from other people's points of view. People often see things differently than we do. Trying to understand how others are seeing things can give us important facts we might never have if we only looked at things from our own point of view.

5. Look for clues in the surrounding events. Clues can often be found in the events that come before and after a social mystery. For that reason, a good social detective must always think about the events that surround the puzzle he is trying to solve.

6. Always check the facts. A good detective always checks to make sure he or she has the facts straight. You can do this by asking other people how they saw situations, to see if what they saw matches what you saw.

Five Steps for Making Sense of the Facts

Once we have the facts, we can use them to give us clues that will help us solve our social puzzles. There are five steps you can take to help you find the clues that might be hiding in the facts.

1. Break things down into pieces to make them more manageable and easier to understand. There are often lots of facts surrounding social puzzles. Breaking things down into pieces and organizing them can be a great way to keep from getting overwhelmed. It can also help us find clues that might be hidden in the facts.

2. Imagine how others might be seeing the situation.

When we are trying to make sense of the facts, it is helpful to imagine that others might see the same facts differently. This is called "putting yourself in other people's shoes," and it can be done in different ways. One way is to directly ask others how they see things. Another way is to imagine that you are that other person, then try to see things the way they do. Ask yourself how you might feel or what you might think if you were them.

3. Make sure to look at *all* the evidence. Sometimes it is easy to leave out essential information. For example, if we leave out how someone else sees a situation and only see it from our own point of view, we won't have all the facts to help us understand what is going on.

4. Go over the evidence many times and try to see things from as many different points of view as possible. Good detectives know that we don't always notice all the clues the first time we look at the facts. By examining the facts several times, we can avoid missing things that might be important for solving our social mysteries. Imagining how the facts would look from different points of view can also help us find clues we may have missed the first time around.

5. Ask for others' opinions. Two heads are often much better than one, so after examining the evidence, it can be extremely helpful to discuss what you have found with other people to get a fresh perspective that might help you solve the mystery.

Creating Social Remedies

Being a good social detective is not just about understanding why things happen. It's also about finding ways of fixing the problems that are going on in someone's social world. The first step in fixing a problem is to identify what the problem is and why it is happening. Gathering the facts and making sense of them can help do this.

But what do you do once you have identified the problem and used the clues to figure out why the problem is happening? That's where social remedies come in. A remedy is something that corrects a problem. And just as there are some effective strategies for gathering and making sense of the facts, there are also some very helpful strategies for creating social remedies. Here are my top five strategies for creating kick-butt social remedies.

1. Brainstorm lots of choices and pick the best ones. It's always helpful to have choices. After you have identified and made sense of the problem, try to come up with at least three possible remedies. You can do this by first brainstorming as many remedies as you can. Think of all the possible solutions you can imagine. Go crazy. Let your imagination and your detective problem-solving skills run wild. Be as creative, imaginative, and Sherlock Holmes-like as you can. Then once you have thought of lots of ideas, you can narrow them down to your top three choices. You can pick the three that make the most sense.

2. List the pros and cons. The next step is to think of all the pros and cons of each remedy. I like to act out the situation in my mind and think of all the possibilities that might occur if I use the remedy.

3. Get other people's points of view. Another great way of exploring the pros and cons of a potential remedy is to share your ideas with someone you trust. Ask them about the pros and cons that they see. Getting another person's perspective can be helpful in lots of ways. This is definitely true when it comes to deciding if a remedy is worth trying.

4. Test out the remedy. Once you have narrowed your remedies down and picked the best ones, it's time to test them out. You can try testing your top choice first and see what happens.

5. Analyze the results. Once you have tested a remedy, it's time to analyze how it worked. Make sure to take lots of notes about how your remedy was successful and how it was not. You can also notice if your remedy had any positive or negative side effects. Remedies are often not perfect the first time. If yours is not perfect, you can try to learn from what did not go right. Use the facts that came from testing it out to refine your remedy and create a new and better one. Most great successes start with failures, so don't get discouraged if your remedy does not work the first time. Just use what you learned from the test to make it even better the next time around.

The Usual Suspects

Gathering the facts, making sense of the facts, and coming up with social remedies are some of the basic things we do as social detectives. But there is a lot more that goes into these three things. Let's start going deeper with a look at how to identify the suspects in social mysteries.

Any good detective always keeps possible suspects in mind when working on a case. A suspect is someone or something you believe might be responsible for something. In the case of a police detective, a suspect might be someone believed to have committed a crime. For a social detective, the suspects are not usually people. They are usually specific types of problems someone might be having. The problems are the culprits. They are usually what results in the social problem or social mystery being investigated. In addition to coming up with an encyclopedia of social remedies, I have also come up with a list of common prime suspects, or reasons that people often have social problems.

I've also made a list of some of the accomplices in social mysteries. Accomplices are things that might be helping the prime suspects. When a crime occurs, the police might have a prime suspect they think could be responsible for the crime. Similarly, a good social detective might have a prime suspect they think could be responsible for the social problems someone is having.

But what makes the criminal commit the crime in the first place? Why do they cause trouble and break the law? Maybe they were in the wrong place at the wrong time or were treated poorly by people when they were younger. Maybe they got hit in the head by a big rock and can't tell right from wrong anymore. The reason they act in bad ways is what I would call the secondary suspect. The secondary suspect is the thing that makes the prime suspect become the culprit in the first place. With social mysteries, the secondary suspect is the thing that makes the prime suspect become a culprit in the social mystery. This will make much more sense as we go on, but for now, just keep in mind that there are prime suspects and secondary suspects in social mysteries. We will be talking about both kinds of suspects and how to identify them.

Having a good idea about what some of the common problems or suspects are and the possible remedies for those problems are some of the most important parts of being a good social detective. Knowing what the culprit is makes it much easier to make sense of the facts when you are on a case. So, let's get to know some of the prime suspects and secondary suspects and explore some ways to deal with them.

Main Ideas Chapter 1

1) What is a social mystery? P - 13

2) What are the six keys to gathering the facts? P - 13

3) What are the five steps for making sense of the facts? P - 14

4) What is a social remedy? P - 14

5) What are the top five strategies for creating great social remedies? P - 14

6) In the world of social detection, what is a prime suspect? P - 15

7) In the world of social detection, what is a secondary suspect? P - 16

Chapter 2: Attention

PRIME SUSPECT #1:

ATTENTION

The first prime suspect I want to tell you about is attention. Attention is a common culprit in social mysteries. Understanding what attention is and the role it plays in social situations can help you quickly and effectively find the solution to many social puzzles.

So, What is Attention?

We use the word attention all the time, but what does it really mean? Attention has to do with putting your mind on something. People often say "put your mind to it," but what they usually mean is put your attention to it. I like to think of attention as a giant, powerful spotlight shining in the dark. You see what the light is shining on. Everything else is dark and out of view, but the light lets you see the place it is highlighting.

Attention has to do with focusing. When we pay attention, we focus our spotlight. Whatever you focus on is what you are aware of. We might be focusing on particular thoughts, or on something we are looking at or listening to. Through our spotlight of attention, we give mental energy to the thing we are highlighting. This can help us to know, remember, and even understand that thing better.

The Importance of Attention

If we don't pay attention to things like people or events or other things, we will not be able to learn about those things. Socially, this is important because good social relating has a lot to do with taking in information, so we can get to know people and situations better and better.

Good attention is also important in problem-solving. We need to pay attention and concentrate on a problem to find solutions for it. Gathering facts also involves attention, as does making sense of those facts. Without good attention, social detectives would be lost and unable to solve any social mysteries.

But even more than helping us solve social mysteries, attention offers something important to our encounters with others by letting people know we are interested in them. It lets them know we want to be with them and are curious about what they have to say. As you read this book, you will see that showing others we are interested in them is incredibly important in friendships.

Good attention is important not only for a social detective who is trying to solve mysteries but also for anyone who wants to get along well with people in their social world. Because of this, attention is one of the top prime suspects to look for when investigating social mysteries.

Difficulty with Attention

Attention helps us learn more about people. When we pay attention in a conversation, we hear the information being exchanged and are able to respond in a way that makes the other person feel listened to and understood. This is really important for friendships. Attention also lets people know we are interested in them, something that is very important in friendships. People are attracted to people they feel are interested in them. But when we are not paying attention, it can give others the impression that we are not interested in them, which can make them less interested in us. The bottom line is that people like others who give them attention and don't feel as close to those who do not.

DIY: Attention Thought Experiment

DIY stands for "do it yourself." We are going to be doing DIY experiments during our detective training to help make your social detective skills even better. Here is the first one for you to try out.

Imagine we are sitting together, perhaps in the classroom at the Social Detective Academy training facility. Imagine I'm in front of the class and there is a commotion outside. There is a squirrel dancing on a tree branch, tormenting a dog below who is wildly barking at him. In his own squirrel way, he is teasing the dog, saying "nanny, nanny, you can't catch me." It could happen, right?

When this happens, you naturally twist your neck, turning your head to look out the window behind you to see what's going on with the dog and the squirrel. But what if I hold up three fingers while you are watching the commotion, and ask you to tell me how many fingers I'm holding up? If your spotlight of attention is on the crazy dancing squirrel and the dog, will you be able to tell me how many fingers I held up? Will you even hear me ask you about my fingers? Most likely you won't because your attention was elsewhere. You could probably tell me lots about the squirrel and the dog, but not about what I was asking.

Now think to yourself for a minute and see if you can remember a time when you were not fully paying attention to something someone was sharing with you. Most of us have had times when our attention was somewhere else. Maybe you were in class when a teacher was giving a lesson, or with your parents, or with a friend or in a group. See if you can remember where your attention went instead. Do you remember if not paying attention caused any problems?

How We Show Attention

It's helpful to understand a little more about how we show attention in order to tell if attention is the culprit in a social mystery. We can show attention by listening to what others say and by responding appropriately. But there are other important ways we show attention. Eyes can be a very powerful way to show others we are paying attention to them. Where we look affects not only what we see, but also what we are thinking about.

When someone looks at us, they are focusing their spotlight of attention in a very powerful way. This is what might have happened in the DIY above with the dancing squirrel. If you turned your head to look outside, most of your attention would be focused outside as well. Of course, you would not be able to see how many fingers I was holding up if you were looking out the window. But there is a good chance that you wouldn't have heard me, either. Your eyes would most likely have pulled your listening attention away, as well as your visual attention. If you were looking out the window, your attention would probably have been focused completely on the squirrel and dog drama.

What we see affects our attention in powerful ways, and others know it. They feel our attention move away when our eyes are gazing elsewhere. Let's do another DIY experiment to test this out.

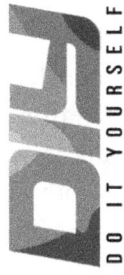

DIY: Showing Attention with the Eyes

Find a friend and ask them if they will do an experiment with you. If they agree, ask them to look away while you are talking to them. Then talk to them about something you like to talk about—something you are interested in, like about what you did over the weekend or about some video game you like to play. They can stare off into space or look at something in their hand. They can look anywhere else, just not at you. Do this for a minute or two to get a sense of what it feels like when their eyes are not looking at you. How does it feel when their eyes are not on you while you're talking? Does it seem as if they are with you?

Then ask them to look back at you. Continue telling them about what you were talking about. Do you notice a different feeling when they are looking at you while they talk? Does it feel like they are paying more attention? Does it seem that they are more interested in you? Do you enjoy talking with them more when they are looking at you?

After you do this exercise, you can try it in reverse. Let your friend talk, but don't look at them. See if this feels any different to you. Do you notice a difference in your attention or sense of connection with your friend when you are not looking at them? Then look at them, and see if you can notice the change. How do you feel when you are giving your friend attention with your eyes? You can also ask them what it was like for them.

Another common way we show attention is with our body language. We are going to talk a lot more about body language later on. But for now, let's just do another little DIY to get a feel for how the body can show attention.

DIY: Showing Attention with the Body

Let's ask a friend to do another experiment. Tell them about something you like to talk about, as you did in the DIY experiment above. But this time ask them to fidget and turn their body away from you while you are talking. They can still keep looking at you but have them move their body and turn away from you.

Notice how this feels. Does it seem they are fully with you? Now ask them to stop and turn towards you. Have them stop fidgeting and just listen. Do you notice a difference in how this feels? Does it seem they are more with you and interested in what you are saying?

Here you can try and switch it up again. This time you be the one fidgeting and turning your body away. Do you notice a shift in your attention when you do this while your friend is talking? You can also ask them what it was like for them so you can get a better sense of their point of view.

Eye contact and body language can have a huge impact on our ability to pay attention. They also can greatly affect what we communicate to others about our attention. The more we focus our eyes and bodies on something, the easier it is for our mind to shine its spotlight of attention on that thing.

Things That Get in the Way of Attention

We know attention is important, and we know a few of the things that can help us show others we are paying attention. But it still might be hard to pay attention. Have you ever been in a situation where you really wanted to pay attention? You might have known it was important and really tried, but no matter how hard you tried, you just could not keep your spotlight of attention on the thing you were trying to focus on. Maybe it was something a friend or your mom or dad was saying. Maybe it was something your teacher was talking about that you knew was important for you to know. But no matter how hard you tried, your attention just kept wandering off.

If you ever have had this happen to you, you're not the only one. It happens to all of us. It's probably happened to me at least ten times today alone. But there are things we can do to keep our attention from wandering off. The first step is understanding some of the things that get in the way of attention. Below are a few common causes that make us lose attention. These are the accomplices that might be making the prime suspect of attention the culprit in a social mystery. Let's take a look at some of the things that might cause problems with attention.

1. Thinking about other things (what our mind is doing)—If our mind is thinking about something, it can be incredibly difficult to pay attention. Our thoughts take up a lot of energy. They often demand that our spotlight of attention shine on them and only them. Understanding when this is happening and finding ways to redirect our spotlight of attention from our thoughts to something different can be very helpful. A good place to start is to ask yourself what kind of things you might think about at times when you want to be paying attention to something else besides your own thoughts.

Sometimes we might be upset with something and thinking about that. Maybe our friend was mean to us and we can't get it out of our mind. Or we may just be daydreaming about something interesting, like playing our favorite video game. Even If what is happening at the moment is interesting or important, we might be more likely to think about something else in which we have a special interest.

There are other times when someone says something that makes us think of something else that is not about what is happening in the present moment. When this happens, it can pull our thoughts to that other thing. This kind of thing happens to all of us. And we often don't even realize it.

For example, a friend might be telling you about something important that happened to them over the weekend. While they are telling you their story, they might mention that they had some really awesome pizza that day. You might be really hungry, and when they mention pizza, your mind starts daydreaming about hot, bubbly, cheesy, good pizza with the cheese melting ever so slowly off the slice as you raise it to your mouth for a big delicious bite...yummmmm!

I do love pizza. And I'm feeling kind of hungry myself. What was I talking about again? Oh, yeah. Pizza, right? Nope. I was talking about getting distracted by other thoughts. Getting distracted by other things...like hot, delicious pizza! Perfect example. This kind of thing happens all the time, so it can be really helpful to be aware of how our attention can get hijacked by other thoughts. Once we notice this is happening, we can more easily bring our attention back to the thing we want to be paying attention to.

2. Looking at other things (what our eyes are doing)—As we talked about above, our eyes not only give others very powerful messages about where our attention is, but they also can pull our attention away from what others are *saying* and focus it on what we are *seeing*.

Our brains are actually built to focus our attention on what we are sensing. If we hear something, we get a strong urge to turn our attention towards it. And if we see something, we do the same. It is a way our caveman and cavewoman ancestors protected themselves from things that might eat them. While a dancing squirrel is probably not going to eat us, seeing and hearing it can still have a powerful impact on where we place our attention.

3. Doing other things (what our body is doing)—We also talked about how doing other things with our bodies can make it difficult to pay attention. While some actions can be done without using a lot of our attentional energy, other actions can make it really hard to focus. Doing the laundry or making a sandwich or building a Minecraft castle might distract us a lot, even if we are trying hard to focus. These kinds of things are likely to take up a lot of our mental energy and not leave much left over for us to focus on the things we want to be focusing on.

There are times when a little physical activity can actually help some people pay attention better. Maybe rocking in a rocking chair or smushing up a gummy eraser or even spinning a fidget spinner might help some people focus better. But those things are not likely to involve us thinking about what our bodies are doing. And we can still do them while facing the other person and without a lot of commotion or interference to get in the way of paying attention. We need to wonder if what we are doing with our body is making it easier or more difficult to pay attention.

But even if we are not distracted by what we are doing with our bodies, others might think that we are distracted. For example, if we are dancing around while someone is talking, they might think we are not really interested in or paying attention to what they are saying. If our bodies are turned away, they may still think that we are not paying attention to them.

A good social detective will consider these things when they are interacting with others or when they are trying to solve social mysteries. All of these things distract us, and distraction is the main thing that interferes with attention. But there are some great tools we can use to help us to be more attentive.

Tools for Paying Attention

Of course, knowing the prime suspects helps us to identify the main culprit and accomplices in a social mystery. But once that is done, a good detective then needs to find remedies to truly solve the mystery. We first identify the culprit, and then we find a remedy to keep that culprit from causing any more problems.

When we determine that attention is the culprit in a social mystery, there are several remedies that can help. Below are some of the remedies and tools for paying attention better.

1) Keeping our eye on the ball—As we discussed, a powerful way to direct attention is with our eyes. What we see often affects our attention. A great tool for staying focused is to keep your eyes on it. I call this *keeping your eye on the ball*. That's something coaches often say in sports. And it makes sense.

If you're playing baseball and someone throws the ball to you when you're not looking at it, it's not very likely you will catch it. We need our eyes to track the ball and keep our attention on it. Similarly, our eyes can help us track what others are communicating to us. If you are having trouble focusing attention, try to deliberately turn your eyes to the thing on which you are trying to focus. Think of the thing you are trying to pay attention to as the ball you are keeping your eye on.

DIY: Keeping Your Eye Off the Ball

Here is a little practice you can do to get your mind used to keeping your eye on the ball and that can help you see how powerful looking at something can be in helping us track it. First get a ball, a soft ball--very soft--for this activity, because you might get hit. Start a nice, easygoing game of catch. Notice where your eyes are focused while you are playing. You might notice that when you throw, you are focusing on the other person. This helps you target where to throw the ball. When you catch, you are probably looking at the ball as it comes towards you. This helps you track the ball as it approaches, so you can catch it.

Now switch it up a little. Look at the ball when you throw it to your friend and don't look at your friend as you throw, even if you want to. Does this affect your accuracy? You may still get the ball to your friend because you are probably still seeing your friend out of the corner of your eye. Some of your attention may still be on your friend, but not as much as when you are looking directly at them. A little attention is better than none, but I imagine you will notice that you are much less accurate and that it is much more difficult to throw accurately when you are not watching the other person.

When your friend throws the ball to you, don't look at the ball. Keep your eyes on your friend as the ball comes towards you and try to catch it. Again, you may be able to catch the ball because you might be seeing it out of the corner of your eye. But you likely will not be as good at catching it as you would be if all your visual attention was on it. It's the same with most things. The more attention we pay to something, the better we will be able to track and respond to it.

Now let's try a more extreme version of this. Make sure you have a really soft ball for this one, and don't throw too hard. Close your eyes and throw the ball to your friend. You may do alright because you probably have a sense of where your friend is. But I'll bet you're not as accurate.

Next have your friend throw the ball to you while your eyes are closed, and try to catch it. If you can catch the ball when you do this, the Force is probably really strong in you, and you should seriously think about enrolling in Jedi training!

It's really hard, if not impossible, to track a ball that is being thrown to you when you can't see it. We need to be able to see it to follow it. This is often true for many things other than balls. If you want to know where a mosquito lands so you can swat it, it will be much easier to do if you follow its flight with your eyes. Or if you want to follow what your teacher is teaching you, it will be much easier to do if you keep your eyes on her. What we see affects where we place our attention. See if you can practice keeping your eye on the ball in things you do, and notice if this affects how well you are able to stay focused.

2) Spotlight of attention—We have talked about the idea of our attention being like a spotlight. Wherever we point that spotlight is where our attention goes. This idea of attention as a spotlight can help us if we use it intentionally. You can keep the image of a spotlight in your mind, and imagine yourself shining it on the thing you want to pay attention to.

This is kind of like keeping your eye on the ball, except the ball is in your mind rather than in the outside world. Looking with our eyes helps us pay attention to things outside of us. But we can also look at things inside of us, like our thoughts. This might seem a little confusing because we usually look with our eyes. When we think about something and keep our thoughts with it, we are looking with our minds. The spotlight of attention is a great way to direct where we look with our minds. It's a great way to keep our mental eyes on the mental ball of our thoughts.

Ask yourself where your spotlight of attention is to get a better sense of whether you are focused or distracted. Ask yourself where your thoughts are. Are they on the thing you want to be paying attention to? Are you keeping your "eyes on the ball?" Or are they on something else?

Being aware of our attention and of what we are focusing it on can give us a lot of power and control over our attention. See if you can use this idea of attention as a spotlight to become more aware and in control of where you are placing your attention.

DIY: Spotlighting

Take a flashlight and turn the lights off in a room. Turn the flashlight on and pay attention to whatever it lights up. Let yourself think about what is in the beam of the flashlight. Let the spotlight of your mind focus on whatever the flashlight is lighting up. Let's say you are in your room, and the spotlight lights up your bed. Let your thoughts stay with your bed as the light is on it. You can think of snuggling up in it, or about the color of the sheets on it. Or you might be thinking about how long it has been since you washed the sheets, and that you better get them in the laundry before they start growing mushrooms on them. Once you have spent a little time on the object of your focus, turn off the light, and let your mind wander.

When the light is off you can think about whatever you want. Daydream a little. Then turn the flashlight on again and shine it somewhere else. Do the same thing. Let your mind and thoughts focus on what the flashlight is shining on.

Notice how the light highlights one thing while everything else is dark. Notice how your thoughts are focused on what the flashlight is lighting up, and how other thoughts fade into the background. When you turn the light off and give yourself permission to let your thoughts wander, your thoughts can go lots of other places. This is how we want to use our attention.

Sometimes it's wonderful to let our thoughts wander, as long as we can control them when they do. We want to be able to focus them when we want and to let them roam at other times.

3) Laser focusing—Another tool for paying attention that is similar to using the spotlight of attention is laser focusing. Instead of a spotlight, imagine you have a laser that highlights things you want to pay attention to. Lasers are more intense spotlights, and they are more focused than spotlights. When you want to focus even harder on something very specific, you can use your laser focus, instead of using your spotlight of attention.

Imagine the laser beam coming from the middle of your forehead, pointing at the thing you want to pay attention to, such as something you are thinking of or something outside of you. When the laser is focused on something, that is where your attention is focused, too. If you are doing this and still getting distracted, try imagining the laser beam becoming brighter and more concentrated. Let the image of the beam glow brighter in your mind, and imagine it lighting up an even smaller area for you to focus on.

4) Having a conversation with your mind—Even when you are keeping your eye on the ball, using your spotlight of attention, and focusing your laser, it still may be difficult to pay attention. Sometimes our mind does not seem to do what we want it to, and it wanders even when we are trying to keep it focused.

At times like this, it can be helpful to have a nice conversation with our mind. Having a conversation with our mind may sound a little strange, but the practice of having regular conversations with our mind can help us gain a lot of control over our thoughts and attention. And when we have more control over our mind, we become the mind's master and our mind becomes our loyal servant.

So how do we have a conversation with our own mind? It's simple. Just talk to your mind. Ask it questions. Tell it what you want. For example, if you are in class at school, you can ask your mind if it is paying attention to what the teacher is saying. If it is, praise it for doing a good job! If it's not, tell it you want it to pay attention. You can also remind it to focus when you notice it getting distracted.

All minds wander at times. That is part of human nature. It happens to all of us, and there is nothing wrong with that. The trick is to do our best to notice when it wanders and to guide it back to what we want it to be focusing on.

You can imagine your mind as being like a sweet little puppy. Puppies are easily distracted. But if we want to get the puppy's attention, we talk to it. We call its name nicely or tell it to sit or stay, which helps bring its attention back. We can do the same kind of thing with our minds. When our mind wanders, all we need to do is remind it to bring its attention back. It's ok if we remind our mind over and over to bring attention back.

If your mind wanders ten times but you eventually bring it back on the eleventh time, you have succeeded. The key is to keep noticing when your mind gets distracted. Even if you have to remind your mind a thousand times, it's ok. Just keep bringing it back when it drifts away, just as you would the excited, distractible puppy.

Every time you bring your mind back you are creating better communication with your mind and letting it know who is the boss. When you do this, you are strengthening your ability to put your attention where you choose to put it, rather than letting your mind be the master.

A very simple yet powerful way to bring our attention back is to just say to ourselves in a friendly voice, "pay attention." If your mom or dad or teacher tells you to pay attention, it probably works, at least for a little while, so it makes sense that it would work when we do it with ourselves.

We can also be specific when we want our mind to pay attention. For example, we can say, "Pay attention to Joe" or "Pay attention to the teacher." We can get even more precise and tell our mind things like, "Pay attention to the main topic, because Joe is sharing" or "Pay attention to Joe's body language."

Later we will talk about things like the main topic and body language and why it's so helpful to pay attention to these kinds of things in our detective training. For now, it's just good to know that we can help our minds get better at paying attention by reminding them to do so on a regular basis. And it's also helpful to know that we can be specific about exactly what we want our mind to pay attention to, like the main topic or body language. We are going to explore having good conversations with our minds in the DIYs below.

DIY: Mind Mastering

In the following four do-it-yourself detective training exercises, we are going to practice some things that can help us master our mind by getting to know it better and learning how to have good conversations with it. Getting to know our mind better helps us to have better communication with our mind. And better communication with our mind helps us to know it better. The two go hand in hand.

The four DIY practices we are going to practice here are: a) finding our thoughts; b) labeling our thoughts; c) noticing the flavor of our thoughts; and d) having conversations with our mind. Let's do a little practice for each of these four things.

a) DIY: Finding Our Thoughts

In this DIY detective training exercise, we are going to locate where our mind actually is. For now, let's call the mind the place where our thoughts happen. This is the place inside where we talk to ourselves. Let's locate this place inside of us.

Get in a comfortable sitting position and close your eyes. Take your spotlight of attention and shine it right into your mind. You want to look for the place inside of you where you talk to yourself. For many people, this is right in the center of their heads, between their ears.

You can test out where your talk is by doing a simple experiment. Start saying the alphabet to yourself. Don't say it with your voice. Just say it inside. Think it. A,B,C,D....Where do you notice yourself thinking the alphabet? Is it in the middle of your head? Is it to the side? Or is it somewhere else? Just let yourself notice where you are thinking or hearing it inside.

When you locate the place where your mental talk is, let yourself shine your spotlight of attention right there. Let yourself shine your spotlight of attention on the place where your mind is reciting the alphabet.

Once you have your spotlight of attention shining on your mind you can stop reciting the alphabet. Don't stop shining your spotlight there. Just stop reciting the alphabet. Now just watch and wait. Just wait to see what comes up next in your mind. All you need to do now is keep your spotlight of attention on your mind and watch. Something is bound to come up in that space.

If nothing comes up in your mind, you are either a master at quieting your mind or you have fallen asleep. Minds are seldom completely quiet. It might also be that you have gotten distracted and are not noticing anything in your mind. Your spotlight of attention is completely off, and you are not even thinking about noticing what's going on in your mind. I know this one well.

I can't tell you how many times I have started off trying to notice what's going on in my mind and ended up thinking about some cool video game or something like that. Sometimes it is a long time before I realize I am supposed to be noticing what is going on in my mind.

But have no fear if this happens. It happens to everyone. The trick is to come back if you get distracted. Remember what we said before. If you get distracted ten times but come back to what you are trying to pay attention to on the eleventh time, you win.

So just keep coming back to your mind. Keep bringing your spotlight of attention back to that space in your mind where you think things, and see if you can notice when thoughts arise. You can even have a little conversation with your mind to remind it that you are the boss, and you need it to keep your spotlight focused.

b) DIY: Labeling Our Thoughts as Thoughts

Another great strategy to help become more aware of our thoughts is thought-labeling. To do this, all you need to do is say the word "thought" out loud every time you notice a thought rising up in your mind. You don't have to say what the thought is or how it makes you feel. All you have to do is say the word "thought" as a way of making a note to yourself. This can help keep us from getting lost in the stream of thoughts that we often get lost in.

c) DIY: Noticing the Flavor of Our Thoughts

Something else that can help us to master our mind is to notice what I like to call the flavor of our thoughts. Do your thoughts have a happy flavor or a sad flavor? Are they stressful thoughts or calm, peaceful thoughts? Are they thoughts that make you feel more confident or less confident? There can be many different flavors to our thoughts, and getting a sense of the different qualities of our thoughts can be very helpful.

d) DIY: Having Conversations with Our Mind

Once we are more aware of where our thoughts are, when they arise, and what flavor they have, it becomes much easier to have good conversations with our mind. After you have experimented with these first three practices you can try to get to know your mind even more by having some regular conversations with it.

We have already talked about telling our mind where we want it to focus. But let's go a little deeper into having conversations with our minds. You can start by just saying "hi," as you would to a friend. You can ask your mind how it's doing. You can ask it if it is clear and focused, or fuzzy and distracted. You can ask it if it is awake and alert, or sleepy. If there is no one else around you can even do this out loud, but it's perfectly fine to do it silently.

It may seem a little strange to ask your mind things like this, but it can help to develop the ability to have good conversations with your mind. And being able to have good conversations can make it much easier to tell your mind what to do. It can make it easier to communicate to your mind that you are the boss, and it needs to listen to you.

After saying "hi" and asking your mind some questions, you can tell your mind what you need from it. You can tell it when you need it to pay attention to something. You can tell it to stop daydreaming when you need it to be clear and focused. You can even tell it to think more positive thoughts if it is being negative.

You can tell your mind you need it to listen up and respect your authority. Tell it to pay attention when your teacher is talking or when you want to get your homework done. You can also tell it to slow down or stop thinking so much when you are trying to relax or go to sleep. See if you can do these things every day and notice if it helps you to become a better master of your mind. Getting to know my mind better and having conversations with it has helped me so much. See if it helps you, too.

5) The Dot Method—We have talked about some things that can help you have better focus and attention and become the master of your own mind. But like most skills, building attention and becoming the master of your mind takes regular practice.

It's easy to forget to pay attention, even when we have lots of tools to help us. How many times have you told yourself to pay attention to something, but before you knew it, you had forgotten to pay attention and your mind was somewhere completely different? It happens to all of us. But there are ways we can remind ourselves to keep our attention on something.

There are some common ways people remind themselves to do things. In the past, people would tie a string around their finger to remember things. Today we might use sticky notes and stick them on the door or our desk to help us remember. We might put a reminder in our phone or set an alarm. These are all great methods for reminding.

But there is another very simple and effective way to help you remember things. It's called the Dot Method. All you need to do is draw a dot on the back of your hand with a pen and tell yourself that whenever you see the dot, you are going to remember to pay attention.

Every time you notice the dot on the back of your hand it reminds your brain to focus. When you see the dot, you can have a conversation with your mind, reminding it that you are the boss and that you need it to focus on what you are doing.

You can also use the Dot Method to help you remember to practice your other attention-building strategies. The dot can remind you to use your spotlight or laser to focus, as well as remind you to notice your thoughts and ask your mind questions. The dot can help you remember lots of things.

6) Removing distractions—One final trick for helping you pay attention better is getting to know your opponent. An opponent is someone or something that competes with you. When it comes to focusing, the opponent is anything that tries to compete for your attention. It distracts you from the thing on which you are trying to focus.

Some competitors for attention might be our thoughts and daydreams. The tricks we talked about above can help us with the mental competitors for attention. But there are some other very straightforward opponents that we can deal with pretty easily.

For example, we can get distracted by the things we see or hear. Maybe kids are playing outside the window while we are trying to study. Maybe the television is on in the background, and we get pulled to stare at it, even if the sound is off. Or maybe the sound is on, and we can't help listening to a show that someone is watching in the other room.

We also might get distracted by the temperature. It might be too hot or too cold, which might make it hard to pay attention. Maybe there is a distracting smell. Maybe your mom or dad is making dinner, and you are really hungry, and the smell makes it hard to pay attention to something you are reading because the smell makes you think about eating.

Many things in our environment can be distracting. But once we identify the opponent to attention, we can do something about it. If it is a visual distraction, we can turn our eyes away. If it's some kind of sound that is distracting us, we can move away from it or maybe even wear earplugs. Whatever it might be, once we identify it, we can try to find ways of removing it.

The Case

Time: Saturday afternoon, 3:14 PM

Place: West Valley Mall food court.

Alan and Karina were sitting having burgers and chatting about the awesome new virtual reality game they had just played in the mall. It was at one of those hi-tech video game places where you go in a room and wear full haptic suits, virtual reality glasses, fight aliens, and go on cool adventures. "I loved how realistic that was!" Karina said enthusiastically. "That was so awesome! And when the spaceship bumped into an asteroid, the haptic suit made it so you could totally feel it!" Alan replied. You could tell they were both enjoying hanging out together.

As they were talking, a group of kids from their school came in and sat down at the other end of the food court. "Check it out. It's Samantha and her friends," Alan said, casually pointing to the group. Karina looked behind her and smiled. "Did you hear about her?" she said. "You mean Samantha?" "Yeah!" Karina replied excitedly. "No, what's up?" asked Alan. "Well, the other day Dale asked her if she wanted to be his girlfriend!" Karina went on to tell Alan all about how Dale had asked her and about how Samantha had responded.

Alan kept looking at the group of kids while Karina talked. He would move his eyes back and forth from Karina to the group while she was talking. After telling Alan all the gossip she knew about Samantha and Dale, she asked "So, what do you think about all that?" Alan responded to her question with "Uh-huh. Yeah. That's cool." Karina's face lost its excitement. But Alan was looking at the group of kids and didn't notice. "Hey, check out what Darren is doing," pointing to one of the boys in the group who was trying to juggle french fries.

Karina was silent. Then Alan started to laugh as Darren lost control of the flying french fries and they landed on Samantha. "Check it out," he said to Karina, pointing again to the group. "Samantha did not look amused," he said laughing again.

"I think I'm going to head home," Karina said. Alan brought his eyes back to Karina and looked surprised. "What? I thought we were going to look around the mall together." "I think I should be getting home," Karina said in a voice that was much less enthusiastic than it was before. "Maybe you can go walk around with them," she said, pointing at the group of kids. "Uh, ok. I guess I'll see you on Monday?" Alan said. "Yeah, sure," Karina said as she walked away. Alan was really confused. "We were having a really good time," he thought to himself. "Why did she suddenly leave?" he asked himself.

Can you use your social detective skills and figure out why Karina might have left so suddenly?

The Facts

Alan knew this was clearly a social mystery, so he started where Johnny always said you should start--with the facts.

- Karina and I are good friends.
- We had a great time at the virtual reality place.
- We were enjoying each other's company and having a good conversation.
- Some other kids came into the food court and sat down at a table near us.
- Karina started telling me about Samantha and Darren.
- I was listening to Karina. But I was also watching what the other kids were doing while Karina was talking.
- Karina asked me what I thought about what she was saying.
- I started talking about how Darren was juggling french fries.
- Karina's mood changed and she said she was going to go home.

When reading about Alan's social mystery and thinking about the facts, does anything stand out to you? Do you have a sense of what prime suspect might be the culprit here?

Cracking the case

"Karina's mood changed after the other kids came," Alan thought to himself. "Maybe there was something about that that affected her." Alan thought back to his training and remembered the first prime suspect Johnny had told him about--the prime suspect of attention. He remembered that attention is really important in friendships. It lets others know we are interested in them and that they are important to us. Good attention helps people enjoy our company.

Remembering this, Alan asked himself if he had done anything that might have interfered with his attention. In asking himself this, he remembered some important clues that might have contributed to Karina leaving early. "I stopped looking at Karina when the other kids came. I was still listening to her, or at least, I think I was. But if I wasn't looking at her, she might not have known I was listening." Alan also remembered what Johnny had said about how where we look can affect our attention. Maybe he hadn't been listening as well as he could have, because his eyes were focusing on something else. Alan realized that when Karina had asked him what he thought about Samantha and Dale, he did not respond in a way that showed her he was paying good attention to what she was saying. "Maybe that made her feel like I was not interested in what she was saying," he thought.

Then he remembered something else. He remembered that he changed the subject and started laughing about Darren juggling the french fries and dropping them on Samantha. "Wow. I bet that made Karina feel bad. She probably thought that I was more interested in Darren and Samantha than I was in her." Alan felt bad about this, but he remembered that good social detectives can fix problems by having good social remedies. He started thinking of ways to remedy this situation and make sure it didn't happen again with Karina.

Key Culprits in the Mystery:

Prime Suspect #1: Attention

Social Remedies.

The first thing Alan did to make sure this would not happen again was to think back to what Johnny had taught him about making sure you keep good attention. He remembered the importance of keeping your eye on the ball and not changing the subject. These were two things that he did not do with Karina when he got distracted by the other group of kids. He remembered that we can keep better attention by doing things like using the spotlight of attention and laser focus, having a good conversation with our minds, and trying to remove distractions. He kept all these things in mind when he saw Karina at school on Monday.

Time: Monday, 12:07 Pm

Place: School cafeteria

Alan found Karina sitting at the table where they usually had lunch together. "Hi, Karina!" Alan said in a voice that showed he was happy to see her. Although Alan had been a bit hurt when Karina left so abruptly on Saturday, he had done his detective work, so he had a better understanding of why she might have left. He could take it less personally, which made it easier for him to show excitement about seeing her. "Hey," Karina said in a somewhat flat voice. "Karina, I wanted to say that I'm sorry if I seemed a little distracted Saturday. I imagine that felt bad." When Alan said that, Karina smiled. It feels good when people acknowledge things like that. "Thanks for saying that, Alan. Yeah, it did feel kinda bad." "I can imagine. Sometimes I get a little distracted, but it's not personal. I love hanging out with you," he said. Karina's face lit up when he said this. "I like hanging out with you too Alan," Karina said. "Well, if I ever get distracted again you can let me know, and I'll do my best to give you all my attention." "Thanks, Alan. That means a lot to me."

Alan took out his lunch and started eating, but he made sure to keep his spotlight of attention on Karina. They talked about what they had done for the rest of the weekend and even talked more about Samantha and Dale. At one point, some other kids started dancing while waiting in line for their lunch. Alan noticed himself getting distracted by them, so he had a little conversation with his mind and reminded himself how important it was to keep his attention with Karina. He turned his spotlight of attention into a laser beam to help him con-centrate even better. And at one point he even tried to remove distractions by moving to another seat, so he would be facing away from the group of dancing kids. The two of them had a great conversation, and Alan could tell Karina was in a good mood. Alan was happy he was able to solve his social mystery. Karina was a really good friend and he would never want to do anything to hurt their friendship.

Main Ideas Chapter 2

1) What is attention? P - 17

2) Why is paying attention important? P - 17

3) What is the spotlight of attention? P - 18

4) How do we show we are paying attention? P - 18

5) What things make it hard to pay attention? P - 18

6) What are some remedies for attention problems? P - 21

7) What are the four practices for mind-mastering? P - 24

PART TWO

Verbal Communication:
Listening and Responding

Chapter 3: Verbal Listening

How we listen and take in what others say is very important. Listening increases the likelihood that we will be good at responding to others. Listening helps us to figure out what we are supposed to respond to.

Good attention makes for good listening. If we are paying attention, it is much more likely that we will be able to really listen to what others are saying. When we are considering verbal communication suspects, it's always a good idea to consider attention issues first.

You can review Prime Suspect #1 (Attention) from the last chapter to make sure you are taking attention into consideration when working on a social mystery. Once you know that attention is not the main culprit, there are several other prime suspects we can look at. Let's look at some of the suspects that involve our ability to really listen and take in what others say.

PRIME SUSPECT #2:

TOPIC MISSING

When trying to listen well, it is very helpful to get a sense of the main topic of a conversation. A main topic is an idea or theme someone is trying to share or the most important central idea someone is trying to express. Topic missing is often a main culprit in social mysteries. We always want to consider this suspect when doing our social detective work.

Identifying the main topic can sometimes be a challenge. When someone is talking, there are many things they include in the conversation that are what we social detectives like to call "extraneous details." When something is extraneous it means it is not a very important or necessary part. Extraneous details are pieces of information that are not very important or necessary to get someone's main point across. They may be details that help to set the stage for the main topic, or they may help give a clearer picture of things, but they are not really the essence of what the other person is trying to convey to you.

Here is an example.

"Beth went to the beach yesterday to go surfing with her new surfboard. It was a really hot day, and she got some pizza at Joe's Pizza Shack to take with her down to the beach. When she got down to the water, she saw a giant shark chasing someone just offshore, but before she could scream, it bit the person. An ambulance came, and fortunately, the guy was not badly injured, but it was really scary. You don't see many sharks at the beach, and she had never seen a shark outside of an aquarium or on television before. Seeing one right there where she was just about to go surfing was shocking."

What would you say the main topic is? What is the most important piece of information being shared with you, and what are some of the extraneous details? If you said the main topic was seeing a shark attack, you're right. Some of the extraneous details were things like going surfing, getting pizza, and it being a hot day. These extraneous details help to set the stage for the main topic, but they are not the main, most important point.

Sometimes people can give way too many extraneous details, and that can be a suspect in itself, but we will come back to that later. For now, the main topic of our discussion is...well, the main topic is the idea of the main topic. Getting a sense of the main topic helps us focus and pay attention to the most important information that the other person is sharing with us.

People sometimes say a lot. It can be hard to keep track and remember all of what they said. But if we have an idea of what the main topic is, we can focus on the other things more easily. Knowing the main topic also helps us in responding to the other person. We will talk more about that in a little bit.

But for now, the main point is that it is very helpful to look for the main point or main topic in a conversation. By doing so you will become a better listener. When doing your social detective work, it's always good to ask yourself if *topic missing* could be a prime suspect in a social mystery.

How to Figure Out What the Main Topic Is

People often share a lot of information when talking, so finding the main topic can be challenging. But there are questions good social detectives ask themselves to determine what the main topic might be. Here are some of those questions:

1) Is there something in what the person is saying that seems most important?

You want to be careful to separate what is *most important* from what is *most interesting* to you. Sometimes the most important thing someone is trying to share may not be the most interesting to you. Sometimes those two things are the same, but often they aren't.

For instance, in the example above you might be more interested in pizza or surfing than in the shark attack. But you don't want your interests to keep you from listening for the main topic. Sometimes people might listen more to the parts they are most interested in, and in doing so, not give enough attention and listening energy to what is most important to the other person.

2) Is there something the other person is saying that they seem to be focusing on and coming back to, or repeating, as they talk?

This is often a great clue about what the main topic might be. Extraneous details often get mentioned but not repeated a great deal, but the main topic is often repeated or elaborated on several times during a conversation. For instance, in the example, Beth mentioned the shark and things about the shark encounter more than the other things, like surfing or pizza.

In trying to identify the main topic, a good detective looks for this kind of clue. They know people repeat or give a lot of details about what is important to them, and that might be the main topic they are trying to communicate to the listener.

3) Is there a part of what the person is saying that has more energy or emotion than others?

Often the main topic might have an emotional charge, so you can listen carefully for emotion words or look for signs of emotional reactions around certain topics. In the example above, Beth used the words "really scary" and "shocking" when describing the shark encounter. These words communicate emotional charge and are great leads to what the main topic might be.

We will talk more about all the ways you can look for emotional clues. For now, just keep in mind that strong feelings about a particular topic can be a clue that it might very well be the main topic.

4) What is my summary of what the other person is saying?

In your mind, try to summarize what the other person is telling you, and ask yourself what it is the other person is trying to communicate. When we summarize, it often helps us sort out in our minds, not just what we are most interested in, but what is most important in what the other person is saying.

DIY: Identifying the Main Topic

Write a short paragraph about something you might like to talk about with a friend sometime. Make sure you have the main topic or main point in mind before you start writing. Also, make sure to add some extraneous details that help describe or set the stage for the main point you want to share. Switch papers with someone else and see if you can figure out what the other person's main topic is. Tell the other person why you think that is their main topic. What were the clues that brought you to your conclusion? See if what you were thinking matches what they were thinking.

PRIME SUSPECT #3:
MOOD MISSING

Another prime suspect in many social mysteries is *mood missing*. People often have problems in social situations because they miss the feeling or mood that someone is trying to share. While someone may be good at listening to the details someone is sharing, and may even be really good at identifying the main topic, they may have trouble listening for the feeling or mood someone is trying to convey. And if we miss the mood or feeling we are missing a big part of what someone is trying to share with us.

For example, we might understand that Beth's main topic had to do with the shark attack. But what is the main mood of what she is communicating? Can you identify the clues that help us know what the main mood or feeling she was conveying might be? Did she seem happy about the shark attack? Did it seem funny or amusing to her? The emotional charge or energy of what she was saying helps us to figure out the mood.

If we just get the main topic but miss the main mood, we are missing a big part of what is being communicated. Missing important things like mood can affect our friendships with people in significant ways. We will talk more about this when we talk about verbal responding. For now, it is helpful to remember that getting the mood someone is trying to express is very important in social interactions. A good detective will always keep mood missing in mind when looking for suspects in social mysteries.

How to Identify Mood or Feeling in What Someone is Saying

There are many ways of identifying the mood or feeling in what someone is communicating to us. Believe it or not, many of these ways have very little to do with the actual words the person is saying. They are more about nonverbal communication. We will talk more about those very interesting nonverbal ways of understanding people later. For now, let's talk about some of the clues we might discover about people's moods in the actual words they use when talking to us.

1) Specific Emotional Words

Sometimes people use specific words to communicate a mood. In the example, Beth used the words "scary" and "shocked" when talking about the shark attack. These emotionally descriptive words not only help to identify the main topic but also help us to figure out the mood.

Can you think of some words that might give us clues about the mood? Here are some of the basic mood words people might use: happy, sad, angry, scared. We also use other words like excited, frustrated, tense, stressed, relaxed, restless, calm, agitated, hopeful, hopeless. Take a look at Appendix Y (Feelings List) for a longer list of words we can use to describe moods.

Many words specifically tell us the feeling someone is trying to express. There are other words that can express feelings, even though they are not exactly feelings themselves: heavy, down, bubbly, chilled, bright, dark, turbulent, gentle, chaotic. For example, someone might say, "there was a dark cloud surrounding Joe that day," or "Things seemed bright when Joe thought about his future." There are lots of words that a good social detective will look for to get clues about the mood of the person they are working with.

2) Emotional Ideas

Sometimes there may not be specific words, but there is an overall tone to what someone is saying that helps us get a sense of what they might be feeling. Making sense of the overall tone of what someone is saying can be more difficult than identifying specific emotion words. But with practice, we can become skillful at identifying mood overtones in what someone says. Being able to do this can be a very powerful tool, so it is well worth the practice.

Here is an example for you. "It was a slow day. Not much to do. I just sat around. I spent two hours doing homework and then realized I had done it all wrong and had to do it over again." Can you speculate what feelings the person saying this might be having? What gives you clues about the feeling tone?

"It was a slow day. Not much to do. I just sat around." You can probably imagine that this is something someone who was feeling bored might say. And this: "I spent two hours doing homework and then realized I had done it all wrong and had to do it over again." While the speaker never says they are frustrated, this seems like the kind of thing that might make someone feel frustrated.

Here is another one. "The doctor said I had to get a shot. I knew I had to do it. But the needle was so big! It was like a knife and it made me think of one of those movies where someone is getting chased around by a bad guy who is trying to kill him!" What might the mood of this communication be? And what would give you clues about the feeling tone? For me, the way the person is describing the doctor and shot experience gives me the sense that it was a stressful experience.

In both of these examples, there are no specific emotion words, but you can get a sense of the tone and of what the person might be feeling just by the situation. One thing that can help us figure out what the mood is when there aren't any specific feeling words, is to imagine how you might feel in the situation being described.

Imagining yourself in the other person's shoes like this is a great thing for a detective to do. It can help you in your detective work in many ways, which we will talk about as we go on. But for our purposes right now, it can be a great way to get a better understanding of the mood being expressed.

SOCIAL MYSTERY 2

The Case

Time: Thursday, 5:32 pm

Place: Noah's bedroom

Noah was very excited about the new phone he just got. Up until now, he had used his dad's old dinosaur flip phone. He could make calls but it was pretty much useless for anything else. It took forever to text with it, and he couldn't be a part of any group chats with people. But now he was totally legit, and for the first time ever he was invited to join a group chat with his friends Sal and George.

Here is some of their text exchange.

Noah: "Hey, guys!"

Sal: "Hey, Noah!" Sal included a happy face emoji.

George: "Nice to have you in the group chat, Noah!"

Noah: "Thanks. Great to be here."

Sal: "Hey, I have to tell you what happened to me this weekend."

Noah: "What happened?"

Sal: "Well, my family and I went to the book store. Mom said we could all get a book. I love going to the book store. So many books to choose from. When we go, we spend a lot of time there before we decide which books we want to get. I really like books from the Star Wars universe and found this great one about Yoda when he was young. I was reading and guess who came along?"

George: "Who?"

Sal: "Billy!"

George: "Billy is such a jerk." George added an angry face emoji.

Noah: "He always picks on me. Last week he knocked my lunch off the table in the cafeteria.

Sal: Yeah, he is a total jerk. So, I was sitting there minding my own business and Billy came up and grabbed my book, and said 'What, you like to read? Reading is for nerds.' 'Why are you here then Billy?' 'Because you're stupid that's why I'm here.' Billy answered, laughing at what he said as if he was so funny. I didn't want to let him get to me so I just said 'whatever'."

George: "He was there because you're stupid?" George replied this time adding a confused face emoji to his text.

George: "That makes absolutely no sense. He thinks he is so funny. But it's just annoying and immature."

Sal: "Yeah, totally. He annoys everyone. But of course, in typical Billy style when he could not get a rise out of me, he took it to the next level. He grabbed my book and flung it on top of the bookshelves. And those bookshelves are really high. There is no way I could have gotten it."

George: "Seriously?"

Noah: "Did they have another copy of the book? Yoda is so cool. I'd love to read a book about his early days."

Sal: "Can you believe he did that?"

George: "Yeah, I can. It's a total Billy move. What happened next?"

Sal: "Ok, this is where it gets good. One of the people who work in the book store saw Billy throw the book. He asked Billy why he did that and he actually said that I did it. Can you believe that? The guy told Billy he had to leave the store. It felt good that the bookstore guy did that but I was really shaken up. I mean I am so sick of Billy."

Noah: "Did you get the book back?"

George: "Why were you so upset, Sal?"

Sal: "I hate when he acts like that. He messes with everyone. I was just quietly sitting there minding my own business, feeling good, and he comes in and totally messes with my mood."

Noah: "But did you get the book back? Yoda is so cool."

George: "I get that Sal. He does the same to me."

Sal: "What has he done to you, George?"

George: 'Billy kept trying to trip me in the hallway and I fell into Katie and Billy said 'Are you trying to kiss her?' Then for the rest of the day, he went around school saying I had a crush on Katie. It was so obnoxious. And Katie felt embarrassed too."

Sal: "That is so messed up! Sorry that happened George."

George: "Yeah and I'm sorry that happened to you too Sal."

Sal: "Thanks, George. Did you end up telling on him?"

George: "No, but my math teacher, Mrs. Rudimentary, heard him and you know she does not tolerate that kind of stuff. She let him have it."

Sal: "That's good. He deserves that."

Noah was feeling left out. He had talked about how Billy was a jerk to him but no one responded. But when George had talked about how Billy was bullying him, Sal asked him all about it. And no one even acknowledged his questions about the Yoda book. Noah was confused. Fortunately, he had his social detective training to fall back on. He remembered that when you are confused about something socially it usually means that there is a social mystery to solve. So, Noah put on his detective hat and tried to figure out what might be going on. In trying to crack the case, the first thing Noah did was to gather some important facts:

The Facts

- Noah had just gotten a new phone and was finally able to be a part of group text chats.
- Noah was texting in a group chat with his friends, Sal and George.
- His friends seemed happy to have him in the group chat.
- At first, they were all chatting in a way that seemed to include everyone.
- As the conversation went on, his friends began to respond less and less to him.
- The conversation was about the bookstore, Star Wars books, Yoda, and Billy being a bully.

When reading about Noah's social mystery and thinking about the facts, does anything stand out to you? Do you have a sense of what prime suspect might be the culprit here?

Cracking the case

Since Noah's friends seemed happy to have him in the group when they started chatting, Noah thought this mystery might have something to do with the details of the conversation. He remembered some really important prime suspects that had to do with verbal responding, so he thought that he would look for clues there. He read through the text thread and noticed some clues. You might want to take a look back over their text exchange to see if you can find the same clues Noah did.

Noah tried to see if there was a main topic in their conversation. He thought about some of the keys to identifying what the main topic is. He asked himself:

1) *Is there something in what the person is saying that seems most important?*
2) *Is there a part of what the person is saying that has more energy or emotion than others?*
3) *Is there something the other person is saying that they seem to be focusing on and coming back to or repeating as they talk?*
4) *What is my summary of what the other person is saying?*

When Noah asked himself these questions, the main topic became clear. The main topic was Billy being a bully to Sal. When Noah realized this, he read through the text thread again and, in a flash, knew why his friends were not responding to what he was saying. He realized that there were actually two related prime suspects that were the culprits in his social mystery. They were *topic missing* and *talking off-topic*. Noah was focusing on Star Wars and Yoda instead of Billy being a bully to Sal. He did mention that Billy had been a bully to him, but it was at a time in the conversation when Sal was still telling his story. So even though it was on the topic of Billy being a bully, at that point the topic was still about Billy being a bully to Sal in the bookstore. When George later talked about Billy being a bully to him, too, the timing was right. At that point, Sal had finished telling his story about Billy, and there was space to make a slight shift in the conversation. George kept the topic on Billy being a bully but shifted it slightly to how Billy had bullied him. Noah shifted too soon. He did it before Sal had finished his story, which probably gave his friends the sense that he was not really on the main topic. It might have given his friends the impression that Noah was more interested in talking about himself than in listening to Sal's story.

When others sense that we are not staying with the main topic, they may feel as if we are not paying attention. And as a result, they may respond to us less. This made sense to Noah. He felt bad for missing the main topic, but he felt better about his friends not responding to him because he realized it was not personal. It was about a problem he had with his verbal responding. And because he could identify this problem, he felt confident he could do something to fix it in the future.

Key Culprits in the Mystery:

Prime suspect #2: Topic Missing

Prime suspect #4: Talking off Topic

Social Remedies

The next time the three boys were in a group chat, Noah was extra careful to identify the main topic and have his verbal responses match what everyone was talking about. And it had a huge effect. His friends were very engaged with him and responded to the things he was saying. They even mentioned at the end of the next chat how happy they were that Noah got a phone and could be a part of their group text.

Main Ideas Chapter 3

1) What is a main topic? P - 31

2) What is an extraneous detail? P - 31

3) What are some questions you can ask to determine what the main topic is? P - 32

4) What is mood missing? P - 33

5) What are some ways you can identify mood or feeling in what someone is saying? P - 34

Chapter 4: Verbal Responding

The way we respond in verbal exchanges can really affect the quality of our social interactions. The way someone responds in conversation with others affects many suspects. As we talked about before, good listening and attention help us become better responders. But that is only a part of what it takes to be a good responder. Let's take a closer look at some important verbal responding suspects.

PRIME SUSPECT #4:

TALKING OFF-TOPIC

This suspect is closely tied to the idea of missing the main topic, which we talked about in the last chapter. Talking off-topic happens when someone's response to what another person said doesn't have to do with the main topic. When it comes to talking off-topic, people can have huge misses or smaller misses. A huge miss happens when the response has absolutely nothing to do with what the other person just said. Someone might be talking about a class in school, and then out of the blue, the other person responds with a comment about a video game. Total misses like this are obviously problematic in relationships with others, but they are usually easy to identify. When someone's miss is that huge, it stands out.

The trickier misses are the smaller ones. These happen when someone's response is somewhat related to some part of what the other person was communicating, while still missing the main idea. While this does give the other person the impression you were kind of paying attention, it also conveys to them that you are not fully understanding them. People like to be understood and to feel that the other person knows what is important to them. In other words, they like it when the other person shows that they are getting the main idea.

Sometimes the responder misses the main topic the speaker is trying to communicate because they were not listening well and truly missed the main topic. Or maybe they were listening but just did not get it. You can see Chapter Two for a refresher on identifying the main topic.

Other times people might know what the main topic is and still not talk on-topic in their response. There can be many reasons for that. For example, maybe the responder does not realize the importance of talking on-topic. They may not really get how talking off-topic can give someone the message that you are not interested in what they are saying or that you don't get them. And they may not realize how much this can interfere with building friendships. If this is the case, you can help point out just how important responding on-topic is to good friendships, and how much of a prime suspect talking off-topic can be.

It is also possible that the person talking off-topic does realize the value of talking on-topic, but they don't do it because they are so excited about something, that they can't hold themselves back. Sometimes it can be hard to hold yourself back when there is something you really want to talk about.

For example, let's say that you were talking to Beth about her experience with the shark we described in Chapter Two. If you recall, the main topic was how she saw the shark and how it was scary for her. But let's say you really love pizza and like knowing about all the pizza places in town and how good they are. If that was the case, you might be tempted to go straight to asking Beth about the pizza she had at the beach, even though you might get that the shark attack was the main idea she was trying to communicate to you.

So, what do you do when there is something you want to talk about, but it's not related to the main topic that the other person is trying to communicate? What should you do when you know you should stick with the main topic but are just itching to talk about something else? In a situation like that, what can you do to resist scratching the itch?

Social Remedies for Resisting the Itch to Talk Off-Topic

1) Using the Mind to Resist the Itch—One of the most effective ways to resist the itch to talk off-topic is to call upon one of our most powerful allies—our own mind. Our mind can keep us in check and help us make good choices if we use it right. But we often don't. We often act without consulting our mind and allowing it to help us think through things.

This is often true when it comes to urges. For example, if you have an itch because a fly landed on you, you probably don't think, "I'm going to scratch that itch now." You probably just do it. It is an impulse or an urge, and you act on it without engaging your mind to think about it.

Sometimes acting on an urge without thinking is fine, like scratching the place where the fly tickled you. Sometimes it's even helpful. If you accidentally touch something hot, you don't think, "Maybe I should pull my hand away now." You just do it without thinking. And in a situation like that, it's good to do it without thinking, because by the time you thought about the pros and cons of pulling your hand away, you might get a really bad burn.

There are other times when thinking is really important. For example, let's say your mom just baked a delicious apple pie, and it looked really good and you wanted to eat it. If you acted without thinking and just followed the urge and took a big bite out of it, it might cause problems. But hopefully, before acting on the urge, you would think to yourself something like, "It's not my pie, and if I take a bit out of it, I might get in big trouble." And that thought would help you resist just gobbling it up instead of asking your mom if you could have a piece.

Similarly, if you can get yourself to think about responding in a conversation before you act, it can help you to make good choices in how you respond. If you think about the pros and cons of responding off-topic it will help you make a better choice. If it's really clear in your mind that topic missing might make the other person feel like you were not paying attention or do not get them, it might make it easier for you to resist the urge to talk off-topic.

The problem is that urges are often quicker and sneakier than our thoughts. They can slip in and make us act before we even get the chance to think. But habits can be even faster than urges and impulses. A well-practiced habit does not have to be thought about. You just do it. You might have a habit of turning the light on when you come into a dark room or covering your mouth when you sneeze. Those things are so well practiced that you don't need to think about them.

I imagine you have covered your mouth before sneezing so many times that it has become automatic. Turning on the light, or covering your mouth, or swinging the bat at the baseball, or pedaling the bike just right so you don't fall off – these kinds of things are all habits you learned and practiced so much that you don't have to think about them anymore.

Using your mind to think before you act can become a habit too. It may take a little time to form the habit, but just like riding a bike, once you get it, it becomes second nature. See if you can create the habit of using your mind to remind yourself of the importance of responding to the main topic and resisting the urges to respond off-topic.

2) Mantras—One of my favorite ways of turning something into a habit is to use a mantra. A mantra is a thought, idea, or intention we repeat over and over in our minds. It can take the form of a simple statement we say to ourselves. For our purposes here the statement might be, "I'm going to listen for and respond to the main topic." This is something we can get in the habit of saying to ourselves before we speak. It can be something we repeat in our minds every time we are having a conversation with someone. "I'm going to listen for and respond to the main topic."

By saying this repeatedly throughout the day, we are highlighting that intention in our brain. And we are making a habit of the idea of looking for and responding to the main topic. Now it may be a little hard to remember to say that mantra at first. We need to make a habit of repeating the mantra so that the mantra can help us make the habit of listening for and responding to the main topic.

So how do we make a habit of saying our mantras to ourselves regularly? We can write it down on our to-do list. We can set an alarm on our phone for every hour or so, and every time it goes off, we know to say our mantra. We can even enlist the help of people close to us to remind us to say our mantra. You can have a special code word with your mom or dad or friend or teacher. Maybe they can say "detective" and that can remind you to say your mantra to yourself. Or they can just say the word "mantra"

If you practice saying your mantra regularly, you will start to notice the habit you are forming getting stronger and faster than the urges or impulses. Give it a try, and see how it works for you.

3) The Power of the Pause—Another trick you can use to keep an urge from making you do something before you have time to think is to get in the habit of pausing before you speak. Pauses also help you to formulate your ideas so you can verbally respond in ways that get your message across to others in the best way possible.

To help yourself get in the habit of pausing before you respond, you can use a simple mantra that consists of the single word, "pause." That single word repeated throughout the day can help you to slow down and take some time before you respond. And this little extra time can give you the space you need to let your thoughts, rather than your urges, determine your responses.

4) Getting to Know Your Body Better—Getting to know your body better can also help you to make better choices. We often feel urges in our body. And urges can be very powerful things. They can be like a giant magnet that pulls us to do things, even if those things are not the best choices for us. By getting to know your body better, you can gain more control over your urges, and in doing so, make better choices.

It can feel really uncomfortable in your body when you have a strong urge and don't act on it. For example, if someone was talking with Beth about her experience at the beach and really wanting to talk about pizza rather than the shark attack, it might feel physically uncomfortable to not act on the urge to talk about the pizza. It might feel like having the itch that desperately needs scratching and not being able to scratch it.

Just as we often scratch an itch without even thinking about it, it is all too easy to go off topic without even thinking about it, even if we know it is not good for our friendship to do so. But understanding our bodies can help us. By being aware of our body's reactions, our urges, or itches, we can choose whether or not we want to scratch. By being aware of our bodies, our decision to scratch is not just an automatic response that we engage in without wondering if it is the best thing to do. It is a conscious choice.

The best way to get to know your body better is to pay attention to it. And as we discussed before, a great way to pay attention is to use the spotlight of attention. Before, we used the spotlight of attention to get to know our thoughts better. Here we can use the same skill to get to know our bodies better. Below is an exercise called "body scan" that uses the spotlight of attention to get to know our bodies better.

DIY: Body Scan

At first, it's helpful to do the body scan in a quiet place with your eyes closed, so you can focus on what is going on inside your body without getting distracted by what you hear or see. But once you get the hang of it, you can do it almost anywhere, as a way of checking in with yourself.

Start by getting in a comfortable position. You can sit or even lay down if you like. Close your eyes and imagine your spotlight of attention. Shine that spotlight on your feet so that all your attention focuses on your feet. Let everything else go dark except the place where your spotlight is going. And as you do this, allow yourself to notice what it feels like in your feet.

Are your feet hot or cold? Do they feel heavy or light? Is there a comfortable feeling in them, or do they feel uncomfortable? Or maybe there is just a neutral feeling. Be poetic in how you describe the feelings in your feet. Maybe they feel bubbly or tingly, or like there is a little river of energy running through them. Maybe they feel as if they are tightening or releasing. It might feel like static in there, like when the radio is not tuned in properly. Or like water flowing, or feathers tickling, or little rubber balls bouncing up and down in there. Let your words and your imagination find ways to describe what it might feel like in your feet.

You may also find that as you shine your spotlight of attention, the feeling seems to have a shape or color to it. It may seem like the feeling is moving in a certain direction or as if it is very still. It may seem like your feet are as hard as steel or as soft as tapioca pudding. It may even feel as if the sensation is stronger in one spot and weaker in other spots of your foot, or as if there is one specific spot the feeling is starting at and then radiating out to other places.

For some people, it may be hard at first to sense what it feels like in your feet. If this happens, you can wiggle your toes and see what that feels like. Our bodies can feel things in lots of ways. They can physically feel things, like when we wiggle our toes and sense them rubbing against our shoes. We can also feel things in deeper, subtler ways, like when we feel emotions or more quiet sensations. But sometimes sensing these more subtle, quieter feelings takes practice. Doing things like wiggling our toes can help us to focus our spotlight of attention on our bodies better so that we get better and better at sensing subtler feelings and sensations.

And it's important to remember there is no right or wrong way to do the body scan. If we are focusing our spotlight on our body, we may feel many different things. Success here is not about what you feel or how much you feel. It's about how well you can build your ability to shine your spotlight on your body so that you can get to know yourself better.

Once you have spent a little time shining your attention on your feet, let your spotlight move up to your lower legs. Do the same thing here that you did with your feet. Notice if there are comfortable, uncomfortable, or neutral feelings. Notice temperature and tension. Be poetic in your description of what you are feeling in the same way you did with your feet. After spending some time with your lower legs, move your spotlight to your upper legs, then to your waist, and then your stomach and chest.

Often people feel a lot of the more subtle sensations, like emotions and tensions, in their chest, so make sure to give some special attention to this area. Keep moving the spotlight slowly to cover all the places in your body. From your stomach and chest, you can move up to your throat, then to your shoulders and arms, then to your back and up the back of your neck, all the way to the top of your head. Come to the front again, and let your spotlight shine on your face and eyes and mouth. Notice all the different flavors of sensation you might be feeling in your body in different places.

https://www.socialdetectiveacademy.com/body-awareness-practice/

Befriending our Bodies

Something that can be really interesting is noticing if your feelings shift and change as you pay attention to them. Often the simple act of paying attention can have a powerful effect on the way we feel. Just as someone giving us attention when we are feeling bad can help us to feel better, giving our own body attention when it is feeling bad can help us feel better. This is another way that something like the body scan can help us with urges. Paying attention to our body not only helps us think through the pros and cons of acting on an urge in order to make a better choice. It can also make the urge less uncomfortable. It can make the urge not itch as much. And we are less likely to act on an urge that does not itch as much.

The bottom line is that when we befriend our bodies, our bodies treat us better. And this whole idea of befriending is really important to a social detective. A good social detective helps build good relationships. If you build a good relationship with someone who might bully you, there is less chance that there will be conflict and bad feelings in that relationship. Good relationships with other people make us feel good. The same is true for our relationship with our bodies. If we build a good relationship with our bodies, there is less chance it will cause us suffering.

We build a good relationship with people by exchanging information and by showing interest in getting to know the other person. We build a good relationship by paying attention and listening and responding, and all the other things we have been talking about. The same is true for our relationships with our bodies. By paying attention and listening to the information our body is sending out, it becomes our friend. And the more it becomes our friend, the less likely it is that it will bully us and make us feel things or even do things that are not in our best interest.

Give it a try. Try to befriend your body every day, and see how it treats you back. The body scan is a great way to strike up a conversation with your body. It is an excellent tool for any social detective to have in their bag of tricks. By practicing it yourself, you will be able to help others learn it, so they can manage their urges better, too.

The more you practice the body scan, the better you get at it, and the more powerful an effect it has. At first, it's helpful to practice it with your eyes closed in a quiet place. But once you get the hang of it, you can do it almost anywhere, and it can have just as powerful an effect.

Fear of Forgetting

We talked above about some of the secondary suspects that might lead to people talking off-topic. These might be things like not getting or understanding the importance of the main topic, or being very excited about talking about something else.

But there is one more important secondary suspect that can result in people talking off-topic. It's the *fear of forgetting*. People often talk off-topic because they fear that if they don't say what they want to say right then, they will forget and it will be lost forever. This is a big problem for a lot of people. But there are some great things you can do to help with this.

First, you can try to tell yourself that if what you have to say is really important, it will come back to you later. This is a nice idea, right? But it may not always work. We may not really believe that it will come back to us. What if that strategy does not work? Well, you could turn your idea into a mantra, and just keep repeating it over and over in your head until there is a good time to talk. The problem with that is that if you are focusing on remembering too hard, you will not keep up with the conversation, and may either miss the right moment to say what you had to say, or completely miss other important parts of the conversation, and end up being totally left out of the conversation and miss opportunities to talk on-topic and have a good conversation with others.

So, what else? Maybe you could write down a short note to remind yourself. Sometimes this might work. And if it's on paper, you can free your attention up to listen and respond to the flow of the conversation and stay with the main topic. And this is bound to help you in your relationships.

But what can you do if it's not a good time to take notes, or you don't happen to have a pen and paper? In these situations, I like to use memory techniques. One of my favorite memory techniques involves making mental connections. This is a cool way of remembering things by connecting the thing you want to remember something else, like an image or another idea in your head. When you connect something you want to remember to an image or to another idea, it can help you to remember much better.

It's kind of like tying a string around your finger or using the dot method to help you remember. But instead of a string or a dot, it's an idea or picture in your head. Let's say you want to remember to tell your friend about this new video game you heard is coming out. You can make a picture of the game in your mind and imagine you and your friend playing it. Or you can think of a single word to help you remember. For example, if the game is the new Super Smash Brothers, you can say "smash" in your head and just try to remember that word. You can just say "smash" in your head every few minutes while the conversation continues. This way it's not taking up all your attention, so you can keep up with the conversation.

PRIME SUSPECT #5:

NOT RESPONDING TO MOOD

Another very common suspect in social mysteries has to do with the way we respond to the mood someone is communicating. We have been talking a lot about the importance of talking on-topic. Missing the topic can be problematic in making good social connections. But it can be even more problematic when we miss the mood or feeling tone that is being communicated. If we miss the facts, details, or ideas someone is expressing, it can be annoying. But facts and ideas are usually not as deeply tied to the soft tender parts of us as feelings often are.

When someone misses our feelings, especially if they are sensitive feelings, it can feel really bad and feel like the person does not get us. It might even seem like they don't care about us. People like to be understood around their feelings even more than they like to be understood around their thoughts and ideas. Getting feelings or moods is very important. But while missing moods can cause problems in friendships, getting moods can be an incredible way to build a friendship and create what I like to call "social equity."

When someone builds equity, they are building value. When someone has equity in a home they own, it means that they have value in it. And that value can translate into actual money. Social equity has to do with the value we have to others, as a result of what we have invested in our relationships with them. The more we invest in our relationships, the more value there is. People with a lot of social equity are often valued more by other people. This often translates into being more popular and liked by others.

Being skilled at responding to people's moods is one of the prime ways we invest socially and build value with others. Really, all the tools we have been and will be talking about are ways of building social equity. But responding well to others' moods is a particularly powerful way to increase our social equity with others.

In the last chapter we discussed mood missing, and how to pay attention and discover what the mood of a conversation is. But the real test for any social detective has to do with implementation. Implementation refers to how we take something we have learned or are aware of and use it in the real world, or in other words, how we demonstrate what we have come to know.

The difference between being aware of something and demonstrating that awareness is huge. I've had many cases where my client was great at understanding someone's mood, but despite getting the other person's mood, they were not able to effectively communicate their understanding to the other person. They were not able to respond effectively. So, let's talk about a few of the things that might get in the way of responding to mood, to increase the chances of building social equity by demonstrating to others that we get them. And of course, these would be secondary suspects that contribute to the prime suspect of *Not Responding to Mood*.

Things That Might Get in the Way of Responding to Mood
1) Lack of interest

Someone may be capable of reading the mood of another person accurately but just not be interested in engaging with the feelings of the other person. As a result, they may ignore the mood, and change the subject to talk about something else other than the mood. When this is the case, it's helpful to remind the person how important it can be to communicate that they get the mood of others. Hopefully, the motivation to be a good friend will be stronger than the motivation to talk about something more interesting, and the person will spend some time acknowledging the other person's mood before moving on.

It's important to remember that responding to someone's mood does not necessarily mean you have to spend hours discussing their feelings. While you may be a social detective, that does not mean you have to be someone's therapist. There may be times you want to spend some extended time discussing someone's mood with them. But that is not an essential quality of a good friend. Often you can just give a little acknowledgment and then move on.

If someone is expressing something good that happened to them, you might just need to say something like "That's awesome," or "That must have made you so happy," to show them that you understand. If they are expressing a negative mood, you might just need to say "That sucks," or "That must have felt bad." But the point is that you want to let them know you get what they were expressing.

2) Discomfort

Someone may be capable of reading the mood of someone else but feel uncomfortable with the mood and want to avoid it. There are many reasons someone might feel uncomfortable with the mood someone is trying to express. The other person's mood may bring up bad feelings in them. For example, if someone talks about a bad feeling they have or something that upset them, it may stir similar feelings in the listener. For example, If someone talks about how they were laughed at in school and how it made them feel bad, it may stir feelings in the listener about a time he was made fun of, and it might bring up all the bad feelings the person had themselves. Or maybe someone shares something positive, like how they got an A on a test they studied really hard for. While this is a positive thing, it may bring up feelings in the listener about a time they did poorly on a test or did not study enough.

Someone's first reaction to something like this is often to avoid and change the subject. While that might give the listener some relief, it can make the person who was communicating the mood feel bad. Just as in situations in which someone has a lack of interest, it can be very helpful in situations like this to remind ourselves that good friends respond to moods. And hopefully, the motivation to be a good friend will be stronger than the motivation to avoid the uncomfortable feeling.

Another thing that is helpful to remember in situations like this is that often one of the best ways to deal with negative feelings is to face them, rather than avoid them. While avoiding uncomfortable feelings that might come up in a situation like this might help you push those feelings away, actually facing them can help you not just push the bad feelings away, but change the bad feelings. Responding to your friend's mood by listening and letting them know you get what they are feeling is a way of supporting them. And supporting them can actually help you feel supported yourself. For example, if you say to your friend who was laughed at, "That must have felt terrible," it can help them feel not as alone. That can help you feel good about yourself, and help you not feel as bad about the times you were made fun of. Give it a try sometime. It really works.

Another thing that often makes people feel uncomfortable is that they may feel a need to make the other person feel better. They may feel like it's their job to fix the other person's feelings, but may not know what to say to make things better, and as a result, they may say something that misses the mood. If they don't know what to say to make it better, they may end up saying nothing at all.

But the truth is that when people are sharing a less than positive mood with you, what they often need most is not someone to "fix it." What they need is someone to "feel it." Fixing a negative mood often involves trying to offer a solution or telling someone that they should not feel the way they do. While this can sometimes be helpful, it can make someone feel that the other person does not really get them. If someone says they are sad because their dog dies, and we try to fix it by telling them they should just go get another dog, we are missing the real point, which is that they are sad. If we try to fix it by telling them they should not feel bad because it was only a dog, not a person, they will not feel understood by us.

What people often need in a situation like this is for us to just feel it–to just hear how they are feeling and reflect it back to them. For example, some good things to say might be saying something like, "That must feel so bad to have lost your dog. That would make me sad too." Or "I'm so sorry that happened." Those would be great ways to "feel it" with the other person. You are not trying to make them feel better or offer some solution. You are just showing them that you get their mood.

Sometimes hearing that we get the mood can be the best way to help someone. And the good news with that is that when we focus on feeling it rather than fixing it, we don't need to come up with some big solution to their problems. We don't need to fix it. We just need to feel it and not try to take the feelings away. Knowing this can make it much more comfortable to respond to people's moods because we can relax and realize it is not our job to make them feel better. It's just our job as a good friend to let them know we can understand how they feel. And the ironic part is that sometimes the best way to "fix it," is to not try to fix it. The best thing may be to just "feel it."

Techniques for Effectively Responding to Mood

Once we recognize the mood and are motivated to respond, even if we are not interested, and we deal with our discomfort and don't feel the need to fix it for them, what then? What do we say or do to effectively show someone we get their mood? There are some very easy things we can do to show someone we get them. Some of these things were demonstrated in the examples above, but let's go a little deeper into them.

1) Reflecting

The first thing we can do to show someone we get their mood is to reflect. When we look in a mirror, we see a reflection of ourselves. A good mirror will accurately reflect back to us what we look like. When we are reflecting another person, we become a mirror, in a way. We reflect back to them, not what they look like, but what they are communicating to us. Reflecting their mood back to someone is a great way to show them that we get what they are feeling.

In the last chapter, we talked about how people sometimes use specific emotion words to let us know the mood they are trying to communicate. They may say something made them happy or sad or angry or scared. When someone uses direct emotional words, we can reflect back to them by using the same words they used. For example, if someone says, "I got so mad at school today when we were playing basketball in gym class. I was just about to make a shot, and Joey pushed me on the ground. He didn't even get called for a foul! Can you believe it?" You can reflect the feeling of this simply by saying, "I can see Joey pushing you down and not even getting a foul made you really mad."

Other times someone might not use a specific emotional word, but by using the tools we discussed in the last chapter, we can use our detective skills to solve the mystery of what they might be feeling. For example, someone might say, "I just got my math test back, and I got a D on it. I can't believe it. I studied so hard for that test." From what the person said, you might conclude that they feel bad and disappointed about their low grade, so you might reflect back to them by saying, "I bet you were disappointed about that."

2) Validating

You can often make a reflection even better by adding a validation. Validations are a great way to show someone that not only are you getting the mood they are communicating but that you also are getting why they are having the mood. In the example above, you can take it a step further by adding a validation. You can simply reflect to the person by saying, "I can see that Joey pushing you down and not even getting a foul made you mad." This shows you got what the person was saying.

But we can add a validation onto that response by saying, "Wow, I can see how that would make you really mad when he pushed you down and did not even get a foul!" This not only shows that you understood his mood, but that you also can *understand* how getting pushed down would make him mad. This mirrors even more information back to the person. It mirrors back that not only did you understand what they felt, but also why they felt it, that you get how that would be upsetting.

3) Empathizing

When we can get what someone is feeling and why they are feeling it, it helps us to get closer to really understanding their mood, not just intellectually, but emotionally, too. It's possible to intellectually understand that someone is feeling something, but not really understand it emotionally. To understand what someone is feeling emotionally, we need to be able to feel a little bit of the same feeling. If we are not able to feel even a little twinge of what they are feeling, we are not fully getting the other person.

It's kind of like if someone tells you chocolate ice cream is delicious. If you have never had chocolate or ice cream, you really couldn't relate to how good it tastes. You might intellectually understand that they like it, but because you have never had the experience of the wonderful taste, you can't know just how delicious it is. (And as you hopefully know, it is very delicious!)

If someone is upset because they were pushed down in a baseball game, but you have never had any experience like that, you might intellectually understand from the person's words that they are upset.

But you might not have any clue about what it really feels like because nothing like that has ever happened to you.

Being able to emotionally get what someone else is feeling helps us to empathize with them. To empathize with someone means we not only understand with our minds what they are feeling but that we also can share in the feeling they are experiencing. Of course, intellectually understanding what someone is feeling is a great thing and can be very helpful for friendships. But being able to share a little bit of what someone is feeling can be so much more powerful. It can help them feel understood in a much deeper way.

Sometimes it's easy to empathize. If you have tasted chocolate ice cream, it's going to be much easier to imagine the sense of deliciousness that comes from eating it. Or if you have also been pushed down while playing baseball, and the person who pushed you also did not get fouled, it will be much easier to feel a little of what your friend is feeling, because you have experienced the same thing.

But what do you do when someone is telling you about something you have never experienced? How do you share in the feeling someone is having when you have never experienced it directly yourself? One thing you can do in a situation like this is *approximate*. To approximate means to come close to something.

Approximating means to find something similar even if it is not exactly the same. Maybe you have never had chocolate ice cream but maybe you have had vanilla pudding. While they are not the same, they are both desserts, and you can approximate how delicious the ice cream is by remembering the deliciousness of the pudding.

Or maybe you have never been pushed down in a baseball game, but maybe your big brother shoved you in the hall the other day and did not get in trouble for it. Again, it's not the same, but the feeling you had with your brother might approximate how your friend felt getting pushed down while playing baseball.

While it's true we might not always have had the same experiences as other people or may not have the same feelings they do, we can often approximate by trying to find situations in our own lives that were somewhat similar to theirs.

Once we find a similar experience, we can recall it and remember what it felt like for us when that happened. We might even want to share that similar experience with the other person. Sometimes sharing our similar or approximate situation can help others feel even more understood.

After we reflect and validate, we might want to offer a relating statement that shows we share some of the same feelings. In the example above, we might start with a reflection and a validation like this: "Wow, I can see how Joey pushing you down and not getting a foul would make you really mad!" Then we could add something to show we empathize with them. "That never happened to me, but the other day my brother pushed me down. When I told my mom, she just told him not to do that, and he didn't get in trouble or anything. It felt so unfair. I imagine that what happened to you might have felt really unfair too."

SOCIAL MYSTERY 3

The Case

Time: Monday, 7:58 AM

Place: School

It was another Monday in the seemingly endless sea of Mondays that marked the school year. Melody was neither a morning person nor a Monday person. And the combination of the two made Monday mornings her least favorite part of the week. But one thing she did like about Mondays was getting to see her friends. As she entered homeroom, she saw her friend Brittany already seated. She called to her, "Hey Brit!" in a voice that was as cheery as a Monday morning would allow. Brittany glanced over and gave her a little nod and then turned her gaze away and stared off into space. Something did not seem right with Brittany. She was usually the cheeriest one in the room. Even on a Monday morning, she was always bubbly and bouncy. But today it seemed that all the light had been sucked out of her. She sat slumped over her desk with a pained look on her face.

After class Melody asked Britany how she was doing. Asking people how they are is a great way to show you are interested in them. And being a well-trained social detective, Melody knew this. Brittany looked up and met Melody's gaze. As she did, tears welled up in her eyes. "Floppy is really sick," she said, the tears running down her cheeks as she spoke. Floppy was Brittany's childhood dog. They named her Floppy because her ears were so big that she couldn't lift them, and they flopped all over the place, covering her eyes and getting in her mouth. "Oh no!" Melody said. "What's wrong?" "The vet isn't sure," said Brittany. " She's sleeping a lot and doesn't want to eat. The doctor said she might just have an infection but I'm so worried it might be something really bad! I mean, she isn't a puppy anymore. I love her so much! I've been so anxious all weekend! I can't imagine her not being here. I would be devastated if something bad happened to her," she said with even more tears.

"Well, hopefully, it's nothing. Don't worry about it. And you know what?" Melody said in a deliberately cheery, positive voice. "If she dies, you can always get a new dog." Melody smiled and patted Brittany on the back. But this did not seem to cheer Brittany up. In fact, she started crying even harder, making sobbing sounds as she ran off. Melody was a little shocked by her response. She usually had lunch with Brittany but that day Brittany was nowhere to be found. Melody tried Snapchatting her after school, but she didn't respond. She could tell Brittany saw her message because it said it was read. But Brittany was silent. Ghosting is what they call it when someone does not return your messages and ignores or avoids you. And it was clear to Melody that Brittany was full-on ghosting her.

Brittany always responded to Melody's messages. Melody was confused and upset that her friend would ghost her like this, and she had no idea why. Melody knew she had a full-fledged social mystery on her hands. Fortunately, she was trained for just this kind of situation. So, she sat down and did what all good social detectives do when starting on a social mystery. She gathered the facts.

The Facts

- Brittany is usually cheery, even on Mondays.
- This day she was not, because her dog was sick.

- Melody and Brittany are good friends.
- Brittany told Melody about what was happening with Floppy.
- Melody tried to cheer Brittany up.
- During their conversation, Brittany got even more upset and ran off.
- Brittany and Melody usually have lunch together, but Melody could not find Brittany during lunch.
- After school Melody tried to Snapchat Brittany, but Brittany did not respond even though she read Melody's message.

When reading about Melody's social mystery and thinking about the facts, does anything stand out to you? Do you have a sense of what prime suspect might be the culprit here?

Cracking the Case

Melody thought it would be helpful to run through some of the main prime suspects to see if she could find any helpful clues. She started by asking herself if she gave Brittany her full attention during their conversation. "I think I was pretty attentive to Brittany. I don't think that's the culprit," she thought. Then she asked herself if she was on topic. "I know the main topic was Floppy being sick. And I stayed with that topic the whole time we talked," she thought. "So that wasn't it either. How about mood matching?" she asked herself. She went through her list of strategies for identifying moods, asking herself the following questions:

1) *Did Brittany use specific emotional words in what she was saying?* Melody recalled her using the words "worried," "love," "anxious," and "devastated."

2) *Did Brittany share specific emotional ideas?* In thinking about their conversation, Melody could see that Brittany was clearly communicating how upset she was about Floppy being sick.

When Melody answered these questions for herself a huge, giant light went off in her head. "Oh no!" she said out loud. "I totally mood missed!" She realized that her friend was really upset. It was so clear to her now. But the truth was that Melody had recognized those things at the time Brittany was sharing with her, so she actually didn't mood miss. But she didn't respond in a way that was sensitive to her friend's mood. She saw the signs but did not respond in an emotionally sensitive way to her friend. It was clear to her that the culprit in her social mystery was the prime suspect *not responding to mood.*

"Why didn't I respond to her mood even though I was aware of how upset she was?" she asked herself. "I knew she was upset. But I didn't respond well to the mood she was in. Instead, I responded to her being sad and worried by being cheery and positive. And I even joked about it and minimized her feelings by saying she could just get a new dog. That was so insensitive of me!" she thought. Melody felt bad about this and now understood why her friend might have ghosted her for the rest of the day. But she also knew that with her good social detective skills she could make this right. First, she needed to figure out why she had acted the way she did.

Melody remembered how Johnny had taught her to identify things that might get in the way of responding to mood. Johnny had said that in addition to mood missing, other things can get in the way of responding to someone's mood. These things were 1) lack of interest and 2) discomfort.

Melody definitely did not have a lack of interest in what her friend was feeling. She cared a lot about Brittany and loved Floppy too. She wanted to be a good friend to her. So that was not it. Then she asked herself if she had any discomfort when Brittany shared how upset she was, and she realized that she did. When Brittany started getting teary-eyed, Melody could feel it. She started to feel upset too. And she remembered that when she had lost her dog, Roger, a few years ago, it had been really hard for her. Hearing Brittany's fear about losing her dog brought up the feelings Melody had when Roger died.

She wanted to help her friend feel better. But she didn't know what to do to make it better. She remembered how Johnny taught her that when we feel responsible for other people's feelings, we sometimes try to fix it by talking them out of their feelings. People don't need us to fix how they feel, they need for us to just feel it with them. Melody realized that because she felt uncomfortable, and because she wanted to help her friend feel better and didn't know what to do, she tried to fix things rather than feel things. She tried to fix her friend by taking her out of her feelings rather than just feeling the worry and sadness with her. And this resulted in her not responding to her friend's mood.

When Melody realized this, she knew what she needed to do. She needed to have a do-over with her friend. She recalled how Johnny had taught her that reflecting, validating, and empathizing were great ways of letting others know you understand how they are feeling. She kept those things in mind and made a plan for making things better with Brittany the next day.

Key Culprits in the Mystery:

Prime suspect #5: Not Responding to Mood

Social Remedies

Time: Tuesday, 7:56 AM

Place: School

Tuesday came, and Melody got to school early to see if she could catch her friend before class. As luck would have it, Brittany had got to school early too. Melody called to her and sped up to catch her. "Hi Brittany," she said. Brittany turned, but when she saw Melody, she looked down and said hi in a voice that told Melody she was still upset. "Brittany, I wanted to say that I'm so sorry about how I responded to you yesterday." Brittany's face softened when Melody said this. "You were so upset about Floppy and instead of really listening to you, I tried to talk you out of feeling upset." Brittany smiled a little. "It's ok, Mel," she said. "No," said Melody, "It isn't. The truth is, I just wanted to help you feel better, so I tried to cheer you up. But that's not what you needed. You were upset for a good reason," she said, validating Brittany's feelings. "Floppy being sick and not knowing what was going on must be so hard," she added, validating more while she reflected back what Brittany had told her. "I totally get how that must feel. When I lost Roger a few years ago, it was the worst thing that had ever happened to me," she added, showing empathy and understanding. Brittany looked right in Melody's eyes. She paused a little, taking in what Melody had said. "I really appreciate you saying that, Mel. It has been so hard. I'm really scared." The girls hugged each other and continued talking as they walked to class. Melody felt good that she could make things better with her friend. She was relieved that she was able to solve this social mystery and make things right with Brittany.

PRIME SUSPECT #6: UNDER-RESPONDING

and

PRIME SUSPECT #7 OVER-RESPONDING

Two more very common verbal responding suspects have to do with how much or how little of a response we give in our interactions with others. They are Suspect #6: *Under-responding* and Suspect #7: *Over-responding*. It can be tricky to find just the right amount of response to give in our conversations with others. But when we do, it can bring a lot of value to our social interactions. And of course, that means building more social equity. Let's go into these two suspects.

Under-responding

Under-responding happens when we do not give enough information back to the other person when we talk. This can result in the person feeling like we are not interested in them or that we don't really get them. They may think we are bored or don't really care enough to put effort into having a conversation with them, or that we just don't understand.

Also, under-responding can make interactions boring. Imagine playing catch with someone who does not know how to throw the ball back to you or only throws it back after a long time. They may catch it, but then they don't throw it back. You may go take the ball from them and try again. You might keep throwing for a while, but very soon that game is going to get old. It's the same with conversations. We want to keep the ball going back and forth at a nice pace to keep it interesting. Like the game of catch, not enough back and forth can make conversations very dull.

There are some good tricks for assessing if we are under-responding in our interactions with others. Tuning into the feedback others are giving is a great place to start. Remember, a good detective always gathers the facts, and the feedback others give is a great source of facts.

Sometimes when we under-respond to what someone said, the other person may not respond to us right away. They may be waiting for us to say more. This delay in responding might take the form of an awkward pause. Awkward pauses can happen for many reasons and might not necessarily be feedback that we are under-responding. If the other person is an under-responder themselves, there may be an awkward pause after you speak because they are not throwing the conversational ball back to you, as is often the case with under-responders. They just may not know what to say back to you. But it is also often the case that an awkward pause may occur because the other person is waiting to see if you have more to say. A good detective thinks about all the possibilities when they are faced with an awkward pause.

Another way to assess if we are responding enough is to notice if the other person is repeating themselves. Under-responding can sometimes result in what I like to call *the repeater effect*. When someone does not feel like the other person has heard them, the effect can be that they repeat what they have said, in hopes that the other person will get it the second or third or fourth time they say it.

Just like the awkward pause, this repeater effect can be the result of many things. It can happen when we respond off-topic or off-mood. It can also happen when the other person is really enthusiastic about what they are saying. But it often is also a good clue that we may be under-responding. When we under-respond we are not giving enough information back to the other person to let them know we get them. And people like to know you get them, so they may repeat what they have said until they feel understood.

Another clue that you might find in the other person's feedback is their level of energy. Sometimes when people don't feel like the other person is interested in them or they don't feel understood, their enthusiasm for the social exchange goes down. This might take the form of them talking less. It might also take the form of them giving you nonverbal signals that they are not as energized about your interaction as you are. We will talk more about these very important nonverbal aspects of communication in a later section. But for now, it's helpful to know that when the other person gives us feedback that they are not as engaged in the conversation, it might be because we are under-responding. Again, it could be because of other things, but under-responding is often a prime suspect when this happens.

In addition to gathering facts about the feedback people are giving you, it is also helpful to gather facts about how you are interacting with others. Being aware of ourselves and our actions is one of our most powerful tools for solving our own social mysteries. With talking off-topic and talking off-mood, one of the main social remedies we discussed was being more aware of whether or not we were accurately getting the other person's main ideas and main moods. Our awareness is a big asset in being more socially successful around those things. Similarly, by noticing things in ourselves that might be signs of under-responding, we become more skillful at finding a good balance in our exchanges with others.

One of the main things we can try to be aware of is how much we are talking in our exchanges with others. Are we using single word responses or short sentences in response to what the other person is saying? This can be a very measurable way to assess if we are responding in a balanced way. If they are talking in paragraphs and we are only giving very short responses that do not convey an adequate amount of related information, it might be a sign that we are out of balance in the exchange.

There are times in conversations when one of the people takes up more talking space for a period of time, and that can be fine. It does not mean we are under-responding. You don't always have to match every response in length. But it can be helpful to notice if responses are generally similar in length. Sometimes someone might be telling you a story or might be very enthusiastic about something, and you might be listening more than responding, and that can be fine. But you usually want an overall balance, which might mean you can talk a little more later.

Remedies for Under-responding

There are some good tools you can keep in your detective bag of tricks that can help if you become aware that under-responding is the culprit. If you're not sure what to say, you can use your skills to identify the main topic and main mood to help you think about how to respond. Even if we can't think of much to say, but are responding to the person's main idea and main mood, we will be giving a significant amount to the conversation. One or two sentences that convey that we are interested and getting the other person is worth a thousand sentences that just ramble aimlessly and miss the essence of the conversation. When in doubt about what to say, you can just reflect the main topic and mood in your responses.

You can also use the strategy of *shifting the flow of the conversation*. If it feels like a conversation is not going anywhere and you don't know what to say, you can always gracefully try to change the subject. You want to make sure not to change the subject in the middle of a discussion. That could be topic missing. But knowing when to change topics is very important. We will talk about this more later, but for now, know that shifting the flow of a conversation by changing the subject at the right time can often help us respond in a balanced way.

Another thing you can do when under-responding is an issue is to remind yourself to elaborate. Elaborating means to describe something in more detail. When we elaborate on something we said, we give more details than we did in our first response. You can ask yourself, "Can I elaborate on what I just said to contribute in a more balanced way to the conversation?" For example, if your friend tells you about going to the beach and seeing a shark, you might respond with "Cool!" You might want to elaborate on that response, and say something like "Wow, that's cool seeing a shark. I mean, it's scary but also kind of cool." This response gives more detail by communicating to the person that we heard what they were saying, and that we also can imagine what it might have felt like in their situation.

Another great tool to use when having trouble responding is asking relevant questions. While this may not provide an equal amount of talking, it is showing interest and investment in the conversation. Equal responding does not always mean just saying the same amount of words; it's more about showing the same amount of investment of energy in a conversation. Asking the other person questions can be a great way of responding that does not involve having to come up with lots of things to say. One way you can respond is by asking the other person to elaborate more on something, like when you asked your friend more about the shark at the beach. This not only shows that you were listening to what they were saying, but that you are interested and would like to know more.

If you notice under-responding going on and it's hard to find words to respond, it can also be helpful to communicate nonverbally. The truth is, you can get away with not saying much if you have good nonverbal communication. Much of how we show people that we are interested and attentive comes from how we respond nonverbally. We are going to talk a lot more about nonverbal communication in the chapters to come. For now, it's good to keep in mind that if we are having trouble finding the words, we can help to balance that out with our nonverbal responses. Using things like good eye contact, attentive posture, and appropriate head nodding can let others know we are interested, engaged, and getting them.

The end goal is that we want some overall balance in our exchange. We want to feel and want the other person to feel like we are playing ball as much as they are. We want to make sure that we are catching the ball by listening and giving the other person space to talk. We also want to make sure we are throwing the ball with our responding, and that we are throwing the ball accurately by responding in ways that show we are getting the other person.

Over-responding

While it is important that we don't under-respond in our exchanges with others, there is also something called "too much of a good thing." Responding to others can bring us closer to them. It can show we are engaged and interested, and it can bring energy and life into our social interactions. But too much responding, or *over-responding,* can cause many of the same problems that too little responding can.

Over-responding can give the impression we are not interested and not really getting the other person. It can also make an exchange really boring and result in the other person losing interest. Remember, the best game of catch is when the ball is going back and forth. It's problematic if the other person is always throwing us the ball and we are not returning it, but it can be just as problematic if we are always throwing and never receiving. When we respond too much, there is no room for the other person to have their say. And the game of catch between two people interacting with one another turns into a game of pitch, where one person is throwing the ball at the other person without much mutual exchange.

Over-responding happens when one person is taking up too much of the conversational space in a social interaction. Just as with under-responding, there may be times when one person is talking more than the other person and it may not be a problem, so it's important to assess not only how much each person is throwing the conversational ball, but to also assess if any imbalance is creating problems. There are some good clues to help you assess if over-responding is a problem and should be considered as a prime suspect in a social mystery.

Feedback from the listener often gives us a lot of valuable information about this. Is the person who is listening trying to say something but not able to get the space to speak? Does the listener seem content to listen, or does it seem as if they are just looking for a space in the conversation to say something? Does the listener start to glaze over and lose attention or energy as the speaker continues to talk? Does the listener's body language communicate that they are involved, or do they seem bored or frustrated?

Talking fast is also a sign of over-responding, as is crowding. Crowding is when someone does not allow much space in between things they say as if they don't take a breath in between sentences. This does not allow space for the other person to join in a conversation and is often a big clue that over-responding may be happening. We will talk more about this later as well, but for now, it's helpful to keep this in mind when trying to determine if over-responding is a culprit.

You can also think about the amount of information being offered in an interaction, as well as the content of the information, to help get a sense of the balance in the exchange. For example, it's helpful to assess if we are elaborating on what we say the right amount. As we talked about above with under-responding, elaborating more on what you are saying can often be helpful, but with over-responding, elaborating can often be the problem. There is a balance we want to find with how much we elaborate.

The over-responder elaborates too much, which results in giving too much information. In figuring out if someone is over-responding, we can look to see if they are giving too many details or going off on tangents. To go off on a tangent means to wander off the main topic and drift endlessly onto other things. There may be a connection to the main topic at first, but the person quickly starts rambling about things that are way off track.

Here is an example of going off on a tangent that one of my social detective clients did. Someone asked him if he played Minecraft and this was his response: "Yeah, I love that video game. I like building cities in it. I built this really cool city the other day…."

So far so good right? Reasonable response. But it doesn't stop there. He goes on into rambling tangent land: "I used diamonds to build it. I really love building things. I have a huge collection of model airplanes and rockets I have built. I also love building Star Wars models. I built a huge Death Star last month. Basically, anything Star Wars and I'm all over it. I saw *the Empire Strikes Back* 47 times. I know every line in it. My favorite part is where Han Solo…." His answer turns into a blow by blow account of a good ten minutes of the movie, with scenes being described in great detail and lines the characters said being recited. He probably would have continued to the end of the movie had I not stopped him.

This example is a good description of two things. It's a description of going on a tangent because he started with Minecraft, went on to models, and then ended up on Star Wars movies. There is clear wandering off the main topic here, but the other thing he does is overelaborate.

Too much elaboration with lots of unimportant details can result in what is known in the world of social detecting as *TMI* or *too much information*. TMI can be a huge problem in social interactions. If you want to make sure you bore people and have them lose interest in a conversation, giving *too much information* is a great way to do it.

Basically, TMI is exactly what it says it is. It's when someone gives way too many details in their interactions with others. We have all seen this happen or even done it ourselves. It's rarely done with bad intentions. People don't start by saying "I'm going to talk way too much about something, so I can hog up all the conversational space and annoy other people." They usually over-respond, elaborate too much, and give TMI because they are excited about something. But even though the intention is not bad, the effects of TMI can be very negative.

TMI often goes along with one of the most powerful and treacherous of the over-responding culprits–the *monologue*. Known far and wide as a notorious culprit in social mysteries, the monologue has been responsible for countless bad social interactions. At this very moment, there are probably thousands and thousands of unwanted monologues going on around the world.

A monologue is when someone talks for a very long time without letting anyone else talk. A very long time. Very, very, very long time. Without any room for a breath and no space for anyone else. A monologue is basically a speech at a time when a speech is not appropriate. It is a lecture to those who have no desire to be lectured. It is a relentless game of pitch-the-conversational-ball over and over to someone who was really just expecting a nice back-and-forth game of catch. Now if you are watching a Shakespearian play or an interesting television show or a standup comedian or even a teacher in class, a monologue can be great. Those are times when long speeches might be called for and wanted.

There are other times when monologues might not be wanted, but might be more or less appropriate. At least that's what my dad thinks every time he lectures me about something he thinks is vitally important for me to know right then and in excruciatingly painful detail. But that is a whole other conversation.

The point here is that there are situations in life where one person talks and talks and talks, and the other person just listens, and it is completely appropriate. But that is usually agreed upon in some way by the individuals involved. There is some understanding that one person will be talking a lot and the other will be listening. In these situations, it is clear to all involved that it is not really going to be a conversation.

A monologue is not an interaction in the same way a conversation is. It's one-sided to the extreme. It's not just a little over-responding; it's total domination of the conversational space.

Remedies for Over-responding

Once you identify that over-responding is a suspect, there are many things you can do to shift the conversational balance back to a place where it feels good for all involved. Let's take a look at some tools for over-responding.

1) Questioning the Suspect

Just as in the case with many other prime suspects, *self-awareness* is a powerful tool in keeping over-responding in check. When the police have a prime suspect in an investigation, they usually bring them in for questioning to see if they are the culprit. It's the same for a social detective. We want to bring our prime suspects in for questioning so we can gain more awareness about whether they are the culprit in our social mystery.

Here are some good questions you can ask to gather important facts and clues to see if over-responding is the culprit in a social mystery.

A) How long are the responses?

B) Is the response a good summary of the topic or is it TMI?

C) Is the speaker going off on tangents?

D) Are there lots and lots of details?

E) Is one person talking much more than the other person?

F) Is the speaker giving a monologue?

G) Does the listener seem to be getting bored?

H) Is the speaker talking really fast?

I) Is the listener trying to speak but getting talked over?

J) Is there interrupting going on?

Once there is more awareness of how over-responding is at play, there are things that can be done to find a more balanced amount of responding.

2) Timing Our Responses

Timing responses can be a great way of increasing our awareness to see if over-responding is a culprit. If you have ever watched a debate on TV or at school you might recall that people are allowed a certain amount of time to give their opinion or respond to what someone else has said. They are timed, and when the buzzer goes off, they have to stop talking. In addition to helping increase awareness, this can help people use their talk time wisely, prioritize what is the most important thing to say, and try to say it in the least amount of words possible.

You can time the other person's response and try to match it lengthwise. There might be times when you could do this with an actual stopwatch or by watching a clock on the wall. You obviously want to be careful doing something like that in a conversation, because that could seem strange to others and make them feel you are not interested in what they are saying, and it could interrupt the natural flow of a conversation. But there may be times when you can discreetly do this by glancing at a clock.

Even when there is not a clock in sight to glance at, you can still time by trying to keep track of the passage of time in your mind. When we think about time it can often make us better at accurately assessing how much time has passed, so see if you can notice the passage of time in ways that do not interrupt the flow or distract you too much from what the other person is saying.

3) Identifying the Main Topic

A lot of over-responding happens when people go off on tangents. A great way to make sure we don't go off on tangents is to be able to identify and stick with the main topic. We discussed this at length in Chapter Two, so I won't go over it too much here, other than to say that when you are responding, it's good to remind yourself what the main topic is. Try to stick with only talking about the main topic if you think over-responding might be a culprit.

4) The Art of Summarizing

A summary is a brief statement or account of the main points of something. A good summary avoids needless details and gets right to the heart of the matter. Being skillful at summarizing is a great way to make sure there is not too much information in responses. You can practice the art of summarizing in many different ways.

The most direct and logical way to practice this is in your interactions with others. After someone says something, you can ask yourself what the main point or points were. What was the main topic, and what information did the other person express to let you know what the main topic was? After you ask yourself, "What was the main topic?" you can ask yourself, "What would be a good summary of that topic?"

A good summary will take the keys points the other person said about the main topic and string them together in a way that shows you understand what the main topic was. It will get right to the heart of the matter with as few words as possible.

You can often give a summary about something someone says, even if the other person goes off on tangents and gives TMI. For example, you could summarize the tangent ramble my client gave when asked if he likes Minecraft like this: "Building diamond cities sounds cool. And building a Death Star is awesome. You really must like Star Wars if you watched it 47 times."

This is a straight-to-the-main-points account of what the other person said. If my client had given this kind of to-the-point response, it still would have been a tangent because he switched to talking about Star Wars. But it would not have been TMI. And a little tangent without TMI makes the tangent much less annoying.

There are some other good ways to practice summarizing. If you watch a movie or a television show, you can try to summarize the main points after it's over. How would you clearly describe the show to someone else who has not seen it, in as few words as possible? What were the main points in the show? What happened in the beginning, middle, and end? What general feeling did the characters in the show have? You can ask yourself questions like this and see if you can answer them in a clear way that uses as few words as possible.

You can do the same thing about something you learned in class. In your mind, or with someone else, see if you can give a short summary that describes what you learned in class that day. Not only will that help you practice the art of summarizing, but it will also help you keep what you were taught in your brain, so when it's time for the test you won't have to study as hard.

You can even practice the art of summarizing when your parents give you a lecture. If your parents are anything like mine, this may be a challenge. While I respect my parents and know that they often have a lot of wisdom to offer, they also are world-class champions at rambling, tangents, and TMI, not to mention being expert monologuers.

If your parents are anything like mine, there may be lots and lots of "main points" to summarize. And there may be lots of extra details and way too much information surrounding those main points, so it might be more of a challenge to find those main points amid all the monologuing lecture debris. But if you can find and summarize the main points in an epic parent lecture you will be sharpening your summarizing skills. You will also get loads of extra brownie points with your parents by summarizing what they said back to them because just like all of us, parents like to feel that they are being paid attention to and understood. A good summary is an excellent way to do it.

Even if we are not talking to other people, we can always practice summarizing in our heads. Just as we can summarize what we learned in class or saw on television in our head, we can also summarize other things just for practice. We can summarize what we did over the weekend, what we did when we got together with friends, what our favorite video games are about, and what we like and don't like about classes in school. The things we can summarize are endless. And the more we practice the art of summarizing, the better an artist we become. So, a good detective always encourages their clients to practice the art of summarizing.

5) Putting on the Brakes

Even when we are aware that we are taking too long, we know what the main topic is, and are skilled at the art of summarizing, we may still have trouble stopping ourselves from over-responding. Sometimes people get so excited about something that it's almost painful for them to not say everything they want to about it. It's like we talked about earlier when we discussed how our impulse to do something can be so strong that it can override what our mind knows would be the best choice. If we are excited about something, we want to scratch the itch by saying as much as we can about the thing that we are excited about. But if we scratch without letting the mind have its say and help us find a balance in how much we respond, we may get caught up in over-responding.

When the impulse to over-respond gets the best of us, we can use some of the strategies we talked about earlier, about resisting the itch to talk off-topic. Some things that can help are: a) using our mind to think through things, b) having mantras, c) harnessing the power of the pause and, d) getting to know our body better with tools like the body scan. Take a look back to the section on *resisting the itch to talk off-topic* to refresh yourself with these tools and see if you can find ways to use them when you or your potential client are having trouble resisting the impulse to over-respond.

SOCIAL MYSTERY 4

Time: Friday 8:18 PM, just after the Homecoming football game

Place: Dale's Pizza and Sub Shop

Sari saw Tommy bounce through the front door of Dale's Pizza and Sub Shop and strut over to the table where she was sitting. She could tell by the look on his face and the way he was moving his body that he was on top of the world. "Hey Sari!" he said to her as he approached the table. She got up to hug him and he literally picked her up and spun her around in a circle. "Hey, Tommy! Congratulations!" Sari said.

Tommy was the quarterback for their school football team, the Chipmunks. The Chipmunks had just won the homecoming game against their longtime rivals, the Hawks. Sari and Tommy's group of friends were meeting at Dale's to eat and celebrate their victory. Nothing expresses a high school sports victory more than pizza and sugary carbonated beverages.

"That was such a close game!" Tommy said as he sat down across from Sari. "And did you see the size of that defensive lineman on the Hawks? He had to be a ringer. He looked like he was 20 years old. He was either held back more than once or has a serious case of gigantism. He looked like he could be in the NFL. I thought he was gonna kill me!" "Uh-huh," Sari said without much enthusiasm. She loved going to the school football games and loved supporting Tommy and her other friends when they played. But as for the game, she could take it or leave it. She didn't even know all the rules. "That guy just knocked over our offensive linemen like they were bowling pins." "Uh-huh," Sari said in a somewhat flat voice. She really did not get what he was talking about. She often felt that way when conversations were about the specifics of sports. But she did not want Tommy to see how much she did not know about the game so she just listened. She planned on just waiting it out until he was done talking about the game so they could move onto topics that were more interesting to her.

"Did you see that Hail Mary?" he asked her. When he asked this, Sari froze for a minute. She had no idea what he was talking about. The weather out was pretty nice. There was no hail or snow. In fact, there was not a cloud in the sky. And she searched her memory for anyone named Mary who might have been at the game that day, but couldn't think of anyone she knew. She just stared at him as the pause in their conversation got longer and more awkward.

But this did not stop Tommy. It seemed to almost fuel his intensity and he talked even faster and louder. And while he seemed enthusiastic his face started looking tenser and tenser. Tommy went on to repeat what he said about the Hail Mary play two more times. And Sari said "Yeah" again both times. Then Tommy jumped to talking about the Superbowl last year and how the game was so close and about the statistics of the players. Sari was getting more and more lost and the more lost she got the faster Tommy seemed to talk and the tenser his face looked. And the more details he gave about NFL players statistics.

Finally, Tommy stopped talking and took a deep breath. "Anyway," he said. "Yeah, that's cool," Sari said in an effort to try and respond to the flood of sports statistics he had just thrown at her. Tommy's enthusiasm had disappeared, and he looked at Sari seemingly not knowing what to say. "Yeah, cool," he said. The two sat there staring awkwardly at each other, neither seeming to know what to say next.

Eventually, some other friends came and sat down with them at the table. Even though Sari was looking forward to hanging out with Tommy and was hoping they would have some time alone before the others came, she felt relieved that the others had arrived. The group conversation went back to the Chipmunks victory that night. They all talked about the giant ringer linebacker and about the deep pass to Stan with ten seconds left on the clock. The others at the table seemed as enthusiastic as Tommy was, and they seemed to understand what he was talking about, adding in other details about the game.

Sari noticed that Tommy also seemed to relax as the conversation went on. He talked slower and not as loud. And the tension she had noticed in his face faded. After a little while, the conversation naturally shifted to what everyone was going to do over winter break. This was also a relief for Sari because that was something she could talk about. She joined in the conversation and felt comfortable again, and she could tell that Tommy was much more relaxed as well. But she still did not feel great.

Something had gone wrong between her and Tommy. They were usually very comfortable with each other, but she could tell he had not been comfortable in their conversation, and she hadn't been, either. In fact, as their conversation together went on, she got more and more uncomfortable. She knew Tommy was going to walk her home that night but was worried about the awkwardness between them because she did not understand what had happened. This clearly was a social mystery for her. But she was a long-time student of Johnny's and knew that if she used her social detective skills, she could figure out what had gone wrong and how to remedy the problem. So, like all good social detectives, she started with the facts.

The facts

- Sari and Tommy are good friends.
- The two are usually very comfortable talking with each other.
- That evening at Dale's their conversation was very uncomfortable.
- Tommy was very excited about the big Homecoming game win.
- Sari did not understand a lot of what Tommy was saying.
- Sari did not want Tommy to know she did not understand all the football terms.
- The conversation became increasingly uncomfortable.
- Tommy kept talking about the same plays he made, over and over.
- Tommy was talking loud and fast.
- Sari felt relieved when their other friends came over.
- Eventually, the conversation changed to something she was more interested in, at which point she felt more relaxed.

Solving the case

Sari thought it would be a good idea to go through some prime suspects to see if any of them might be culprits in this case. Since attention is the basic building block of good social exchanges, she thought she would start there. "How was my attention?" she asked herself. Even though she hadn't understood a lot of what Tommy was saying, she felt pretty confident she had been paying attention. Next, she asked herself if she was topic missing. "I didn't change the subject when we were talking, even though I wish I could have. I was trying to stay on the topic of the game because I knew it was important to Tommy and I wanted to be a good friend and celebrate the win with him." Next, she asked herself about mood missing. "Hmmm," she thought. "Maybe. I know I was not as enthusiastic as Tommy was, but I could tell he was excited. I didn't miss that, but I guess I wasn't as excited as he was. Maybe I didn't match his mood very well. I don't think that was the main culprit though." She had a feeling that the problem might have had something to do with the way the conversation was going, so she thought about some of the verbal responding prime suspects that Johnny had taught her about. As she started thinking about the verbal responding culprits, she had a hunch. Excited to see if her hunch was correct, she asked herself the following questions:

- Did it ever seem like Tommy was not responding back to me right away? Were there awkward pauses?
- Was Tommy repeating himself?
- Did Tommy start under-responding or talking less?
- Was the conversational ball being tossed back and forth in a balanced way? Was I talking as much as Tommy?

Sari recalled that there were several times where she did respond to what Tommy had said and that after she did there was a long pause that felt very awkward and uncomfortable to her. She also remembered that Tommy kept repeating himself and that towards the end of the conversation he pretty much stopped taking. "In thinking about it, it was not a balanced conversation," she thought to herself. "In the beginning, he was talking a lot and I barely responded. He talked in long sentences, even paragraphs, and I gave one or two-word responses. I just did not know what to say," she thought.

Sari remembered how Johnny told her that sometimes when someone is under-responding in a conversation, the other person ends up trying to fill up more space in the conversation to deal with the lack of balance in the verbal exchange. She also remembered that when we are having verbal exchanges with people who are under-responding, we can sometimes repeat ourselves because we don't feel like that other person got us. "Well, Tommy certainly was repeating himself. That could be the reason," she told herself.

In asking herself these questions and thinking over her conversation with Tommy, it became clear to Sari that she was under-responding. "That explains it!" she thought to herself. She also realized that her under-responding also may have resulted in not responding appropriately to Tommy's mood. She was excited the Chipmunks won and was happy Tommy played so well and that he was so pleased about the game. But her short responses probably gave him the impression that she was not happy about the game in the same way that he was. Once Sari was able to see what had been happening, she felt confident that she could come up with some social remedies to help keep this from happening again.

Key Culprit in the Mystery:

Prime suspect # 6: Under-responding

Time: Friday night, 9:30 pm

Place: Walking home from Dale's Pizza and Sub Shop

Sari and Tommy lived on the same street, so they often walked home together from school and get-togethers with friends. After the two of them had their fill of pizza, soda, and socializing with friends, they started their journey home together. "Hey, Tommy, I wanted to say something." "I wanted to say something too," Tommy said back. "Tommy, I just wanted to say that I'm sorry if I was a little quiet earlier when you were talking about the game." Tommy stopped and turned to look at her. "Yeah?" he said. "Well, you were talking about all these plays you made in the game, and about the different players' positions of players. And actually..." She stumbled on her words a little. "Well...Uh...You know...Actually, I don't know a whole lot about football...." she said, looking down and blushing a little.

"I didn't realize you didn't know that much about football. You played it off well," Tommy replied, smiling. "Yeah," she replied. "I didn't know how to respond, so I just didn't say much." Tommy smiled. He said, "That makes sense. I think I assumed you knew more about it, but I shouldn't have assumed that." "I should have told you," she said. "I just didn't want you to think I wasn't interested, because I am. Well... mostly I'm interested in being there and watching you and the others play. And I love the cheerleading too. I really enjoy going to the games and having us all there. I just don't get football that much." "That's ok!" Tommy said. "Maybe you can explain the game a little more to me. Like who is Mary and why were you talking about hail when there was not even a cloud in the sky?" Tommy let out a big laugh. "It's really not that complicated," he said.

"Do you want me to explain it a little now?" Tommy asked. "Yeah, that would be great!" Sari said. On their walk home, Tommy explained what a Hail Mary was and what the different positions did, like offensive and defensive linemen, wide receiver, and quarterback. Sari asked questions and reflected back to Tommy some of the things he was saying to show him she was with him and also to make sure she was getting it right. After a little while, there was a pause. And that seemed like a good time for Tommy to share with Sari what he wanted to tell her. They continued to talk on their way home. Sari felt really good about telling Tommy what was going on with her. It helped her to be more engaged in the conversation. And she felt like it brought them closer together as friends.

Main Ideas Chapter 4

1) What is talking off-topic? P - 39
2) What's the difference between a huge miss and a small miss? P - 39
3) What are some reasons someone might not respond to the main topic? P - 39
4) What are some social remedies for resisting the itch to talk off-topic? P - 40
5) What is a mantra and how can it help us? P - 41
6) What are some things you can do to remember to use your mantra? P - 41
7) What is the power of the pause? P - 40
8) What is the body scan? P - 42
9) What are some ways to deal with the fear of forgetting? P - 43
10) What is not responding to mood? P - 44
11) What is social equity? P - 44
12) What are some of the secondary suspects that can get in the way of responding to mood? P - 45
13) When responding to mood, what is the difference between trying to fix it and trying to feel it? P - 46
14) What are some techniques for effectively responding to mood? P - 46
15) When it comes to empathizing with others, what does it mean to approximate? P - 48
16) What is under-responding? P - 52
17) What is over-responding? P - 52
18) What is the repeater effect? P - 52
19) What are some remedies for under-responding? P - 53
20) What is TMI? P - 54
21) What is a monologue? P - 56

Chapter 5: Verbal Dancing

There is another group of suspects that also involve things that happen in our verbal exchanges with others. I call these the verbal-dancing suspects. When we discussed verbal listening and responding, we were talking about the *content* of a conversation. The content of a conversation has to do with the actual information we exchange with others.

Verbal dancing is all about *the way* we exchange information, rather than with the actual content or with the verbal information we exchange with others. It's about how we communicate, which is often referred to as the *process* of communication. The process we use to exchange information with others is kind of like a dance.

Good dance partners take turns following and leading. They respond to each other so that their movements flow smoothly and gracefully together. To dance well as a team, the partners need to be tuned in to one another. They need to be aware of the speed and rhythm and movements of one another. A good dance involves an exchange. It involves collaboration and an intention to work together towards a common goal.

Good conversations are the same. The people talking need to speak about the same topic and have a similar speed, rhythm, and feel in their responses to one another. They need to work together to make adjustments in the conversation, so they can flow gracefully across the conversational dance floor.

When this does not happen, conversations are awkward and uncomfortable and often leave one or both people dissatisfied. Because of this, learning to dance well in conversations is a very important skill. A good detective will look for clues to see if a problem with verbal dancing is a culprit in a social mystery. So, let's take a look at some of the prime verbal dancing suspects, shall we?

PRIME SUSPECT #8:

FAST TALK

The first of our verbal dancing suspects is *fast talk*. When people are in a rush to get somewhere, they often drive faster than they are supposed to. This can happen in conversations as well. Sometimes we want to get to a point in a conversation or get in all of what we have to say before the other person stops listening. And sometimes we just might be super excited about something, and the excitement makes us race really fast as we talk.

The result is that this can make us speed in our conversations with others. Conversational speeding can be problematic for many reasons. First, just as driving too fast in a car can make you miss the signs along the side of the road, talking too fast can result in missing important signs from the other person in the conversation. If we are talking too fast, we might not be able to read the cues the other person is giving off, and we may miss important feedback from the other person. As we talked about above, not reading the feedback from our dance partner usually results in an awkward dance where the dance partners are not moving in sync with one another.

Talking too fast can also make the other person feel uncomfortable and nervous. It can also interfere with the other person's ability to take in and think about what it is we are saying. Thinking deeply about what another person is saying requires time. The more time we have, the more we can think and feel about what is being said, but if the conversation is whizzing by at lightning speed, there is no time to think deeply about what is being said, because the conversation moves onto something else.

What ends up happening is that the listener spends all their mental energy trying to keep up with the rush of the conversation, rather than spending their energy thinking about and appreciating what is being said. That does not make for good conversation.

Verbal speeding can also increase the chance for prime suspect #9: *Verbal Crowding* to show itself. Let's take a look at that suspect next.

PRIME SUSPECT #9:

VERBAL CROWDING

Have you ever been in a busy place with lots of people all around, and it feels like you're going to suffocate? Like there is no room to breathe or move freely? One of the ways we often describe a place with lots of people or the feeling of no space is to say that the place is crowded, or that we are feeling crowded. Conversations can get crowded too. This happens when the conversational space is too full, and it feels like there is no room for us. It can feel as if we are being suffocated by an endless stream of words.

There are a few different things that can create crowding in our verbal dancing. As we mentioned above, fast talk and verbal crowding often go together. When we talk fast, there is less space between words and ideas. There is less space to think or feel. If we are the listener, it can feel as if there is less space for us to participate in the interaction, which can make us feel crowded out of the conversation.

Fast talking is not the only reason people might feel crowded. Not having pauses between sentences or ideas can also create crowding. Even if someone isn't talking particularly fast, not pausing can make a conversation feel very crowded.

We often wait to talk until we sense two things. The first is that the other person is done with the idea they are communicating. When someone is over-responding, it can be hard to determine when they are done with an idea. An over-responder often keeps going and going, giving more and more detail. Because of that, they may not actually be done with their "idea" until next week. But when there is a balance in responding, we can get a good sense of when someone is done with an idea and it is an appropriate time for us to respond.

The second thing we often wait for before responding is a pause. In well-danced conversations, people pause after an idea has been presented. This allows a few important things to happen. First, it gives the opportunity to really think and feel into what the other person just said. Second, it allows the other person to join in the dance and respond to what was communicated. Remember, good verbal dances involve leading and following, just as a good game of catch involves throwing and catching the ball. But if there is not a pause, the conversation becomes crowded. Not only is there no room to think and feel into what was said, but there is also no space for the other person to participate in the verbal dance.

Crowding can lead to several different outcomes. It can make someone feel overwhelmed and suffocated, and they may deal with this by removing themselves from the conversation in order to get space. I call this *checking out*. Checking out may be subtle and take the form of not talking or paying attention to what the other person is saying. The person feeling crowded may drift off into other thoughts and not really be present. They may go into their own inside space. They may think about other things, in order to create mental space in a situation that feels too crowded for them. Checking out can also be more obvious. The other person may physically leave to get space. Or they may choose not to get together in the future as a way of gaining space.

Another response to crowding is to *claim space* by moving forward instead of away. Instead of checking out, the other person may push forward into the conversation more aggressively, to claim conversational space. This is the equivalent of putting your elbows out and physically pushing others away in a crowd to make some personal space.

In a conversation, this often takes the form of interrupting. If someone is crowding us, and we choose to deal with it by claiming space rather than checking out, we might try to cut the other person off and start talking ourselves. We won't wait for a pause or the end of an idea. We will just jump in and elbow our way into the conversation. We might also try to make space by talking faster and louder, in order to claim our territory in the conversation. Just as a monologue is the extreme form of TMI, interrupting is the extreme form of verbal crowding.

As you might imagine, these strategies to claim space often make things worse. It's possible that if someone responds to crowding by crowding back, the first person will take the feedback and slow down. They might realize that the other person needs some space to talk, and they will give it to them. But usually, that's not what happens. Usually, the first person starts to crowd even more. They respond to the interrupting by interrupting back. They respond to the faster, louder talking by talking faster and louder themselves.

When this happens, the dance that could have been a beautiful, cooperative conversation becomes a sumo wrestling match, in which each person is trying to push the other person out of the ring. And this is no fun for anyone. The point here is that when not handled well, crowding can result in more crowding and turn something potentially wonderful into something that is no fun for anyone involved. It would be worthwhile for us as social detectives to be able to recognize some of the signs of crowding and have some strategies for putting these culprits in their place and keeping them from turning a good social dance into a wrestling match.

Remedies for Fast Talking and Crowding
1) Being Aware

As is often the case, self-awareness is a great place to start when coming up with social remedies. So how do we become more aware of fast-talking and crowding? When we are driving a car, we can look at our speedometer to tell us how fast we are going. Of course, there is no such thing as a "speakdometer" that tells us our Words Per Minute (WPM) the way our speedometer can tell us our Miles Per Hour (MPH). We need to develop our senses so we can notice our WPM ourselves.

When we are in a car, we have ways of determining our speed other than the speedometer. We can look at how fast things seem to be moving outside the car. We can feel the pull on our bodies as the car accelerates, which lets us know our speed is increasing. We might even get a sense of our speed by the way the car rattles and shakes as it goes faster. And we might notice how the sounds around us change as we are driving faster. These kinds of things can help us get a sense of our speed without using the speedometer.

Tuning into our senses can help us become more aware of our WPM in a similar way. Asking yourself the simple question of "How fast am I talking?" can be a powerful tool. When we ask this question, we tune into our talking speed. People often are quite capable of sensing when they are talking fast, but they just don't think about it. This simple question can help us think about it.

We can also try to compare our talking speed to others. When people are driving, they get clues that they are driving too fast by noticing that their car is whizzing by all the other cars on the road. They compare their speed with the speed of others. We can do the same thing in conversations, and it can help us to be more aware of our WPM.

We can also listen to our own voice as we are speaking to get a sense of whether we are talking fast. When we are driving faster, our ears can hear that the engine of our car is going faster, the wheels are moving faster on the road, and the wind is sounding different. Our ears can also help us sense when we are talking faster if we listen carefully to ourselves.

We can also tune in to our bodies to get a sense of our talking speed. Just as a car rattles and shakes a little as we drive faster, our bodies have a certain feeling when we are going fast. If you pay attention to how your body feels when you are talking slow, compared to when you are talking fast, you can develop a better sense of what it feels like when you are going fast. It can help you be more aware of your WPM.

Once we notice we are talking fast, we can do things to slow down, like taking our foot off the gas pedal and putting it on the brakes. We can deliberately try to speak extra slow as a way of decelerating. We can also try to add pauses in the conversations. Not only do pauses in our verbal dancing help us slow down, but they also create space.

2) The Power of the Pause

Intentional pauses can be powerful things. When we don't pause, and instead rush to speak, it can give the message that we are not really thinking about what the other person said. It can give the impression that we are more interested in our response than in what they were sharing with us. It can also keep us from enjoying the exchange of information going on in our conversation.

It's kind of like what happens when we eat too fast. Have you ever eaten something you really like? You might love it so much and be so excited about it that you gulp it down and eat too fast. When we do that, we often don't enjoy the flavor of what we are eating, and before we know it, it's all gone. We did not really get to experience it, because we were rushing to get the next bite. Conversations can be similar. When we talk too fast or crowd, there is no room for us or the other people in the conversation to enjoy the flavor of what is being said. We don't have time to savor the words, and the conversation rushes by without it being fully appreciated.

We can increase our ability to use pauses by *reminding ourselves to pause* when we are verbally dancing with others. We can remind ourselves to enjoy the flavor of what the other person is saying as if we would enjoy something tasty we are eating. A *mantra* is a great way of reminding ourselves to pause. Using the word "pause" as a simple mantra you repeat to yourself can help you remember to pause more.

We can also practice *looking for pauses* when we hear others speak. Noticing pauses in others' speech helps us be more aware of the role pauses play in good verbal dancing. Notice when friends pause when talking to you, and be aware of how it feels, compared to when they don't pause. You can notice when a teacher or your parents pause, or when actors in a movie or television show pause. Looking for pauses like this makes it easier to keep the power of pausing in mind in our verbal dances.

Another great tool for helping us pause and slow down and create space is *taking a deep breath*. It's hard to talk when taking a deep breath, so intentional deep breathing can force us to pause. Deep breaths also relax us and are known for their ability to help us slow down and calm our whole body. Being more relaxed and calm naturally leads to slower talking.

3) Taking Time to Think

In addition to pausing, something that can help us talk slower is *taking time to think* before we say something. Thinking about what we want to say has many benefits. It creates a natural pause. When we are thinking about what we are saying, we naturally talk slower. It also helps us say things in a clearer and more organized way and can even help us say more meaningful things.

As we discussed in Chapter Three, thinking before we speak can help us in many ways when we are listening and responding. Things like topic missing or mood missing are much less likely to happen when we take the time to think.

One thing that can help make sure we have time to think is to try and *summarize* the other person's main points in our head before we respond. We can also try to decide how we would like to respond before we start talking. When we are excited about the content of a conversation, we often jump in and start talking without really knowing what it is we want to say. This often leads to a jumbled response that is not really clear or to the point, which can result in things like topic missing or TMI.

Trying to think about what we want to say before we actually say it not only helps us organize our thoughts so we can speak more clearly and meaningfully but also conveys to the other person that what they said is important enough for us to take the time to consider before we respond.

4) Minimizing Interrupting

Finding ways to *minimize interrupting* also helps decrease fast talking and extreme crowding. Making a conscious effort to wait to speak until the other person is done talking and expressing their point is a great way to decrease interrupting. Here again, a *mantra* can really help. The mantra can be as simple as "Are they done?" You can repeat this a few times in your mind while the other person is talking.

If they take a breath or give a slight pause, and you feel the impulse to jump in, you can repeat the mantra, "Are they done?" Are they done with the idea they are trying to communicate? Is the slight pause an indication of being done, or is it just a need for some oxygen? Or are they perhaps trying to take a moment to think about what it is they are trying to say, so they can communicate better with you? The mantra, "Are they done?" can be a great way to remember to notice if it's the right time to speak.

As we discussed, interrupting can be contagious. Even if you are doing things to minimize your interrupting, the other person might keep doing it. It's much more difficult not to interrupt when someone else is crowding, interrupting, or talking too fast. A good social detective has some tools to help them address this kind of suspect.

5) Talking About the Talk

A great way to work with your verbal dancing partner to decrease things like interrupting is to have a conversation about the way you are talking together. I call this *talking about the talk.*

When we talk, we are usually discussing a topic and sharing ideas about that topic. As we discussed above, the ideas we share around a topic make up the content of a conversation, and the way we discuss the content makes up the process. So, we have the content of a conversation, which is what we say, and the process, which is how we say it. A good discussion about how we are talking can be a great way to get better at verbal dancing with our verbal dancing partners.

When two people dance together, they have certain moves and tricks they might be doing on the dance floor. But just as important as the moves are the way the two dancers move together. Do their rhythms match?

Are they in sync with one another? Do they flow nicely and respect each other's space, or are they bumping into each other and stepping on each other's toes? These things can be much more important than the actual dance moves they are doing.

This is the same for conversations. What makes a conversation good often has more to do with the way we verbally dance with each other than what we are talking about. Having a conversation about the process, by talking about the way we are talking, can be very helpful when we notice we are stepping on each other's toes in the verbal exchange.

You can point out in a nice, friendly way that you notice the conversation is going really fast. You can point out that you notice you are both talking over each other and that there does not seem to be much conversational space. Make sure to do this in a nice way so you don't come across as blaming or criticizing the other person. People hear what we are saying much better when they are not feeling blamed or criticized, so you want to make sure to express your observations about the process in a nice, friendly, non-blaming way.

Once you share your observation, you can ask the other person if they notice those things as well, then you can make some suggestions for how you can dance better together in your conversation. You can also ask them if they have any suggestions. You can share some of the things you try to do to make more space in conversation and suggest you do it together.

For example, you can say to the other person, "Why don't we both try to slow down together?" That's a nice, non-blaming way to offer a suggestion. You can also introduce some of the things we talked about above, like taking breaths, talking slower, and pausing more.

If these things seem to be helping create a better verbal dance, you can point out the nicer, slower way you are communicating, and you can let the other person know it feels good to you when you slow down.

Another thing you can do to help slow things down is to say to the other person, "Let me think about what you just said for a minute." As we discussed, thinking about what the other person says helps our verbal dancing in many ways, but when we tell the other person we are thinking about what they are saying, it can help our dance even more.

Letting the other person know we are thinking about what they said lets them know that what they say is important to us. It lets them know that we are taking them seriously, which usually feels really good to people. The other thing this does is communicate to the other person that you need a little space in the conversation. It invites the other person to join you in a pause so you can think. This can be a great way to slow things down with someone without directly asking them to slow down.

6) One Thing Leads to Another

You can probably see how the things we are talking about here are interrelated. Slowing down our talking creates more space and less crowding. More space allows for deeper conversations, and deeper conversations are often associated with slower talking. Deep breathing helps us pause. Pausing makes room for deep breathing, which helps us slow down and relax. And when we are relaxed, we naturally talk slower and think more about what it is we are saying, rather than rushing. All these things dance together, and when we practice one, the others become easier, and our verbal dance becomes much more beautiful and rewarding.

PRIME SUSPECT #10:

TROUBLE MANAGING THE AWKWARD SILENCE

One of the things that makes many people anxious in social situations is the dreaded awkward silence. Have you ever been sitting with someone, and both of you are just staring at each other? Maybe there is a little embarrassed smile or a nervous laugh. Or maybe you just get up and make some excuse and run away, because you have no idea what to say or do. This may or may not be something you are familiar with, but it's something that many people deal with every day. The dreaded *awkward silence*. And that's why *trouble managing the awkward silence* is on the list of most-wanted prime suspects in the world of social detecting.

How do we start up a conversation when we are smack dab in the middle of an awkward silence? What do we do to get things going? How do we know when, how, and what to say when we are just sitting there staring blankly at the other person? This is a mystery I often see with my clients. The good news is that there are some simple, straightforward things you can do to overcome the dreaded awkward silences.

The first thing to do is to be clear on the difference between awkward silence and regular silence. The truth is, sometimes silence is not such a bad thing. There are even times when we are with other people that silence is a nice thing, such as when we know someone really well. When we know someone well, we are often more comfortable if there are periods of silence. If we are doing something together like watching a movie or chomping on burgers or studying for a test, silence is often nice rather than awkward.

But there are other times when conversation seems like the right thing to be happening in a situation, and we just sit uncomfortably in the middle of what can seem like endless silence. When investigating this common prime suspect there are some good questions we can ask. What makes these kinds of silences so awkward? Is an awkward silence really a problem, and if so, why? What things might make it hard to have a nice verbal dance? And what are some remedies for managing awkward silences?

What makes silences awkward?

There are many reasons we might feel awkward when there is silence. One reason has to do with the tendency of people to feel it's completely their responsibility to fill all the space in a conversation. They think that if there is silence, they must be doing something wrong. They may also take the other person's silence as a sign that they are not interested in them.

Silence can also make space for us to think and feel. As we discussed above, space can often be a great thing. It can help us think more about what we want to say and to be more aware of what we are feeling in the conversation. But if we are feeling nervous to begin with, more space to think and feel can lead us to notice any nervousness we might have had to begin with.

Often when we are with people with whom we feel comfortable, silence does not make us nervous in the same way it might with people with whom we don't feel as comfortable. When we are comfortable with people, the space that comes with the silence might make us more aware of the comfort we feel with the other person. But if we are uncomfortable with people, the space can make us more aware of some of the uncomfortable feelings we might already have with the other person. When we are already not comfortable with someone, the space that comes from silence can amplify the awkwardness we might already feel.

What might make an awkward silence a problem?

The truth is, awkward silences are very common, and they are often not as big a problem as we might think they are. Even though an awkward silence can seem as if it is going on forever, it usually passes, and we fill the silence. Over time, as we get more and more comfortable with other people, the natural silences that happen don't seem as awkward.

Silences are a normal part of our verbal dancing with other people. They can actually help give us the opportunity we need to have less crowding and more space. We usually don't even notice silences when we are comfortable with people. They just happen for a little bit, and then we fill them naturally. It's only when they are awkward that we notice them.

There are times that awkward silences can lead to problems, though. Usually, the problems are not about the silence itself, as much as about the awkwardness we feel as we deal with it. Feeling awkward can make us nervous. And sometimes when we are nervous, we might act in ways that can affect how we respond and verbally dance with other people.

Sometimes when people are nervous, they start asking questions that don't fit, and it can make things more awkward. If someone asks questions that are missing the topic or the mood or are not asked in the best way, it can increase the awkwardness. This might also result in the other person not responding well because they don't know how to respond, which can also make things more awkward. Below are some examples of the problematic ways in which we might respond to awkward silences.

1) Going on a tangent: If you just talked about a test you took in school with a friend in your class, and you rush to fill the silence by asking the person if they have any brothers or sisters, it might feel like a tangent to the other person. Remember, a tangent is when you wander off the main topic and drift onto other things.

2) Mood missing: If someone just told you they felt bad about doing poorly on a test, and you rush to fill the silence by telling a joke, you would be missing the mood of the other person.

3) Interrogation: If you try to fill the awkward silence by asking rapid-fire questions, it can make the other person feel interrogated. When we barrage people with a series of questions, one right after the other, it can often feel stressful, even if the questions have no bad intent, e.g., if we ask, "How old are you? Where were you born? What's your favorite color? Do you like pizza? Do you have any brothers or sisters?"

This kind of rapid-fire barrage of questions can feel very overwhelming. First, it jumps from one topic to another unrelated topic, which can make a conversation feel chaotic, because there is no real topic that is being followed. Second, having to answer question after question so quickly, without any breaks or pauses in between, can feel very intense and can make the other person feel put on the spot and pressured to perform.

4) Giving too much information (TMI) and Monologuing: When you try to fill an awkward silence by talking about something and giving too many details, and you fill the space with lots of information instead of trying to get the other person to verbally dance with you, it can quickly lead to *too much information* (TMI). Eventually, it can even result in a monologue.

TMI and monologues often have the opposite effect of what we want when we experience an awkward silence. When we feel awkward in a period of silence, what we often want is more of an exchange. It's not just that we want to fill the silence. It's that we want to feel the other person engaging with us. When we feel the other person dancing verbally with us, and playing catch back and forth with the conversational ball, it makes us feel more comfortable with them. It makes us feel they are interested in us, and that we can exchange information back and forth together in a comfortable way.

While TMI or a monologue does fill the space, it does nothing to show real interest in the other person, and it does not reassure the other person that we are good verbal dancing partners together. Remember, good verbal dancing involves give and take. It involves a back and forth in the conversation, which is not at all what happens when there is TMI. TMI can have the opposite effect we are looking for and can lead the other person to pull back even more. While the silence might get filled this way, the awkwardness usually increases instead of decreases.

5) **The Run Away:** Another very common problematic response to awkward silences is what I like to call *the run away*. Sometimes the discomfort that comes from an awkward silence can be so great that the person just gets up and leaves. Yup. It's true. I can't tell you how many times I've seen this happen. Usually, the runner makes up some kind of excuse for running away. Of course, this often leaves the other person feeling bad.

The other person might think the person leaving is rude, or they might even think they did something wrong. As you can imagine, this makes future interactions more uncomfortable for the person being left behind. And the person leaving usually feels bad, too. They might feel like they failed, which usually increases their discomfort in future interactions with that person. The run-away is what I call *a lose-lose* situation. Everyone involved loses. The person leaving, as well as the person being left behind, is usually worse off. Both people lose.

But please, if this has ever happened to you, do not despair. As is true with most of the prime suspects we have talked about, you can come back from a run away. Think of it as a minor setback that can easily be fixed with the right tools. We will talk about how to come back from a run away in a bit, but for now, just know it does not mean everything is lost.

6) **The Check-Out:** There are less blatant ways that someone might run away when feeling uncomfortable with an awkward silence. Sometimes people run away to their phone or a book or computer. They may stay in the same room as the other person but run away into some other activity as a way to try and manage the uncomfortable feelings. I call this more subtle kind of running away *the check-out* because while the person is not actually running away, they are still removing themselves from the verbal dance. This is not as bad as actually leaving the room, but it can still have negative effects on both people.

7) **Coming Across as Annoyed or Disinterested:** Another thing that can happen when faced with awkward silence is that we can act in ways that give the other person the impression we are annoyed or not interested in them. Even if someone is not annoyed or disinterested, the awkwardness that can come from unwanted silences can give others that impression. Things like body language and voice tone change a lot when we are nervous and can often be misinterpreted by others. I often see people feeling nervous and showing it nonverbally, in ways that others might easily take the wrong way.

It is good to be aware of what we are communicating nonverbally when we feel uncomfortable. We will talk more about this in the next few chapters when we talk about nonverbal listening and responding. But for now, just know that these kinds of things can affect how comfortable people are when there is difficulty having a nice verbal dance.

Things That Can Make it Hard to Have a Nice Verbal Dance

We talked about what can make some silences awkward, and we talked about how the way we might deal with those awkward silences can create problems. This is all good stuff, and we are going to talk more about how to manage the awkwardness in a bit. But the other important question we want to be asking is, why is there silence to begin with?

What makes it so hard to have a nice verbal dance with people? Why is it that sometimes when we want to have a nice conversation with someone, we can't think of anything to say? Or why do our attempts to throw the conversational ball to the other person sometimes fail to lead to a comfortable back and forth exchange?

Using our detective skills can help us to answer these kinds of questions and get to the root of the social mysteries surrounding this prime suspect of trouble managing the awkward silence.

So why? Why, why, why? Why is it sometimes so hard to get a good verbal dance going? Let's explore a few common reasons:

1) **Feeling uncomfortable:** Sometimes it boils down to the simple straightforward problem of "I don't know what to say." There are lots of reasons we might not know what to say when face to face with someone we would like to have a verbal dance with.

Maybe our mind goes blank out of fear. It happens. It's happened to me countless times. With me, it's usually with girls. While I can often think of lots of things to say, and I am pretty good at starting up conversations, girls often seem to turn my brain into jelly. Girls can make me completely forget how to speak, leaving me to rely on primitive guttural utterances like "Uhhh" or "Mmmm" and sometimes even "Duh." Not the best conversation starters.

But the point here is that feeling uncomfortable can make it hard to think, which can make it difficult for us to come up with something to say. And when we can't think of anything to say, there might be even more awkward silence, which can make us more nervous and make it even harder to think about what to say.

2) **Trouble with spontaneous conversations:** Other things can make us go blank and not know what to say. It's not always because we are uncomfortable. Maybe we just are not good at spontaneous conversation. Some people are good at following conversations and adding to them once they are going, but have a lot of trouble starting them. Once there is a topic, all sorts of thoughts might come up in their mind, but they just can't seem to come up with a topic at all.

3) **Fear of being boring:** Other times people might have ideas for what to talk about, but they are worried that the other person will not be interested in those topics, so they try to figure out what the other person is interested in. This can be a great idea. It can help bring the other person into the conversation. It's good to find common interests with other people. Common interests get conversations flowing. But when we don't know the other person very well, we may not know what we have in common.

If we are worried about bringing up a topic that is boring to someone we don't know very well, we might end up afraid to say anything. This dilemma often leaves people feeling stuck. It can lead to them not offering any topics for verbally dancing because they don't know if the other person will like the topic. Being too worried about saying the right thing can lead to not saying anything at all.

4) **Not having many interests:** Another thing that can lead to not knowing what to talk about in a conversation is when we don't have many interests. Sometimes people don't know what to talk about because there is not much that interests them. People who do not have many interests are often better at following others' leads in conversations and are not as good at starting up conversations themselves.

Remedies For Managing the Awkward Silence

Once we have identified that the culprit in a social mystery is *trouble managing the awkward silence*, how do we keep it from creating problems in social situations? What kind of social remedies can we use to decrease awkwardness and its negative effects and also increase our ability to start up a nice verbal dance? And how can we keep that dance going in a comfortable way?

A good social detective will look for remedies to deal with three main challenges that happen with this culprit. They will look for remedies to 1) make silences less awkward; 2) decrease the negative effects of awkward silences when they do happen; 3) help start nice, comfortable verbal dances and keep them going. Let's look at some remedies for these three things.

How to Make Silences Less Awkward

Nervousness is often the cause of the awkwardness we may feel in moments of silence. When we are nervous, it is much harder to do our part in verbal dances. It makes sense that if we can find ways to decrease our nervousness, we will be better at dealing with awkward silences and have more comfortable verbal dances with people.

Sharing Responsibility For the Conversation

As we talked about before, people often feel it's their responsibility to fill all the space in a conversation. They may also think that if there is silence, they must be doing something wrong or that the other person is just not interested in them. As you can imagine, this kind of thinking can make people much more nervous and can make silences much more awkward. A good detective will find ways of dealing with this kind of thinking.

First of all, it's helpful to remember that *filling the conversational space is a shared responsibility*. It is just as much the other person's job to keep the verbal dance going as it is ours. As the saying goes, "It takes two to tango." It takes two to dance, and this is true if you are dancing a tango or having a verbal dance. It is a shared responsibility. Reminding yourself of this in the middle of an awkward silence can help decrease the nervousness that might arise.

It's also helpful to remind yourself that the awkward silence is *not necessarily a sign that you are doing anything wrong or that the other person is not interested*. Remember, a good dance takes two, and it is possible that the other person might be interested in you, but just not know how to verbally dance.

If the other person is not great at verbal dancing, that might mean you may need to take the lead in the verbal dance to get it going. But that does not mean it's completely your responsibility to take the lead. Being able to take the lead in conversational tangos can be a great skill, but it is a skill that is developed over time. You can still be a great verbal dancing partner even if you are not great at taking the lead.

The main point here is that it's not entirely your responsibility to take the lead and keep the conversation going. Remembering this can help you have much more relaxed and enjoyable conversations. It helps to decrease awkwardness, frees you up to really pay attention to the conversation, and helps you be the best dance partner you can be.

Mantras can come in handy here. The mantra can be a simple "It's not all my responsibility to keep the conversation going," or "Awkward silence does not mean I'm doing anything wrong," or "Silence does not mean they are not interested in me," or even "Silence is not a such a bad thing." Simple reminders like this can be very powerful in helping us feel more at ease and comfortable when we are trying to tango with others in our conversations.

Remembering That Silence is Not Forever and Comfort Grows Over Time

Another thing that often makes people nervous when there is an awkward silence is thinking that one awkward silence means a lifetime of awkward silences. We often think that we will never have anything to say and that the friendship is destined to fail just because we can't get the verbal dance going right then. We may believe that just because we don't feel comfortable talking now, that we will never feel comfortable. But the truth is, every friendship has times when there is nothing to say. And comfort in friendships is something that usually grows over time.

We often don't even notice silences when we are comfortable with people. The silence just happens, and then something eventually comes in to fill it. But when friendships are new, we notice the silences more because there is not a foundation of comfort, ease, and familiarity with the other person yet.

It is also true that it can be harder to find things to talk about when we are just getting to know someone. It's unfortunate because silences are often the hardest when we do not know someone very well. And the times when it is hardest to keep conversations going is often when we are getting to know someone. It's a double whammy.

But here again, a mantra can help. A simple mantra such as, "This silence won't last forever," or "It's common not to know what to say when getting to know someone," or "We will find more to say to each other the more we get to know one another," or "We will both feel more comfortable with each other the more we get to know each other," can help us feel less nervous and awkward when trying to verbally dance with others.

Mantras are a great way to deal with the thoughts that we have when we feel nervous. In addition to worrisome thoughts, we can also have nervous feelings in our bodies when faced with an awkward silence. We will talk more about how to deal with nervous feelings in our bodies in Chapter 8.

Sharing Activities

Another thing that can be very helpful when we are dealing with an awkward silence is to *find some activity to do with the other person*. We can take some of the pressure off by doing something other than just talking. Not all dances have to be verbal. Talking is not the only way we can relate to others. Doing things that are not so focused on talking can be fun and can help us to feel more comfortable being with others.

Our caveman ancestors used to go out and hunt together all day long, and they probably went for long periods without saying anything to each other. When you are trying to track down a wooly mammoth, you probably want to be very quiet so you don't scare it off. But even though they did not talk to each other much, they probably felt very close because they were working together as a team.

Today we don't hunt wild beasts like that, but there are many fun things we do with others that can connect us, but do not involve a whole lot of speaking. There are many modern-day versions of hunting a wooly mammoth that we can do with other people. And the cool thing about these activities is that there is room to have a conversation while we do them. There is room to talk if we think of something to say, but if we can't think of anything to say, we can just focus on the activity and not stress about periods of silence. This can help to take the pressure off and make silences less awkward.

The trick here is to find activities that make room for conversation but are not completely focused on talking. Going to the movies can be a place where we don't feel pressured to talk, but there isn't much room to work on our conversational dance if we do think of something to say. Reading books together or surfing the net on our separate computers or phones is similar. There may be times we do things like this with friends, but these kinds of activities are more separate.

I call this type of activity *parallel activities,* rather than *connecting activities*. Parallel activities are things we do while with someone, but that are mostly pretty separate. We are close to the other person, maybe in the same room or sitting right next to them, but we are not connecting with them, like two parallel lines that run side by side but never connect. They go side by side, which makes it seem like they are together, but there is no real contact.

This creates the illusion of togetherness because there is *physical closeness*. But that's not *relational closeness* and does not necessarily make the two people feel more comfortable with each other. Relational closeness usually involves an exchange of information. Usually, this information involves some kind of verbal exchange, but it does not have to.

If you play catch with someone, you are connecting with them as you throw the ball back and forth. If you dance with someone, you are exchanging information about the way your bodies are moving. When people play music together, they are sharing relational closeness without words. They are exchanging musical information, listening to what the other person is saying nonverbally with their instruments, and responding in a way that matches them. Like a good conversation, these kinds of things are *connecting activities,* because there is an exchange of information happening.

Parallel activities don't offer this type of exchange of information and because of this, parallel activities don't really help us get to know the other person better or feel more comfortable with them. For example, you might sit next to someone in class. You might both be focused on the teacher teaching, but never really exchange any information with each other all year. Because there is no information exchanged, you won't really get to know them. You might spend the whole year sharing the parallel activity of paying attention to the teacher in class but never really connect.

Now, if we talk to the person next to us in class during the year or talk with our friend about the movie we are watching or the things we are looking at on our phones, this can be like connecting the parallel lines. But without the exchange of information, these kinds of activities don't help a whole lot when it comes to creating more comfort with other people.

One way to make some of these more parallel things less parallel is to make sure you exchange information about what you are doing. Watching a video on our phone with someone and then talking about it can be more connecting. Videos are often shorter than movies, so we can connect more in between the videos, or you can share the things you are reading about while surfing the net, and even show what you are looking at to the other person.

Video games are something people often do together, and they can either be parallel activities or connecting activities. When we are aware of the importance of exchanging information and know ways to exchange with others, we can turn parallel activities into more interactive connecting ones. For example, we can take turns playing the video game. We can watch the other person while they are taking their turn, and we can make nice comments that show we are paying attention. If we have a goal of being less parallel and more interactive and connective when doing things like this, we can avoid just sitting side by side with others and not really interacting. And this can help a lot to create more comfort with others.

There are many other things we can do with people that are less likely to run the risk of turning into parallel activities, such as things like board games, puzzles, playing interactive sports, and going for hikes or bike rides. Things like these are great for taking the pressure off conversations, while also offering lots of room to interact and exchange information with the other person. A good social detective will encourage a client who is having trouble with awkward silences to find activities like this.

Do Things in Groups

Finally, a great way to take the pressure off filling the conversational space is to *do things in groups*. When there are more than two people in a conversation, there is less pressure to fill all the space. More people mean more voices, which usually means less awkward silence. And when there is a silence in a group, there is less of a sense that you are completely responsible for filling it. It can really take the pressure off.

There are other things that can be challenging when in a group, like knowing when and how to join in the conversation, or knowing how much to say and how to keep up with the flow of the conversation, so you make sure you are staying on top of the main topic and mood and are not topic or mood missing.

Verbal dancing in groups is an art all in itself that we could talk about a lot. But for now, know that groups can help decrease the pressure of knowing how to fill the awkward silence. And if you are having trouble joining in the verbal dance in groups, remember that all the things we already discussed in the verbal listening, verbal responding, and verbal dancing section. They can help in groups, as well as in one-on-one interactions with others.

Next time you are feeling awkward with someone, see if you can use some of the things we have been talking about here. It just might take your friendship to a whole other level of comfort and enjoyment.

How to Decrease Negative Effects of Awkward Silences

Even when we use all of our best social detective skills, there are still going to be times when silence prevails. And there are going to be times when that silence is awkward. But silence is not the end of the world. It does not have to create problems with others.

By being aware of some of the things that can lead to problems created by silence and by taking steps to manage silence well, we can make sure this prime suspect does not have negative effects on our relationships. Let's talk about some things we can do to make sure normal silences that happen between people don't turn into problems.

Take Advantage of the Power of the Pause

As we have discussed, people often ask questions and make comments that don't really fit, as a way of trying to fill the silence. They might ask questions or make comments that miss the topic or mood, which can actually increase a sense of awkwardness instead of decreasing it. To safeguard against this, it's helpful to pause a little before jumping in with your questions or responses.

A little pause gives us time to assess if our questions or responses are in line with the topic or the mood. It can also decrease the likelihood of crowding and interrogations, and it can create more space for depth in our exchanges with others. A nice planned pause can also help us relax and feel more comfortable with the little silences that sometimes happen between people.

Ask Open Questions

Another way we can decrease interrogations and create more comfort, space, and depth in conversations is to be smart about the way we ask questions. When you are trying to get a conversation flowing, it's especially helpful to ask more open questions than closed questions.

Closed questions usually ask for a yes or no answer or a very short response. "Do you like chocolate?" is a closed question. It only asks for a yes or no answer. "What's your favorite color?" is also a closed question because it asks for a very short response. "Purple is my favorite color" is more than yes or no but is still pretty short.

Open questions, on the other hand, invite the other person to talk more. They are often *What, How* or *Why* questions. For example, "*What* kind of things do you like to do for fun?" is an open question. Closed questions can be *what* questions, too, like "What is your favorite color?" But notice that this open "What do you like to do for fun?" question asks for more details than "What is your favorite color?"

Why questions are also great for getting longer responses. For example, "*Why* do you want to be a video game designer when you grow up?" is a great question to get someone talking. Asking someone, "*How* do you get to the next level?" in a video game you both like to play is also a great way to get more information.

Good questions try to ask about something the other person might be interested in, such as a video game they like to play, so a question like this can be great. The main point here is that good questions are open and invite the other person to give a longer response, which will make you run less risk of interrogating them with rapid-fire questions.

Share Some of Your Own Experience

Another thing that can help reduce the chance of interrogating and can increase comfort and connection in conversations is to share some of your own experience after the other person answers a question. This can help the conversation be more of a shared dance. If someone tells you how they got to the next level in a video game, you might respond by saying something like, "That's cool! I'll try that. I tried to get past that level by doing ____ but I get killed every time. I never thought of what you said, but I'm going to try that next time."

A response like this does a number of cool things. First, it lets the other person know you are paying attention to what they said. It also gives space, so you are not just rapidly firing questions at them. In addition, it offers the other person a compliment by suggesting they are offering you a good idea that you had not thought of.

Of course, you want to remember that good verbal dances have a balance to them. They go back and forth, giving both people the chance to speak and listen. But a nice balance of good open questions and responses that don't have TMI can really help conversations blossom and can create a lot of comfort in our verbal dances with others.

Stay Aware of Our Responses to Awkward Silences

We talked about how nervousness can often make us act in ways that come across as disinterested or annoyed. Being aware of how our nervousness can affect the signals we might give others can keep us from acting in ways that give off the wrong impression.

One way to increase awareness about the signals we might be giving off is to ask ourselves questions. For example, we can ask ourselves if we are feeling nervous or awkward, and if so, we can ask how those feelings might be affecting the way we are responding and acting with others. We can ask ourselves if our feelings are affecting our voice tone, facial expressions, and body language in ways that might come across as irritation or lack of interest.

Again, we will talk more about these important nonverbal signals later in the book. But being aware that our nervousness might show up in these ways can be an important first step in keeping our feelings from negatively affecting our responses to others.

It's also helpful to be aware that even if our voice, face, and body are giving off signals which might be taken as negative, we can counteract that with the things we are saying. If our exchange shows interest in the other person and shows that we are paying attention, this will affect the way others interpret the nonverbal signals we might be giving off. And this will make it more likely that if the other person noticed something in our nonverbal communication, they will not think we are annoyed or uninterested in them.

What we say when talking with someone will change the way they make sense of what our voice tone, face, and body might be saying. This is pretty cool if you think about it. It's cool to think about how one piece of information can affect how someone makes sense of another piece of information in a totally different way. I call this idea, *understanding things in context*. We will talk more about this important idea of context in later sections, and you will see just how powerful context can be in our interactions with others.

Starting a Good Verbal Dance and Keeping It Going

We have been talking about what the dreaded awkward silence does to us and how it can make us act in ways that are not the best for our relationships with other people. It's important to make peace with the awkward silence and keep it from interfering with our relationships.

But making peace with something is not the same as being resigned to it. When you are resigned to something, you just accept it and don't do anything to try and change it. Sometimes in life, we might need to be resigned to things we cannot change and accept the way they are. But that's not the case with awkward silences. Making peace with them does not mean we should not ignore or minimize them when it seems right to do so.

It is true that silences in conversations can sometimes be helpful, and that an awkward silence is not the end of the world. But that does not mean you should just accept them and not do things to fill up the space if you want to. Let's talk about some of the ways we can start up conversations and keep them going, if and when we want to.

Below are four things that can help start good conversations and keep them going. These things are: 1) keeping a good mental attitude and staying relaxed; 2) using your detective skills; 3) being creative; 4) taking action.

Keeping a Good Mental Attitude and Staying Relaxed

When we have a negative attitude about silences that happen in interactions with others, it can create a lot of stress. We might think that the silence is our fault or is a sign that the other person does not like us. We might believe that we will never be able to do anything to make conversations more comfortable. This can really create a lot of stress.

When we are stressed and thinking negative thoughts like this, there is not as much energy or attention left to change things and have a nice exchange. A good place to start is to find ways to manage the negative thoughts that might come up.

Here again, awareness is the first step. When we are aware that we are having negative thoughts about awkward silences, negative thinking will not have as much power over us. And when we are aware, we have the opportunity to shift our thinking in a positive direction. Once we are aware, we can do things like practice mantras that can reassure us and help us think more positively. Some good mantras might be: "It's not all my responsibility to keep the conversation going," or "An awkward silence doesn't mean that they don't like me," or "Just because it's awkward now does not mean it will always be awkward."

See if you can notice whether you have a positive mental attitude about silences that happen in your conversations. If you don't, see if you can do some of the things that we have been talking about to relax and reassure yourself.

Detective Work

Once you are feeling more positive and relaxed, you can figure out what to do to get the conversation going. Good detective skills come in very handy here. When solving any social mystery, a good detective starts by gathering the facts.

First, we want to gather facts about what the other person is interested in. If we know about the other person's interests, we have clues about what might be good topics for a conversation. Ideally, you want to find topics in which both you and the other person are interested. Conversations about common interests make things easier because when both people are interested, they are more likely to participate and contribute to the conversational dance.

The trick here is to figure out what the other person is interested in. The most direct way is to *ask them what kind of things they like.* You can ask what they like to do for fun or if they have any hobbies. You can ask more specific questions, such as if they like a certain video game or movie or musical artist. You can ask them about sports or places they enjoy going to. There are lots of direct questions you can ask someone to get a sense of what their interests are. Not only does this help you get to know the other person, but it also gets the conversation going. And it shows the other person you are interested in them, which is a big plus in friendships.

There are other ways we can gather facts about the interests of others. A good social detective is always keeping his or her ears open in case clues come up. *Listen to what people seem excited about when they are talking with others.* Make a note of those things, so that when it's your turn to strike up a conversation with them, you have a sense of things they like. You can also *recall past conversations* you might have had with the person to look for clues. What kind of things did they like talking about in the past?

There are so many ways to gather clues about what others like. Maybe the other person has a shirt with a certain band or video game on it that will give you information about their interests. Maybe they are holding a book that they like, or you notice that they have a skateboard company sticker on their notebook. All of these things can give you clues for conversation starters.

Another thing you can do to gather clues about good conversation topics is *to introduce a topic you're interested in and see how they respond.* Let's say you just got a new video game. You can tell them what video you got and ask them if they have heard of it or if they have played it. Then you can use your detective skills to see if they seem interested. Do they talk enthusiastically? Do they seem curious and ask you questions? Or do they give you a short response and look bored? These kinds of responses are great clues about whether or not a topic is a good one. If it is a good one, you can continue talking about it. If the feedback you are getting from them suggests it might not be a great topic, you can move onto another topic.

It can also be very helpful to *gather facts about current events* happening in the world. Current events can be wonderful conversation starters. Maybe there was a big fire near you, or a recent space shuttle launch, or the summer Olympics. If you are aware of things happening in the world, you can test them out as possible conversation starters. After you introduce the topic, you can see how the other person responds and decide if you want to continue with that topic, or whether you should try to find one that seems of more interest to you both.

It is also helpful to *be aware not just of current events, but of trends in the world.* Are there new video games out there that you may not have played but that you know about? Are there new gaming consoles or new popular music trends? New memes or popular YouTubers? Are there new movies or books? Are there social media apps like SnapChat or Twitter or Instagram that are popular with your friends that might be interesting to talk about? Knowing what trends are going on in society can give clues about potentially good conversation starters.

Being Creative

Finding a good topic to talk about can often get a conversation going. But it can also be helpful to have some tricks to keep it going once it starts. This is where a little creativity is helpful.

Being creative involves thinking of new ideas. In a conversation, being creative would involve thinking of new ideas to spark the fires of the conversation. Once you introduce a topic, it can be helpful to find some new ideas, thoughts, and questions you can bring in to help the conversation continue to unfold. Most creative thinking does not just come from nowhere. It builds on things. Creative ideas are often inspired by other ideas. In conversations, new ideas, thoughts, or questions are inspired by the ideas, thoughts, and questions that came before.

For example, you might bring up the topic of a new video game you have been playing, and the other person might be interested in it. But what comes next? Where do you take the conversation after you say "Hey, have you played this new game?" and they say "Yeah, it's really fun." This is where you may need to be a little creative in order to dive more deeply into the topic. This is where you want to find new ideas, thoughts, or questions that are inspired by what came before.

One way to be creative as a way of keeping things going is to use what I like to call the *tree of association* (see Figure 1.1). When two things are associated, they are related in some way. The two things are not the same but they have some things in common. Look at all of the branches on a tree. The branches are different, but they are part of the same tree. They are different but related, and they all come off of the same trunk.

I like to think of a good conversation as being like a tree. In a conversational tree, there is a central main topic or idea which is like the trunk of the tree. There are also lots of branches of the conversation that can sprout out of that trunk. These branches are associated with the trunk. They grow out of the trunk. And the combination of the trunk and all the branches that can grow out if it forms the *tree of association*. Just as a real tree needs its branches to thrive, a good conversation needs its conversational branches to thrive.

In a conversational tree, there can be many different ideas, thoughts, or questions that branch off from the main topic or idea trunk. These branches are all related to the main topic or idea, but they are also different in some ways. All the branches are new, creative things that were inspired by the trunk. They sprouted out of the main topic like branches sprout from the trunk of a tree. As a conversation unfolds, we jump from one branch to another, which helps the conversation keep going in a nice way.

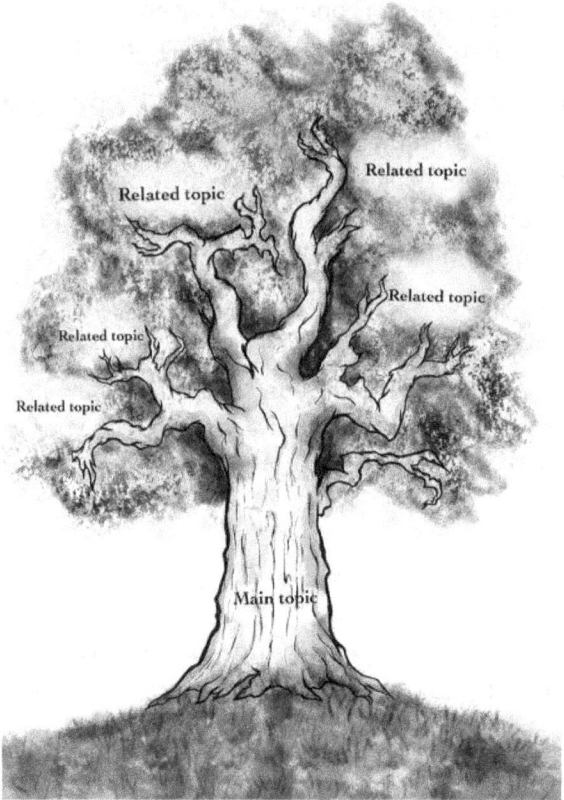

Figure 1.1

Our creative thinking is what helps us grow new branches on the conversational tree. Remember, creativity involves coming up with new ideas. And most new ideas are based on ideas that came before. Part of the goal of a good conversation is to sprout new branches by coming up with new ideas that are associated with the initial idea but are also slightly different. We don't want to be saying the same thing over and over in a conversation. But we also don't want to just jump from topic to topic without anything to connect the ideas.

In conversations, it's best to jump to branches that are close by. Close branches are more associated with each other. They have more in common with the branches next to it. For example, if the main topic or idea trunk of the conversational tree is a video game, such as Mario World, one branch might be, "What are your favorite characters in the game?" Let's call this Branch 1 (see Figure 1.2).

If the other person responds with a character, such as "Mario," his response is Branch 2. A close branch to Branch 2 would be to talk about Mario in more detail. For example, you could ask, "What do you like about Mario?" The question about your favorite character is one branch. The other person's response to Mario is another branch (Branch 2) and the question "What do you like about Mario?" is a third branch. You can see how each branch in this conversational tree is inspired by the last statement or question.

Figure 1.2, *As you can see, the branches are formed by questions and responses. You can see how the question branch of what someone likes about Mario is closer to the person's response branch about liking Mario than is the question about Luigi or about what gaming system they use.*

Another branch would be to ask about a different character, such as Luigi. Let's call this Branch 4. This branch is still related to the trunk and related to Branches 1 and 2 about Mario because Luigi is also a character. But this is not as close to Branch 1 as it would be to ask what they like about Mario. It would still be ok to ask about Luigi, but maybe not as good a question as asking more about Mario. After you discuss Mario a little more, switching branches to Luigi would be great. You want to give each branch proper attention.

In this conversation, you could also ask what other video games the person likes to play. We can call this Branch 5. This question is not closely related to the main trunk of the conversational tree. It's even farther away from Branches 1 and 2 than the branch where we asked about Luigi.

The question about other video games is farther away because it is not about Mario World at all. It is still about video games, and Mario World is a video game, so it is related to the main trunk in some way. But it's not really related to the last branch, and it has much less in common with the trunk of the conversation than the other questions.

"What do you like about Mario?" is the closest branch to the trunk, because it has the idea of Mario and the idea of game characters in common with the last two branches that came right before it (Branches 1 and 2). The question about Luigi has less in common because it does not have anything about Mario in it. But it does have something about game characters in general in it, which makes it closer than the question about what other video games you like because that question does not have anything about Mario or characters in the game in it. The more in common with the last branch a new branch is, the closer it is.

We don't always have to jump to the closest branch in a conversation. But it's helpful to keep in mind how close our responses are to the last branch of the conversation. Keeping this tree of association in mind can prevent us from moving too far from the initial topic when we are trying to be creative and explore other related branches.

You can imagine a squirrel scampering around on a tree, jumping from one branch to another. The squirrel will usually jump from one branch to a nearby one. If he jumps too far, it could be problematic. If the next branch is too far, he might lose his footing and get off balance. Or he might not make it at all and fall off the tree. But if he takes it little by little, jumping from one branch to another one close by, he can make it all the way around the tree with ease.

This is similar to how we can move around the tree of association in conversations. If we jump to a branch too far away, we might throw the conversation off balance or completely lose the thread of the conversation. But if we gradually move from branch to related branch, we can go far and have a great conversation as we explore all the possibilities.

Taking Positive Action

The goal of these things we have been talking about—keeping a good attitude, staying relaxed, using good detective skills, and being creative—is to help shape the way we dance with others to keep a conversation going. But there is a key ingredient we need to help us utilize all these tools. That key is *Action*.

Action lets us take ideas and turn them into real things in the world. We can have lots of ideas about how to be a better friend and a better listener. We can have lots of ideas about how to keep a conversation going and be a better verbal dancer. But without engaging in actions, those ideas will not make any real positive change in our lives. Action is the key.

Sometimes taking action requires a little risk. For example, you may know it's helpful to ask the other person open-ended questions, but you may still sit quietly because you are afraid you might say the wrong thing or not get the response you want. Sometimes action can be scary. But without it, nothing can really change.

A good detective recognizes when action is necessary and looks to see if things are getting in the way of taking the necessary action. When you find yourself in a social situation that could use some improvement, check to see if proper action is being taken.

If you assess that more action is needed, there are things you can do to make this happen. First, use your detective skills to try and figure out what actions you think would help, then ask yourself what is getting in the way of taking that action.

Action is an important part of all the things we have been talking about so far. I am bringing it up here because nervousness about awkward silences often keeps people from engaging in the actions that could decrease the awkwardness. Nervousness can make us avoid engaging in actions that would make things better.

When you get in uncomfortable situations, ask if you are taking action to make things better. If you are, give yourself a high five. If you are not, see if you can push yourself a little. See if you can remind yourself that good action can help.

If nervousness is getting in the way, you can remind yourself that when you take action it does not have to be perfect the first time. You can remind yourself that taking action lets you practice, and practice is what makes you better at things.

Don't be afraid to make mistakes. The most successful people in the world make the most mistakes. Do you know why they make the most mistakes? Because successful people take risks, and because they take a lot of risks, they are more likely to occasionally fail.

But failing and making mistakes does not stop them. They learn from their mistakes and don't give up. They keep trying until they get it right. They practice and practice, and that's why they become so successful. So, remind yourself of this. You can remind yourself if you are worried about making a mistake, that the most successful people make the most mistakes. That is part of why they are so successful in the end.

If you are having some resistance to taking action, it can also be helpful to make a list of the actions you might take to decrease awkwardness and have a better verbal dance. You can even write them down. To do this, you can go over the things we discussed above—keeping a good attitude, staying relaxed, using good detective skills, and being creative—and see what actions you can take to make your interactions better. Once you have the list of actions, you can break each action down into smaller steps to make them less stressful. For example, if the action you come up with is to ask more open questions, you can start by making a list of open questions you might ask. Even if you are not ready to ask the questions, you can think about them. This can help you prepare for actually asking the questions another time.

Give it a try, and see if you can push yourself into action. You might be surprised how at much your nervousness decreases after you do. It has been proven over and over that taking action decreases nervousness. When we do something that makes us nervous, it helps us feel more powerful. It helps us trust in ourselves more. It helps us to realize that we are stronger than our fear and nervousness and that if we just push ourselves a little, we can overcome obstacles. Give it a shot. See if you can push through nervousness and take action. You will be happy you did.

Time: Friday 8:18 PM, just after the Homecoming football game

Place: Dale's Pizza and Sub Shop

Tommy was so excited about winning their homecoming football game. He was proud of himself because he was the quarterback and had thrown the long pass that won them the game. All his friends were planning on meeting after the game at Dale's for some food and celebration. But he planned on meeting his friend Sari there a little before. He was glad he would be able to meet with her first because he wanted to talk about the game with her the most. Tommy really liked Sari and often felt like he wanted to impress her. He thought his great performance in the homecoming game would be a good way to do that. He cared a lot about what she thought of him.

"Hey Sari!" he said in an excited voice as he approached the table she was sitting at. "Hey, Tommy! Congratulations!" she said in an excited voice. They hugged and he sat down. He talked about the scary huge linemen on the other team that kept trying to sack him. And he reminisced about some of the great plays his team made and the Hail Mary he ran and about the final long bomb he threw to Stan that won them the game. But something did not feel right about their conversation. He noticed that Sari's responses seemed short and robot-like. He found himself feeling more and more stressed as the conversation went on, and he found himself feeling relieved when their other friends came to join them.

This confused Tommy because he really liked his one-on-one time with Sari and often tried to spend more alone time with her. He usually felt closer to her after they spent time together, but not today. Today she was acting differently. She did not seem to be responding to his mood and was not saying much in their conversation. Tommy ended up feeling much further away from her by the time the others came to join them. He had no idea why things had gone so wrong. "This is most definitely a social mystery," he thought to himself. He had planned to walk Sari home after their group celebration and really wanted to figure out what had gone wrong before that so they could get back to feeling comfortable with each other. Fortunately, Tommy was also a student of Johnny's so he felt confident that if he put on his social detective hat, he could figure this one out. And like all good social detectives, he started with the facts.

The facts

- Tommy and Sari are good friends.
- The two are usually very comfortable talking with each other.
- Tommy usually feels closer to Sari after their time together.
- Tommy likes to impress Sari. He wants her to see him in a positive way.
- Tommy was proud of his performance at the game and wanted to share his success with Sari.
- Today Tommy felt less comfortable and less close to Sari after their conversation.

Solving the case

Tommy knew that looking at the common prime suspects was always a good place to start when trying to make sense of a social mystery. He remembered that Johnny would often say that when you are personally involved in the social mystery, it's always best to start by looking to yourself first. Johnny would say "Look at how you personally responded, reacted, and made sense of things first." Johnny believed that we don't have much power over other people, but we have power over ourselves and our own actions. "We can't change others but we can change ourselves," he would often say. He said that if we can see how we might be contributing to a social mystery, we can be more effective at finding good social remedies. Tommy shined his spotlight of attention on how he responded, reacted, and made sense of things during his exchange with Sari to see if this could help him make sense of the facts.

"Ok, let's go through some of the prime suspects," he thought. He considered attention. "That did not seem to be a problem." He considered topic missing and mood missing. "Those don't seem to have been a problem, either," he thought. "Was it a problem with our verbal exchange?" he asked himself. He recalled the clues you might see when someone is under-responding. "I was definitely not under-responding," he said to himself. "In fact," A light went on in Tommy's head. Realizing that he was definitely not under-responding helped him become aware of just how much he was talking. He thought he might know what the culprit was, but he needed to be sure. He needed to check out his hunch, so he asked himself the following questions:

- Was I giving too much information?
- Was I monologuing?
- Was I talking too fast?
- Did I allow space for Sari to talk?
- Did Sari seem content listening or did she seem like she was just looking for a space in the conversation to say something?
- Did Sari start to glaze over and lose attention or energy as I continued to talk?
- Did Sari's body language communicate that she was involved or did she seem bored or frustrated?
- Did I go off on a tangent, wandering off the main topic and drifting onto other things?

"Yikes," Tommy said under his breath after asking himself these questions. "*Over-responding* was definitely a culprit in what happened with Sari. I was totally giving way too much information. Maybe not at first but as the conversation went on, I seemed to give more and more details. By the end I was definitely monologuing," he thought to himself. "And the speed of my talking got faster and faster as the conversation went on. This was not only a sign that I was over-responding, it was also a sign that the prime suspect of *fast talking* was also a culprit. I imagine that by the end there was no space at all for Sari to say anything if she had wanted to, so the prime suspect of *verbal crowding* was also a culprit here."

He thought about clues Sari might have been giving off during the conversation. At the time he hadn't thought about that at all, but in looking back he recalled that she did not seem very responsive to what he was saying. "I don't know if I'd say she was glazing over or seeming bored. But when I think back, it's clear that something was definitely up with her. How could I miss that? I must have been so focused on what I was trying to say that I didn't pay attention to her responses. Thinking back, her face definitely seemed like something was up. And her body language seemed tense. How did I miss that?" he asked himself. Then he thought about how he pretty abruptly changed the topic from the game that night to the Superbowl and players in the NFL. "That was a total tangent!" he thought to himself.

Tommy tried to figure out what was going on to make him respond like that. It was not his usual style. He thought back over the conversation and realized that early on there were some awkward silences. He didn't remember the specifics of what had happened, but he recalled both of them sitting in silence staring at each other uncomfortably, not knowing what to say next. He realized that he felt awkward when this happened. Tommy knew silences were not necessarily bad in and of themselves. It depended on how those silences were managed. He realized that part of how he dealt with the awkward silence was by giving too much information, talking fast to fill the space, and eventually going off on a tangent. This made the exchange between Sari and him even more awkward and stressful.

In putting all these pieces together, it became clear to Tommy that he was not only over-responding, he was also fast talking, verbal crowding, and not managing the awkward silence as well as he could have.

"Why did I do that?" he asked himself. "I'm not usually like that," he thought. "Well, I'm not sure exactly how I missed the important clues and why I dealt with the awkward silence in that way. But I do know that my new awareness of how I personally contributed to this situation being stressful can help me do things differently in the future.

Key Culprits in the Mystery:

- Prime suspect #7 Over-responding
- Prime suspect #8 Fast Talking
- Prime suspect #9 Verbal Crowding
- Prime suspect #10 Trouble Managing the Awkward Silence

Social Remedy

Solving this mystery helped Tommy relax, which helped him to enjoy celebrating with his group of friends. After they had all filled up on pizza and soda, Tommy and Sari started their walk home together. Tommy was all ready to talk to Sari about his over-responding when, to his surprise, she started talking about how she had been under-responding. He gave her the space to share and they talked for a while about the homecoming game and about the rules of football in a much different way that felt good to both of them. While Sari was talking, Tommy tried to stay aware of his level of responding. He wanted to make sure he was not over-responding in their verbal dance. Because of what Sari had shared and because of his own better understanding of what had gone wrong earlier, he found it easy to say connected and have a good balance of give and take in their conversation. After their conversation about Sari's under-responding and the rules of football came to a natural ending, Tommy gave a little laugh.

"Ok, so I have to tell you something, Sari." "What's up?" She asked. "Well, I wasn't feeling that good after our conversation earlier, so I did my own social detective work to figure out what was happening. But I came up with a totally different conclusion" he said. "Really?" Sari asked. "Yeah. Remember how Johnny always told us to look at our part first? Well, that's what I did. And I realized that I was over-responding in our conversation. "Yes, I guess I can see that," said Sari. "But that was only in response to my under-responding, I think." "It's so interesting!" Tommy said. "It's interesting to see how we affected each other. You under-responded because you didn't understand the rules of football. And then I started over-responding and talking more and giving too many details, which probably made you under-respond even more." "Yes! What a trip!" Sari said.

"If something like this happens again, I will try to imagine things more from your point of view," Tommy said. "Like with football, I'll ask myself if I think you might know the details I'm talking about." "Thanks, Tommy. I appreciate that. And I will try to speak up if I don't know something, and I'll ask you directly instead of pretending I know. I'm so glad we both trained to become social detectives. It makes things like this so much easier." "Totally!' Tommy said. "Let's make a pact. If we ever feel awkward, like there is some social mystery between us, let's agree that we will bring it up together, and we can solve the mystery as a team." The Tommy-Sari team!" Sari said with a big smile on her face. "I like that!" Tommy said in an enthusiastic voice. "Team Tommy-Sari!" They continued their walk home, talking about lots of fun things. Both appreciated their friendship and their ability to get at the root of social mysteries like this.

PRIME SUSPECT #11:

TOPIC LINGERING

One of the things people often ask me is, "When is it ok to switch topics?" This question comes up mainly with people who have a good understanding of the importance of staying on topic and who have been practicing. It can be confusing knowing when to stay on the topic and when to switch. If we switch too soon, we are topic missing. If we wait too long, we might start going into TMI or we might lose energy in the conversation. We might begin to struggle to find something to talk about, which can increase awkwardness. I call staying with a topic too long, *topic lingering*. Topic lingering is often a prime suspect in social mysteries, especially mysteries that involve problems with verbal dancing. It's helpful to keep this one in mind when on a case.

But how can we tell when we are lingering too long on a topic? How can we tell when we have talked enough about something and the conversational topic has reached its natural end? The ability to sense the natural end of a topic can be extremely useful both for a social detective trying to solve social mysteries, as well as for anyone wanting to have enjoyable, successful social dances. Let's talk about some of the things that can help us to better assess when a topic has reached its natural end.

How to Tell if Topic Lingering is an Issue
1) Balancing the conversational needs

When assessing if it is the right time to shift topics, you want to take into consideration the *quality* of the conversation and the *interest* of the people involved in the conversation. *The quality* of a conversation has to do with things we have been talking about. It is about how the verbal listening, responding, and dancing are going. Is there a nice back and forth of talking, or is one person doing all the talking? Is there new information being added to the conversation, or are the people repeating the same things or struggling to find things around the topic to talk about? Are the things people are talking about stimulating and of value, or has the conversation started to become more about unimportant details rather than interesting thoughts, ideas, and feelings? The *interest* of the people involved has to do with how energized they are and how much they are enjoying the conversation. Do both people seem interested and engaged, or do one or both seem bored and disconnected?

Sometimes good friends will talk about things they might not like because they care about the other person and want them to be happy. So even if one person is not as interested as the other, and even if the quality of the conversation is not the best, you might give a little extra time before changing topics because you know it is important to your friend. Hopefully, your friend would do the same. The trick is to balance the interest levels of the people in the conversation with the quality of the conversation. If the conversation is not very interesting to you, but the quality of the listening, responding, and verbal dancing is ok, you might want to keep it going for a while. But if the quality of the conversation is really poor, then it might be a good time to shift topics, even if it is of great interest to one of the people involved.

2) Taking time into consideration

Even after weighing the quality of the conversation and the interest level of the people involved, it may still be hard to determine if you have been lingering too long and need a shift. Being aware of the amount of time you have spent on a topic can provide additional information to help you decide if it might be a good time to shift topics. If you have been discussing something for just a couple of minutes and feel bored or don't think the quality of the conversation is great, you might want to give it a little more time to see if you can get things going. Some conversations take some time to get going. You can't really tell if they will go somewhere worthwhile until you give them some time. Remember, sometimes it takes a little while to get past the initial awkwardness. Don't rush too quickly to shift topics. If, on the other hand, you have been talking about something for a long time and the quality of the conversation does not seem the best, or one of the people in the conversation does not seem very interested you might want to shift to something else.

How to Shift Topics Smoothly

Once we decide it's time to change the topic, we want to make sure we do so in a good way. Shifting in a clumsy, abrupt way can be disruptive to the flow of our verbal dance. It can also give the other person the impression that we are not interested in or listening to what they are saying. That can increase awkwardness. It's helpful to have some tricks to make the shift as smooth as possible. The four things I find incredibly helpful in making smooth transitions are 1) waiting for the pause 2) making sure an idea has been completed 3) summarizing and 4) making bridges.

1) Wait for the Pause

As we have discussed before, you always want to make sure not to crowd or interrupt others in a conversation. This is even more important when you are about to shift topics. If you crowd or interrupt someone when staying on the same topic it can be annoying. However, the fact that you are staying on the same topic can make crowding or interrupting slightly less annoying This is because staying on the same subject conveys that you are listening and that you are with them in what they are saying even if you are taking up too much of the talking space.

Shifting subjects is delicate. When you shift subjects, you're giving the message that you don't want to talk about the topic anymore. That can give the impression that you are not interested or not paying attention to what the other person is saying.

Making sure not to crowd or interrupt can soften this and make it less likely the other person will take the topic shift personally. Remember, crowding can give the other person the impression you are not really following the dance. When you are sensitive and aware of the verbal dance and demonstrate that by not crowding or interrupting, it helps the other person know that you are still in tune with them even though you are switching the topic. Waiting for the pause is the perfect way to make sure you are not crowding or interrupting.

2) Wait for the End of an Idea

Another thing you want to do when you are getting ready to shift topics is to make sure the other person has finished their idea. Remember, if we are not careful, topic shifts can give others the impression we are uninterested or not listening. And if we cut them off before they complete their idea, it is more likely that they will take it that way. If we are careful to make sure the other person has finished their idea, it helps protect them from getting the wrong message.

Example of waiting for the end of an idea:

Let's take the example we used for understanding what a tangent is on page___ and see if we can smooth it out by waiting for the end of an idea. To refresh your memory, the conversation went something like this:

Person A: "Hey do you like Minecraft?"

Person B: "Yeah, I love that video game. I like building cities in it. I built this really cool city the other day...."

Person A: "Cool."

Person B: "I used diamonds to build it. I love building things. I have a huge collection of model airplanes and rockets I have built. I also love building Star Wars models. I built a huge Death Star last month. Basically, anything Star Wars and I'm all over it. I saw *the Empire Strikes Back* 47 times. I know every line in it. My favorite part is where Han Solo...."

There are major tangents in this example. The first tangent is switching from Minecraft to building model airplanes and rockets. The second tangent happens when he switches to Star Wars movies. If Person B had waited for the end of the first main topic, he could have changed the subject more smoothly. So, the first thing you want to do is identify what the main idea or main topic is. If you want a refresher on identifying the main topic, check out Chapter 3 on topic missing.

Here the initial main topic is Minecraft. If Person B kept talking about Minecraft for a little while, he probably could have found a natural ending or completion of that idea. At that point, he could have started talking about building models and even about Star Wars.

Person B could have asked a few more questions of Person A to show he was following the conversation topic. For example, he could have asked "Do you like building things in Minecraft?" And he could have gone even farther by asking Person A what kind of things he likes to build things in Minecraft. He could also ask what materials he likes to build with. This would have given the Minecraft topic a little time to unfold. Which would have allowed for a more natural, less forced ending of the idea. Once he had talked through a few different things around the main topic of Minecraft, it would have been more likely that there would be a natural ending to the main idea.

3) Summarizing

Summarizing what has been talked about so far is a wonderful way to prepare for a shift in topics. First of all, it demonstrates to the other person that you have been paying attention to the conversation. A good summary reflects what has been said, and that lets the other person know you are really getting it. It can also help to determine if the other person has said all they need to say and have finished expressing what it is they wanted to share. If they are not finished with what they have to say, a summary will often result in them expressing whatever else they want to say on the subject.

The other important thing a good summary can do is help us segue to the next topic. A *segue* (pronounced segway) is a smooth, uninterrupted transition from one thing to another. In good verbal dancing, we segue often, smoothly transitioning from one thing to another. By assisting us in segueing smoothly, summarizing can help us avoid unnecessary awkwardness. You can refresh your memory on the art of summarizing on page __ in the section on over-responding.

Example of Summarizing

Let's take this same Minecraft conversation and use it to illustrate how summarizing can help smooth out transitions from one topic to another. After Person A asks Person B if he likes Minecraft, Person B could ask some questions to get more information as he did in the example above. Let's say Person A says that he likes building tall buildings with skylights in them in Minecraft. And that he also likes using diamonds to build because they are shiny and hard. Person B can summarize that by saying "That's cool. We both like using diamonds. I like how hard and shiny they are too. Skylights are cool too." This summarizes what Person A was saying, which shows that Person B was really listening to him. He could even add this: "With a skylight, you could grow things inside. Most of my cities have small structures in them. I've never made skylights. That's a great idea. Maybe we can build together sometime and you can build some big buildings with skylights and we can grow plants in there." This summarizes and adds some additional information. And it invites Person A into future activities with Person B.

Summarizing like this can help you to see if the other person feels complete with the conversation. If they don't, they may start saying something else about Minecraft. But often summarizing helps to complete the idea and allow for a smooth segue.

4) Bridging

A conversational bridge connects one topic to another. It is what allows a smooth, effective segue. A good bridge takes part of the initial conversation and finds something in it that has something in common with the new conversational topic.

You can think of a bridge as something that connects branches in a conversation. If you recall, we discussed the tree of association in the chapter above. We talked about how good conversations find branches that are a little bit away from the main trunk of the topic. They are a little farther away but are also close enough to smoothly jump from one to the other. We used the idea of a squirrel jumping from branch to branch. You can think of a bridge as something that helps the squirrel easily get from one branch to another, just like walking across a bridge from one branch to another.

When we are talking about a topic, we make little bridges between ideas that are closely related to the main trunk of the topic. When shifting topics, we can still use this same strategy, but the bridges are longer. They reach farther away from the main trunk of the topic we had been discussing.

In the example we used when talking about the tree of association, we explored ideas around the main-topic trunk of the video game, *Mario World,* when we asked the question, "What are your favorite characters in Mario World?" We talked about how asking that question was a close branch to that main trunk. That question created a bridge to the trunk that was fairly close to the new branch.

Figure 1.2

We then asked the question, "What other video games do you like to play?" This branch was farther away but still somewhat connected to the main topic. This question about other video games made a bridge to the main topic in the sense that Mario World is a video game, and the question was about video games in general. But that branch did not have as much in common with the topic as the other questions that were specifically about Mario World, so the bridge was longer. A longer bridge means we must reach farther in our minds to connect this new idea to the trunk of the conversational tree.

This question about other video games is an example of topic shifting. It is shifting from the specific topic of Mario World to the more general topic of video games. This new question might lead to other branches that will take the conversation even further away from the initial trunk by shifting the conversation to a completely different video game.

A topic-shifting bridge would have much less in common with the trunk of the last topic tree than this example, and less in common means farther to jump between branches. It means we must reach farther in our minds to connect this new idea to the previous idea, which means a longer bridge. For example, after summarizing your conversation on Mario World you might say: " I like doing other things besides playing Mario World. I also like playing sports. How about you?"

This question is a bridge between the last topic of video games and the new one of sports. It mentions the last topic (Mario World) and finds a common theme of "things you like to do," but then it moves away from the first topic by talking about sports. There is a bridge, but it is a long one that allows the opportunity to shift topics smoothly. A good long bridge like this can help us keep conversations alive by taking them to new places, and it can do so without awkwardness.

Sometimes a bridge can stretch even farther. Maybe you really want to talk about some of the exciting things you are going to do over summer vacation. Because summer vacation is a much farther branch from Mario World, the bridge between the two will need to be even longer. However, it's possible to bridge things that are not related at all.

After summarizing your conversation about Mario, you might say, "Hey, I wanted to tell you about what I'm doing over summer vacation." This is a total topic switch. Sometimes total topic switches can totally work. If there is a natural pause in the flow of a conversation, it might be easy to switch without even using a bridge.

But what if there is not a natural pause, and you think that if you don't say something, the other person is just going to find more to talk about on the last topic when you want to switch? If this happens, you can try to make an even longer bridge by finding a segue to help smooth things out.

Ideally, a bridge has something in common with the last topic, even if it seems like a stretch. In this example, your summer vacation plans seem pretty far away from Mario World, but you can still find a bridge. You could say something like, "Yeah, I love playing Mario World. I don't get to play much during the week because of school. But summer is almost here, and I will be able to play more. Speaking of summer, I wanted to tell you what I'm doing this summer." A bridge like this one talks about the last topic and also finds a way to make a bridge to a new topic by offering a smooth segue.

There is an art to making bridges between topics that offer smooth segues. It's a great skill to have, and it is a skill that can be developed with practice. A good social detective always practices what he or she preaches. Whether you are working on your own verbal dancing, or whether you want to develop your social detective skills, practicing things like this can help.

Some of these things can seem a little complicated at first. But remember, practice makes perfect. And if you don't completely get something the first time you read it, it's ok. You can come back to it again later and it will most likely make more sense the second time around. Let's come back to the Minecraft conversation one more time to give another example of bridging.

Example of Bridging from Minecraft to Other Topics

Once you have asked a few questions about Minecraft, done some summarizing, and decided it might be a good time to segue into another main idea, you can try to create some bridges between Minecraft, model building, and Star Wars. As we said above, the best way to do this is to find something in common between the different topics. In the initial conversation, there are some commonalities that could help to create a bridge.

There is a commonality between Minecraft and building models since they both involve building. And there are commonalities with Star Wars since there are Star Wars models. If done right, Person B could smoothly bridge Minecraft to models, and then bridge models in general to Star Wars models, and then they could even bridge Star Wars models to Star Wars movies without too much effort.

Let's see how this bridging might look in this conversation.

Person B: Do you like building anything other than Minecraft?

Person A: I build forts in my bedroom a lot. And I've made sandcastles at the beach.

Person B: Oh, that's cool! I like doing those things, too. I also love building models. Have you ever built models?

Person A: Yeah, I built a model airplane once.

Person B: Nice! I love building model airplanes. I also love building model rockets. I even built some Star Wars models.

Person A: Neat.

Person B: Are you a Star Wars Fan?

Person A: Yeah, I've seen all the movies.

Person B: Me too! My favorite is the Empire Strikes Back.

Person A: Oh yeah, that's a great one.

Person B: My favorite part is where Han Solo....

You can see here how some simple bridges brought the conversation to Star Wars movies but in a way that was much smoother than the original version.

Waiting for a pause and the end of ideas and practicing summarizing and bridging can be helpful to make conversational transitions smooth. Give it a try and see how it works for you. And remember, practice makes perfect.

Some Background Facts and Context

Kamila and Lupita have been friends ever since they were kids. Kamila loves Lupita so much. She is like a sister to her. When they were younger, they used to be obsessed with Harry Potter. They both read all the books and saw all the movies. When they got together, they would either watch the movies together or talk about all their favorite parts of the movies. As they got older, Kamila started to become less interested in Harry Potter. She still liked it but she was also developing other interests. Nowadays she likes other kinds of books and movies, and she is really interested in music, YouTubers, and things happening on social media. Lupita, on the other hand, has gotten even more into Harry Potter over time. She was still watching the movies and rereading the books. She is also really into the online Harry Potter video games. Lupita had even started to write Harry

Potter fan fiction where she, along with others, would create new adventures for Harry and his friends. It was really creative stuff. Kamila was really impressed with what a good writer Lupita was. But Kamila was not as into Harry Potter as she used to be. And here is where the social mystery comes in. As Kamila started getting more into other things, she became less interested in spending all the conversational dancing time with Lupita talking about Harry Potter. She actually loved hearing about the fan fiction Lupita was writing, and she didn't mind talking about Harry Potter a little. But it seemed like that was all they talked about these days. She wanted to find other ways to relate to her long-time childhood friend, but she was not sure how.

Here is an excerpt from one of their conversations. It's followed by a description of how Kamila made sense of her social mystery and finding remedies.

Time: Saturday, 2:42 Pm

Place: Lupita's backyard

"I'm so glad you could come over today!" Lupita said to Kamila. "Yeah, me too!" Kamila replied. "We haven't seen each other in a few weeks. What have you been up to?" Kamila asked with wide, cheery eyes and a smile that showed she was really interested in knowing. "I've just been working on writing my alternate ending to the final Harry Potter book." "You mean the Deathly Hollows?" "Yeah, I thought they could have added so much more about what happened after Voldemort died." "That sounds awesome!" Kamila said. "Yeah, it's pretty cool." "What do you think happened after Voldemort died?" she asked Kamila. "What do you mean?" "What do you think happened after they all graduated high school and didn't have to worry about the Dark Lord and all? I mean so many cool things could have happened next," Lupita said. "Yeah, I guess that's true," Kamila added. She thought about Lupita's question, wanting to throw the conversational ball back to her. "Maybe Harry goes off to wizard college and becomes a...what do you call that thing he wanted to be? You know the person who protects against the dark arts?" "An Auror!" Lupita said excitedly. "Yeah, that could be cool." "That's a great idea!" Lupita said. "And maybe he finds out that there was actually another secret horcrux that Voldemort created but hid and he has to find it to make sure he never comes back. "Yeah, that could be cool." "And then there could be a whole other series of books about that. Maybe Voldemort comes back. Or maybe he secretly had a son who grows up and now wants to seek revenge for his father's death." "Yeah, I like it," Kamila said.

Kamila didn't mind talking about Harry Potter. It was kind of fun. But the problem was that Lupita would keep talking about this kind of stuff all day. As the conversation went on and Lupita excitedly came up with more and more interesting ideas about how the story could continue, Kamila found herself getting more and more bored. It was fun at first, but it just kept going. She usually loved hanging out with her friend, but today she found herself looking at the clock, wondering when it would be time to go home.

Finally, after a few hours of brainstorming Harry Potter plots, Kamila heard the doorbell ring. She jumped up from her seat and said, trying to hide her excitement and relief, "That must be my mom." "Aww. That went by too quickly" Lupita said. "We were just getting into it" "Uh... yeah. That's too bad," Kamila replied. "Maybe we can Facetime later and talk more," Lupita said. "Uh...maybe. I need to see what we are doing later," said Kamila. But the truth was that she felt more than done with their conversation and did not really want to Facetime with Lupita later. She loved Harry Potter but she had definitely had her fill.

Kamila felt bad. She had been looking forward to seeing Lupita, but it had not been a satisfying visit. She had recently noticed that she would often come away from her get-togethers with Lupita feeling unsatisfied. "I don't get it." she thought to herself. "I love Lupita. And I love spending time with her. I love Harry Potter too," she thought. "I just find that while I'm excited to see her at first, I get more and more bored, and then at some point, I can't wait to leave. I'm not sure what's going on. This is definitely a social mystery," she thought to herself. Kamila was also a student of Johnny's, so she had some good social detective skills to help her solve this mystery. She knew that the best place to start was with the facts.

The Facts

- Kamila and Lupita had been great friends ever since they were little.
- Over time their interests had changed, but they still had lots in common with each other.
- Lately, Kamila has been feeling unsatisfied with their interactions.
- Kamila often finds herself being excited to see Lupita when they first get together, but after a while she finds herself getting bored and wanting to leave.

Solving the Mystery

Ok, here is a social detective challenge for you! Based on what you have been reading so far, what do you think the first thing Kamila did to try and solve the mystery? If you guessed that she went through the prime suspects, you're right! Kamila actually had a handy written list of prime suspects she used to help her remember. She started with prime suspect number one, attention, and worked her way through the other suspects one by one.

Kamila thought about how her attention had been with Lupita and how Lupita's attention had been with her. "We both usually seem to be pretty attentive with each other," she thought. "I do notice that my attention decreases as our time together goes on. When I first see Lupita, I'm very interested and focused, although I do often notice myself having more trouble paying attention the longer we are together. But my hunch is that attention is not the prime suspect."

Next Kamila thought about topic and mood missing and responding. "We both also seem to be pretty good at staying on topic," she thought. "In fact, staying on topic is something we do very well." She paused for a moment to think about how well they stayed on topic. "We definitely can stay on topic," she said out loud. "We are also both pretty good at noticing and responding to each other's mood. That's something I really appreciate about our relationship," she thought to herself. "We both seem to care a lot about how the other feels and we let each other know." Kamila smiled to herself when she thought about this. She appreciated how comfortable she felt sharing her feelings with Lupita.

Next, she thought about over and under-responding. "Sometimes it does feel like Lupita shares a lot of details. And when she does, I tend to talk less, I think. Hmmm," she thought. "Maybe there is something to that. But we still both seem to throw the conversational ball back and forth pretty well with each other. I will make a note of this, but it still does not seem to be the main culprit."

How about those verbal dancing suspects?" She asked herself as she looked at her list.

- *Prime suspect #8 Fast Talking*
- *Prime suspect #9 Verbal Crowding*
- *Prime suspect #10 Trouble Managing the Awkward Silence*
- *Prime suspect #11 Topic Lingering*

"Neither of us seem to talk too fast. Lupita is often very excited in our conversations. But it does not seem problematic. And she always leaves room for me to respond. In fact, she is good at asking me what I think too. So, I don't really feel crowded in our conversations. And we are comfortable with each other so even when there is silence between us it never feels awkward to me. But when I think about it, I have felt awkward at times. It's not the silence. But I do sometimes feel that I run out of things to say and don't know how to respond. Hmm. I will make a note of that too."

Next Kamila thought about topic lingering and when she did a light went off in her mind. "Oh, my!" she said out loud. "I can't believe I missed this!" Kamila thought about some of the ways to tell if topic lingering is an issue. She remembered how you want to look at both the quality of a conversation and the interest people have in the conversation topic. "Lupita and I usually talk well together. We have a great verbal dance. But I've noticed that as we keep talking about the same topic the quality of our time together goes down for me. While Lupita always seems to find new things to talk about, I start having trouble finding new things. When that happens, I repeat things I've already said. As for the interest in the topic, Lupita seems to have endless interest in the topic but I lose interest after a while. Then I start to get bored and start to feel disconnected from Lupita to the point where I start looking at my watch to see if it's time to go home yet.

When I think about it now, I realize that lately, all we seem to talk about is Harry Potter. We spend way too much time talking about that. I mean I like Harry Potter. But not as much as I use too. And nowhere near as much as Lupita does." She thought to herself. "How could I have missed that?" She asked herself again. "I'm so glad I was able to go through my prime suspect list or I might not have never caught this"

Key Culprit in this Mystery:

- Prime suspect #11 Topic Lingering

Social Remedies

After solving this mystery Kamila thought a lot about how she could remedy this problem with her friend in a way that didn't make Lupita feel bad. She knew her friend loved talking about Harry Potter with her. She wanted to be a good friend and make space for that. But she also wanted to be able to explore other topics in their conversations. And maybe even do other things with her friend. Good friendships can grow and make space for new things.

She decided to start by seeing if she could smoothly shift topics next time she was together with Lupita. She remembered some of the strategies that can help in shifting topics smoothly. Things like waiting for the pause, waiting for the end of an idea, summarizing, and bridging. "If these things don't work then I will tell Lupita directly that I want to spend less time talking about Harry Potter." She told herself. "But I think I can communicate that to her in subtle ways if I use these strategies."

The next time Kamila and Lupita spent time together Lupita started talking about Harry Potter. Kamila went along with it for a while. But when she noticed herself losing interest and getting bored, she started looking for the end of a particular idea. When that happened, she summarized what they had been talking about and then bridged the conversation to a related topic. The related topic was other movies they had both seen. After spending some time talking about other movies, she tried shifting the conversation a little farther away from Harry Potter.

This led to them talking about YouTubers they both liked. Which led to them deciding that they would make some YouTube videos together. Lucida suggested making videos about Harry Potter but Kamila suggested that they think of some other things to make videos about too. And Lupita was totally fine with that. Kamila had worried her friend would be upset but Lupita was totally fine and even excited about it. Kamila felt really good about how things had gone. And felt hopeful that her friendship with Lupita could grow and change in positive ways.

Main Ideas Chapter 5

1) What is the difference between the content and the process of a conversation? P - 63
2) What is verbal dancing? P - 63
3) Describe prime suspect #7: *Fast talk? P - 63*
4) What are some of the problems fast talk can cause? P - 64
5) Describe prime suspect #8: *Verbal crowding P - 64* What things might cause verbal crowding? P - 64
6) What are two things people often wait for before responding to others in a conversation? P - 64
7) What are some ways people might check out if they are feeling crowded in a conversation? P - 64
8) What are some ways someone might claim space in a conversation when they are feeling verbally crowded? P - 65
9) What are some ways we can become more aware of how fast we are talking? P - 66
10) What does the "power of the pause" mean, how can we get ourselves to pause more in conversations? P - 66
11) What does "talking about the talk" mean? P -67 Why might you want to do that? P - 68
12) Define prime suspect #9: *Trouble managing the awkward silence P - 69*
13) What makes silences awkward? P - 69
14) What are some problematic ways we might respond to an awkward silence? P - 70
15) What are some things that make it hard to have a nice verbal dance? - P 71
16) What are some ways to make the silence less awkward? P - 73
17) What are parallel activities? P - 74
18) What are connecting activities and give examples? P - 75
19) What are some ways to make more connections with others while doing parallel activities? P - 76
20) What are open questions? P - 76
21) What are closed questions? P - 76
22) What are some mantras you can use to keep a positive mental attitude when there is an awkward silence? P - 78
23) How can you gather facts to discover other people's interests? P - 78
24) What is the tree of association? P - 80
25) What are some things that can keep us from taking positive action? P - 82
26) What are some strategies that can help us take more positive action? P - 95
27) Define prime suspect # 10: *Topic lingering? P - 95*
28) How can you tell if topic lingering is a problem? P - 95
29) What are some ways to smoothly shift topics? P - 95

PART THREE

NONVERBAL COMMUNICATION: LISTENING AND RESPONDING

Chapter 6: Nonverbal Communication

We have been talking a lot about how we verbally connect with people. We have talked about verbal listening and responding, as well as verbal dancing. When we are skillful at these, we are going to be much better at understanding people and at being understood ourselves. We will be able to communicate to others that we care and are interested and that we get them. Our relationships will benefit tremendously as a result.

But there is more to listening, responding, and dancing than words can communicate. There is actually a whole other world of listening, responding, and dancing that can be even more powerful than the one that involves words. I'm talking about the world of nonverbal communication.

Nonverbal communication involves all the things we communicate without using verbal language. When you look at a painting, the art is communicating something to you without any words. When you listen to an orchestra, all the instruments are communicating to you nonverbally. The painting and music can express something to you without ever using words.

Nonverbal communication can also join with verbal communication to say even more together than the words can say on their own. For example, this happens when the soundtrack of a movie creates another layer of feeling and mood to enhance the story on the screen. It can happen when someone sings along with music. The words alone communicate a message, but when paired with the melodies and harmonies and rhythms of the instruments, the words say so much more. The music expresses a richer layer of feeling and mood than might be captured by the story or words alone.

Our bodies also communicate nonverbally, just like paintings and music and other forms of nonverbal expression. The things our body communicates can have a powerful effect on us, as well as on others.

Part of what can make nonverbal communication so powerful is that we often don't even realize it's happening. It can be like subliminal messages. Have you ever heard of subliminal messages? They are messages that we are not consciously aware of. In advertising, they might flash an image of a product or the words "buy this" so quickly that you do not even realize it is there. Subliminal messages can have a powerful effect on us. They can affect our decision-making and our likes and dislikes, as well as our mood.

Nonverbal communication is often like subliminal messaging. Unless we are tuned into it and using our detective skills, we may not consciously notice it. But just because we don't notice it, does not mean it is not affecting us. In fact, like subliminal messages, it can affect us even more when we are not aware of it.

Have you ever heard someone say something that just does not quite feel right? They may be telling you about how happy they are about something, but it does not feel as if they are genuinely happy. Something about their words does not fit. It is possible that in such a situation you are picking up on their nonverbal communication. Their words may be saying they are happy, but their nonverbal communication is saying something completely different. Because of this, you may be left with a strange feeling without even knowing why. The nonverbal communication may be affecting you without you even realizing it.

A good social detective keeps an eye and an ear out for nonverbal communication. By being aware of this type of communication, good detectives may be able to notice important information to help them navigate their social world.

So much is going on behind the scenes when we are with other people. So much of what is communicated and exchanged is entirely nonverbal. Some people say that 93% of communication is nonverbal. Crazy, right? 93%! That's a lot of percent!

And what is even crazier is that so much nonverbal communication happens without our being aware of it. We are giving off and receiving messages without even realizing it. Those messages are affecting us and others without anyone even knowing it! There is a whole world of subliminal messaging going on all the time that we do not even realize is there.

Can you imagine how amazing it would be if you could fully harness the power of nonverbal communication? If you could be a master at reading those messages and communicating to others exactly what you wanted in those nonverbal ways? You would be some kind of social ninja magician-type person. Well, that is what we aim to do in this chapter. We aim to help you be a social ninja, magician-type person when it comes to the world of the nonverbal so that you can be the best social detective possible.

Sometimes nonverbal communication can be a tricky thing. In some ways, it's not as easy to understand as verbal communication. But I promise you this: Once you begin to master the world of nonverbal communication, your social detection skills will skyrocket.

So, let's jump in. Just as we did with verbal communication, we are going to look at the art of listening, responding, and dancing, but with nonverbal communication rather than verbal.

Nonverbal Listening

To start, I want to clarify something. When I'm talking about nonverbal *listening,* I'm not talking about listening in the regular way. What I'm talking about is nonverbal *sensing. Listening* refers to things you sense with your hearing. Real listening is a type of sensing. It is using the sense of hearing to gather information.

But as you probably know, there are many senses other than hearing that we use to gather information. When we pay attention to what others are saying verbally, we are using our sense of hearing to listen and gather facts and clues. When we pay attention to what others are communicating nonverbally, we are using many senses to gather information.

We do use our sense of hearing to gather nonverbal information and will talk more about this when we discuss all the nonverbal things our voices communicate. But we often use other senses to take in nonverbal communication.

We will soon talk about the different senses in more detail, but for now, let me just tell you what the different senses are. I imagine you are familiar with these five senses - *hearing, seeing, touching, smelling,* and *tasting*. But there are actually three other senses that are not often discussed but which a good social detective uses in understanding their social world and solving social mysteries. I'm going to just tease you with them now, but we will talk more about them soon. The three other senses are *mental sensing, body sensing,* and *relational sensing*. These three senses are incredibly helpful for understanding others and navigating social situations.

I just want to make it clear that when I talk about nonverbal listening, I'm talking about senses other than just hearing. We are using the word "listening" to describe paying attention to the information we are getting through our senses.

Just as with verbal listening, nonverbal listening can help you better understand others. And if you understand them better, you will be able to respond to them better, which will help them sense that you get them and are interested in and paying attention to them. Of course, that will help them feel closer and more connected to you, too. Not only will good nonverbal listening on your part help others feel closer and more connected to you, but it also will help you feel closer and more connected to them. It's a win-win situation. Let's talk about some of the prime suspects that might lead to people missing what is being communicated to them nonverbally.

Nonverbal Listening Suspects

I like to break the nonverbal listening suspects into three categories – facial suspects, body suspects, and voice suspects. You will see that there are many clues we can get from listening to what the face, body, and voice all say. In the next chapter, we will start with a look at the face.

Main Ideas

1. What is nonverbal communication? P - 97
2. What are the eight senses? P - 99
3. What are some benefits of good nonverbal listening? P - 99

Chapter 7: Listening to the Face

PRIME SUSPECT #12:

FACIAL FARSIGHTEDNESS

When someone is farsighted, they can see things far away but have trouble seeing close up. For example, they can see the books on the shelves in the library but may have trouble reading the words on the pages, because they can focus far away but not close up. If they can only see the cover of the book and are not able to read all the words inside, they will be missing out on what the book is really about. They may see the pretty cover but miss out on the story. And as the old saying goes, "you can't judge a book by its cover."

People with facial farsightedness might be great at seeing people's faces from a distance. They may recognize people and be able to see their general characteristics, such as hair and eye color, and things like that, but they have trouble when it comes to seeing people's faces up close.

What I mean by that is they have trouble seeing the little subtle things that faces communicate. They see the whole face. But they can't make out the little gestures and expressions that communicate important nonverbal information. And these little gestures and expressions are like the words within the book that tell the story.

With regular farsightedness, we can just wear glasses to see things better up close. But there are no glasses for facial farsightedness. Fortunately, there are some simple things you can do to be able to read people's faces better close up. As we often talk about, the first step is awareness. The more we become aware of what and how people communicate with their faces, the more our closeup vision comes into focus.

Face Mapping

Faces can give us invaluable information that we can use to create a map of the inside world of another person. A good map of the inside world of another person helps us to understand them much better. And when we understand others better, we are more capable of being a good friend and making good choices when it comes to interacting with them. We will talk more about making maps of others in later chapters. But for now, let's focus on face mapping. And let's pay attention or "listen" with our sense of sight and see what we notice.

There are a few basic things we can look for when trying to navigate the information we get from other people's faces. So, let's start at the top. And I mean that literally. Let's start at the top of the face.

<u>The brow</u>. The brow area includes the forehead and eyebrows. While there are lots of subtle variations in what the brow can express, there are a few basic things that can help us bring into focus what someone's face might be communicating

Below are some pictures of faces. The only thing different in these pictures is the brow area. If you look closely you can see how the little changes in this area of the face can result in the face communicating some very different things. So, let's pay attention or listen with our sense of sight and see what we notice.

But first, let me do a quick introduction to Dan (Fig AA).

Fig AA, Dan

Dan is our digital social detective assistant who will be helping us in this nonverbal section. As all good social detectives know, it's always important to have good introductions when meeting new people. For us that goes for digital people too. Everyone, meet Dan.

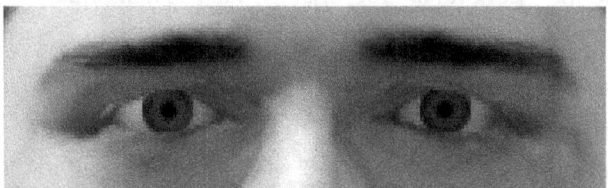

Pic 1

*Picture 1 - **Neutral brow**:*

In Picture 1 Dan's brow is in what I call a "neutral" position. Both the forehead and eyebrows are at rest. Sometimes a neutral brow can mean that part of the face is not really communicating anything in particular. But sometimes it can be a sign of *relaxation or even gentle concentration.*

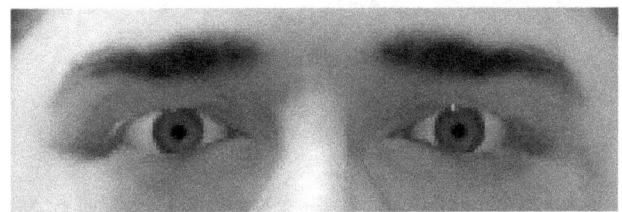

Pic 2

Picture 2 - Brow raised slightly:

In Picture 2 Dan's forehead is up a little and the eyebrows are up as well. You can tell the forehead is partly up because there are a few little wrinkle lines in the forehead. If you notice, the eyebrows are raised somewhat evenly. This could be a sign of *interest or a positive mood.* But because we don't have any other information, it is hard to tell.

This same type of slightly raised brow could be a sign of many things. It could be a sign of someone being happy or sad or anxious. More information is needed to tell. But for now, the main goal is to start to notice the little differences in the parts of the face because these little differences can communicate a lot, especially when they are combined with other facial expressions and gestures.

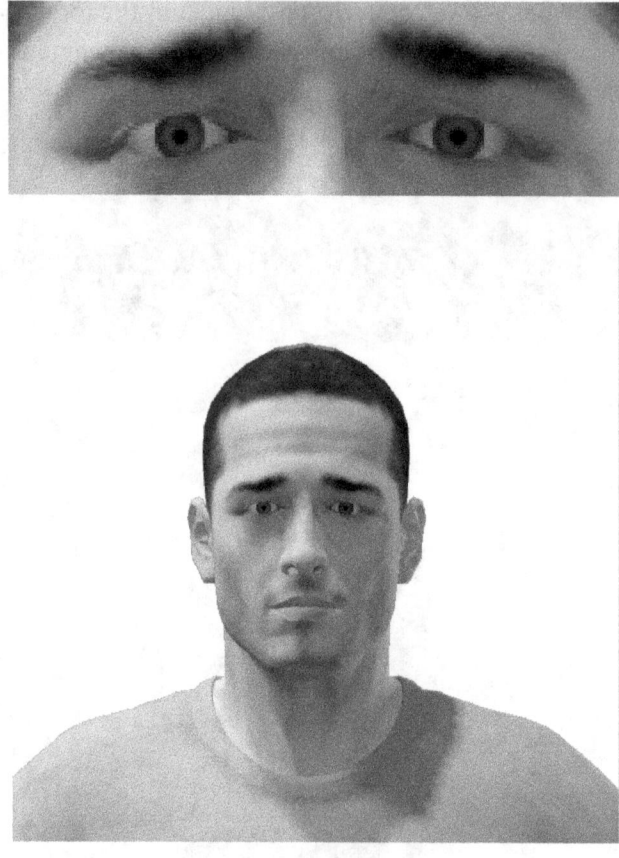

Pic 3

Picture 3 - Brow raised medium with slight peak and furrow:

In Picture 3 Dan's brow is up even more. There are more wrinkles in the forehead, which is a sign that the forehead muscles are being flexed more. In Picture 2 the forehead muscles were being flexed slightly but in this one, they are being flexed even more. More flexing makes the forehead look a little tense. It's not a lot of tension, but it could be a sign of some *mild tension or even sadness.*

The eyebrows also seem to be raised up more in the middle. In Picture 2 the eyebrows were raised more evenly, but here they are pointing or peaking more in the middle. While eyebrows raised slightly and more evenly can be a sign of interest or positive mood when they begin to raise more and peak in the middle that can be a sign of some tension.

The peak of the eyebrows can lead to what is known as a *furrow* in the brow. A furrow happens when lines begin to run up and down in the middle of the forehead as a result of the eyebrows peaking in the middle. Picture 3a shows a furrow in more detail.

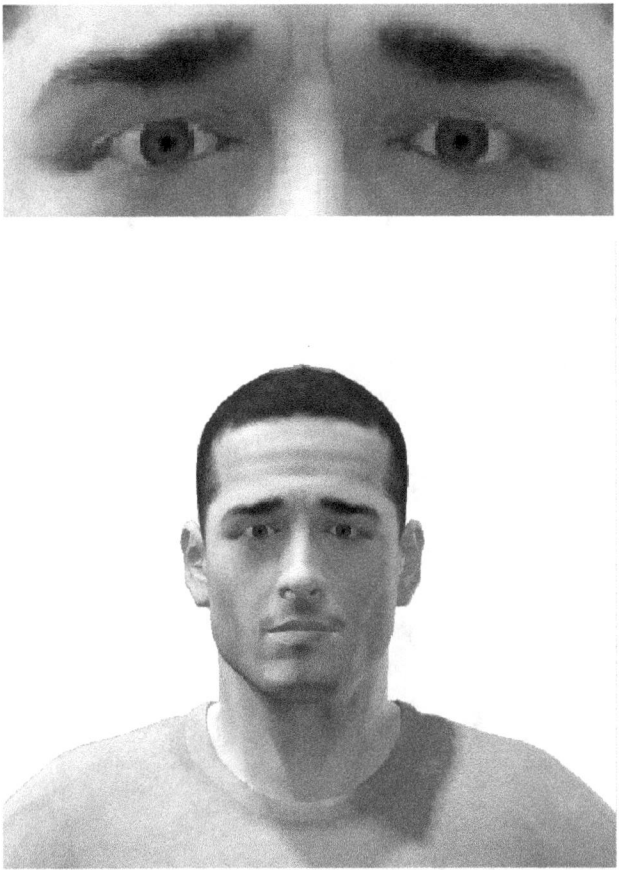

Pic 3a

A furrowed brow is often associated with more tension. This can be a great clue when we are doing our detective work. This level of tension might be a sign of *surprise, mild stress, or worry*.

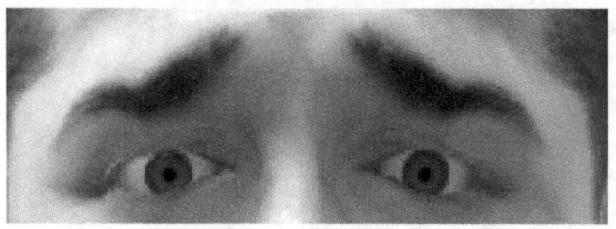

Pic 4

Picture 4 - Brow raised high with significant peak and furrow:

In Picture 4 Dan's forehead and eyebrows are raised even more, and there is a peak in the middle of the eyebrows, which results in a furrow in the forehead.

As the eyebrows raise and peak more, the face begins to communicate that there may be even more tension. This might be a sign of startle or stronger surprise. Or it might be a sign that the person is scared or significantly anxious or stressed.

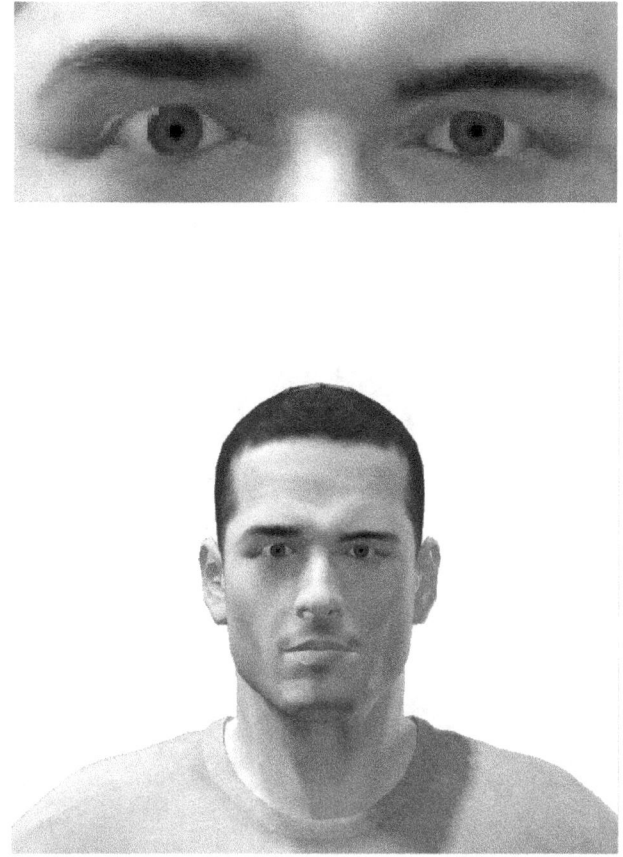

Pic 5

Picture 5 - Brow slightly lowered with more on one side and eyebrows slightly pulled together:

In Picture 5 Dan's forehead is lowered and the eyebrows are pulled together slightly. You might notice that in this picture one eyebrow is a little higher than the other. These things create a furrow in the brow as well, but it looks a little different because the eyebrows are lowered instead of raised. This kind of brow might be communicating that someone is *confused or a little annoyed*.

Note: You want to make sure to be careful with nonverbal communication because you can't always tell exactly what it is being communicated. Sometimes it's not as clear as verbal communication. For example, a slightly lowered brow and eyebrows pulled together can also happen when someone is trying to concentrate and pay attention to something. *A good detective takes all the clues and looks at them together to determine what is going on*. By looking at other clues alongside the clues the face is giving off, you will get a better understanding of what someone's face is expressing.

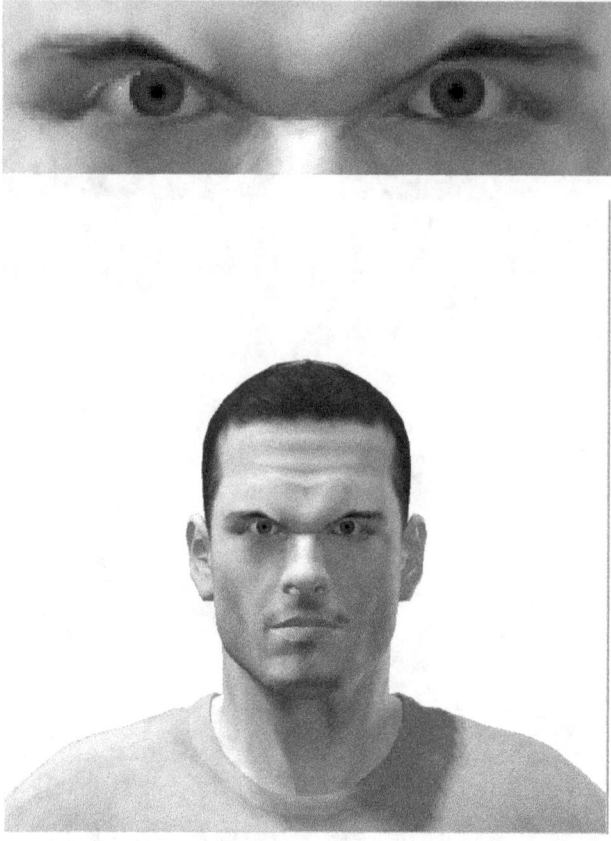

Pic 6

Picture 6 - Brow lowered a lot, eyebrows pulled together:

In Picture 6 Dan's whole brow is clearly pointing down and pulled towards the middle. The furrow is very clear. This brow is expressing a lot, and because of that, it is easier to read on its own than some of the others we have looked at so far. This kind of brow might be communicating *anger or a high level of irritation*.

The Eyelids

Moving down the face, we come to the eyelids. Now as you might be gathering already, many parts of the face work together. You may have noticed in the pictures above that the eyebrows and forehead tend to move together a lot. You might have noticed that even though the rest of the face was the same, the eyelids were partly affected by the changes in the brow. Different parts of the face affect each other.

As you look at the next set of pictures, you might notice how the brow tends to shift as the position of the eyelids change. But our main focus here is the eyelids.

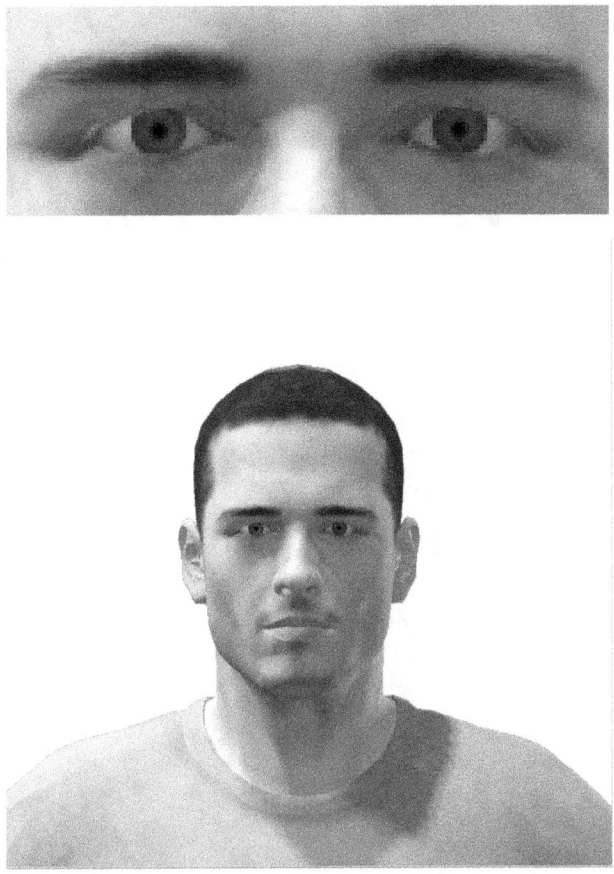

Pic 7

Picture 7 - Eyelids in neutral:

As with the neutral brow in Picture 1, the neutral eyelids here in Picture 7 may not be a sign of anything in particular. But even without anything significant this neutral state of the eyelids could be an indication of *relaxation* or even *gentle concentration*.

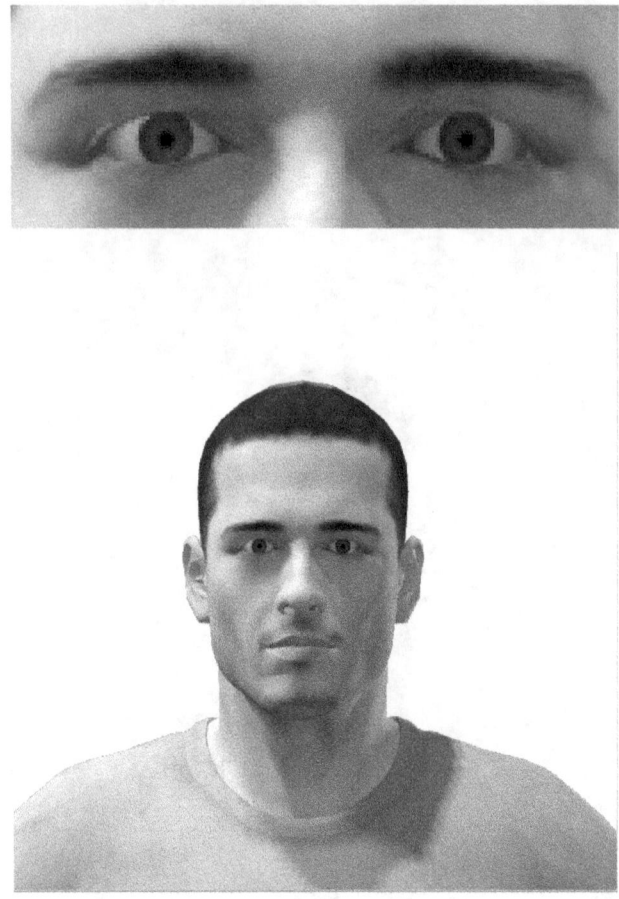

Pic 8

Picture 8 - Eyelids slightly wide:

In Picture 8 Dan's eyelids are open a little more than they are in the neutral position. This is still not communicating a lot but it might be a sign of being *interested or happy.* As with all facial expressions and gestures, this can be helpful information when combined with other things.

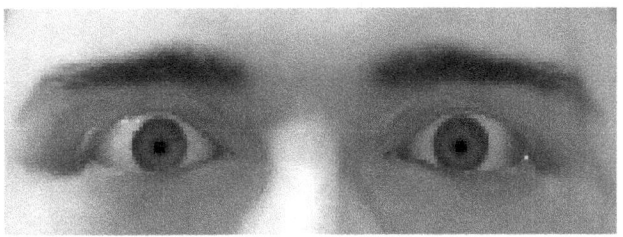

Pic 9

Picture 9 - Eyelids open wider:

When facial features begin to move more and more away from their natural resting position, it is more likely that they might be communicating something. The eyelids opening more in this picture can suggest some tension or emotional distress. Eyelids opening like this can often be an indication of *surprise or even shock or worry*.

Now surprise is not necessarily bad. And wide-open eyelids are not always a sign of tension or distress. They might be communicating *excitement or enthusiasm* just as much as they might be expressing tension or distress. So, you want to take this information and add it together with other clues you are getting from what the person might be communicating to you nonverbally.

Shock eyes: One thing that you might notice in this picture is how Dan's eyes are beginning to look a little freaky. It's not that they are open wide that is making them look that way. It's actually the little bit of white you can see just above the iris of the eye. The iris is the round, colored part of the eye. Usually, the top of the iris is slightly covered by the eyelid. When it's not and you can see some white like in this picture, it can look freaky. I call this "shock eyes" because it's often what you see when someone is shocked or very stressed and afraid. Without any other nonverbal communication from the face, shock eyes can definitely seem strange. But notice the next picture and see if you get a different feeling from the shock eyes.

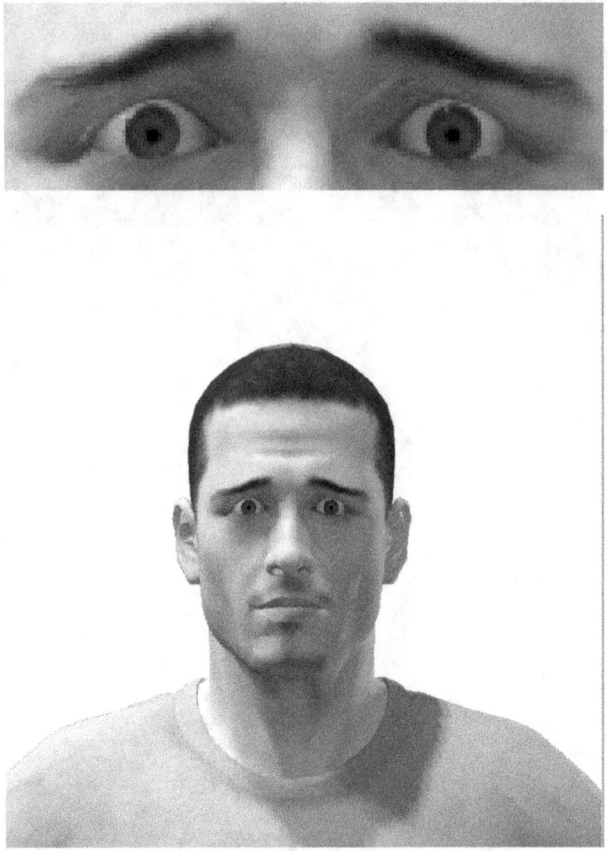

Pic 10

Picture 10 – Eyelids open even wider with eyebrow peak.

In Picture 10 Dan's eyelids are open even wider than they are in Picture 9, indicating even more tension. And here the eyebrows are pointing up in a peak, which is often connected to tension. You can also see there is even more white above the iris, which is a stronger sign of shock eyes.

But the shock eyes in Picture 10 do not look as freaky as they do in Picture 9. Do you know why? It's because the raised brow and peaked eyebrows give you important information that helps you to make sense of the shock eyes. It is very clear in this picture that this person is distressed. This picture suggests *fear, worry, or anxiety*. It could also suggest someone who is about to cry.

The wide eyes and raised brow together make this clearer. And the shock eyes emphasize this even more. In Picture 9 the shock eyes were not as clearly a sign of fear, worry, or anxiety, so it made it hard to make sense of what the shock eyes were communicating. The person could have been angry or crazy, for all we know. All we knew is that they had shock eyes and that it was intense, but we did not know why. Here it is much clearer. Here we get a better sense of what the shock eyes might be expressing.

When someone is communicating a strong feeling with their expression but it is not clear what the feeling is, it can feel freaky and make people uncomfortable. But when it becomes clearer what the strong feeling is that they are expressing, we relax because we get it.

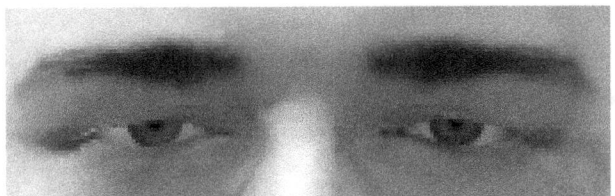

Pic 11

*Picture 11- **Eyelids slightly closed:***

In Picture 11 Dan's eyelids are closing slightly. This suggests more relaxed or tired eyelids, which might be an indication that the person is *sleepy, tired, or possibly bored*.

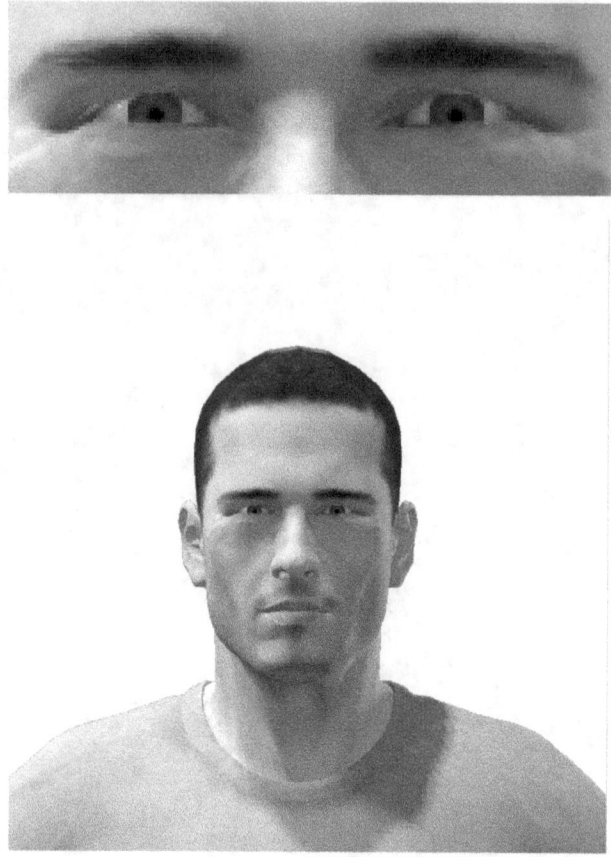

Pic 11a

Picture 11a – Eyes closed from bottom:

Notice how in Picture 11a Dan's eyes seem closed, as in Picture 11. But here it is not the eyelids that are covering up the eyes as much as it is the skin under the eyes that's doing the covering. These little wrinkles, which are called "crows' feet," form in the outside corners of the eyes. While this may seem subtle, it can have a big effect when taken together with other information.

Here in this picture, it may not appear to be communicating a lot. But the crows' feet and the eyes getting covered by the skin beneath often happens when people are smiling. And even if we are not fully aware of that, it can dramatically affect how we read people's faces and interpret the genuineness of their smiles. We will discuss this more later. But for now, just look at Pictures 11 and 11a. See if you can notice the difference in how they look, and maybe even in the feeling you get from them.

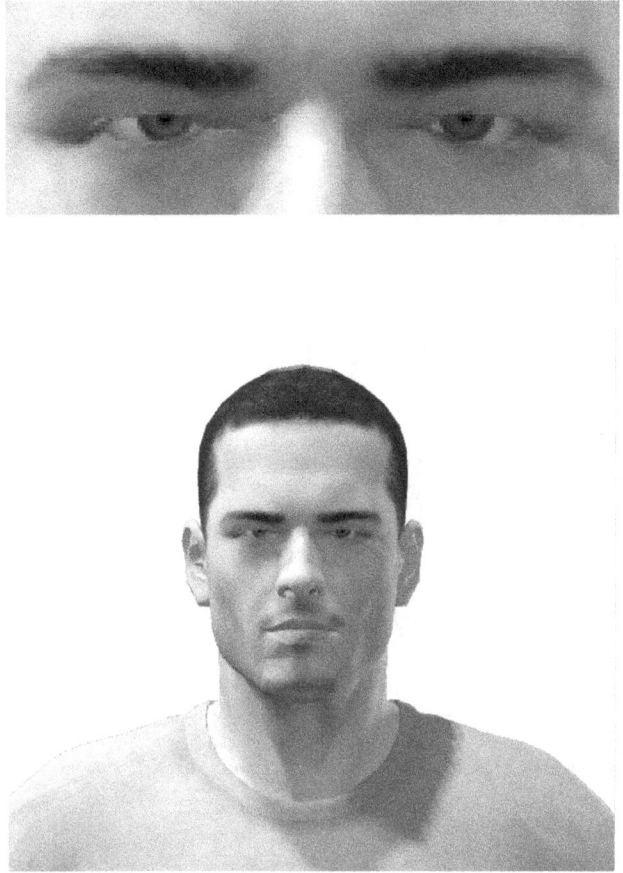

Pic 12

Picture 12 - Eyelids slightly closed and eyebrows pointing down:

In Picture 12 Dan's eyelids are slightly closed like they are in Picture 11. But here the eyebrows are pointing down as well. This gives us more information to help make sense of things.

This kind of eyelid/eyebrow combination might convey sleepy, tired, or bored, as was the case in Picture 11. But the extra information the eyebrows give us might be a sign that there is something else going on. It could be that the person is *concentrating really hard*, or that they are *annoyed or angry*. Here again, we want to consider all the facts when coming to a conclusion.

So many possibilities, right? It can seem overwhelming. But wait until we put it all together. It will become much clearer when we add different clues together.

The Mouth

Continuing to move down the face, we come to the mouth. Of course, the mouth can communicate a lot with what comes out of it. This is where all the verbal communications emerge, but the mouth communicates so much more than what it says with words.

In many ways, the nonverbal communications the mouth expresses can be the easiest of the facial communications to read. And the nonverbal information the mouth communicates can help us a lot when trying to make sense of the information the other parts of the face are communicating. So, let's take a closer look at the mouth

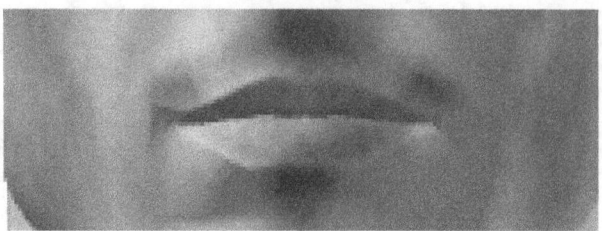

Pic 13

Picture 13 – Neutral mouth:

In Picture 13 Dan's mouth is at rest. It is in its neutral position. As with the brow and the eyelids, this may not be a sign of anything in particular. But it could be a sign of *relaxation* or even *gentle concentration*.

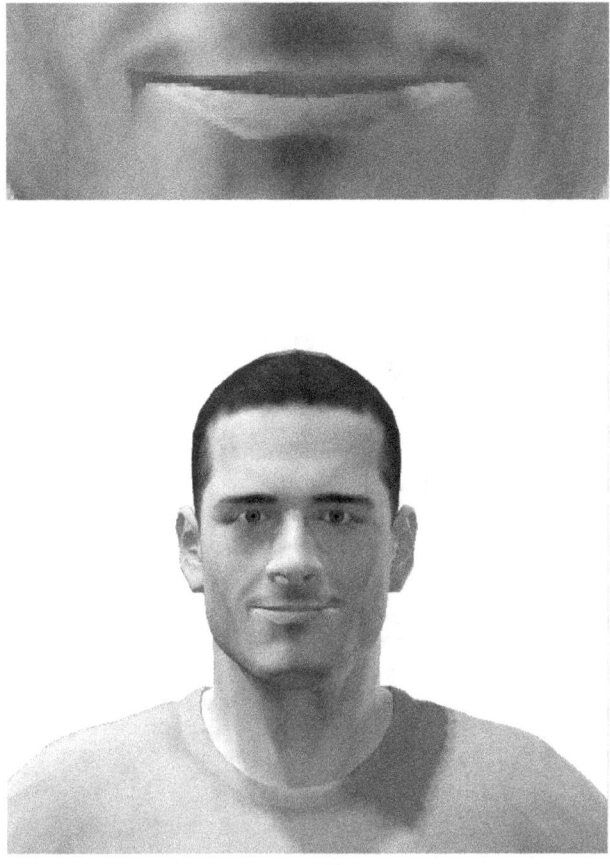

Pic 14

Picture 14 -Corners up slightly in small smile:

In Picture 14 we see the corners of the mouth start to rise a little. This is what happens when people smile, and a smile can nonverbally communicate a lot. When the corners of the mouth go up just a little, it is called a small smile. A small smile is often the sign of a positive emotion like *happiness, satisfaction, or contentment.*

Take a look at Picture 13 and Picture 14. Notice the little differences between the mouths in these two pictures. It can be really helpful to notice the little differences because, even though it might seem subtle, those little differences can communicate a lot. A good social detective develops a keen ability to notice little shifts in facial expressions. It's worth taking a closer look and building your ability to notice little differences.

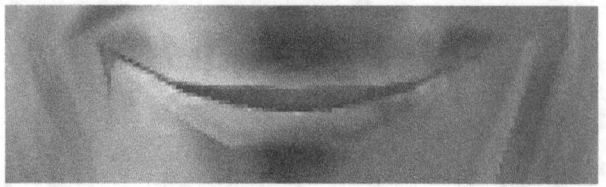

Pic 15

Picture 15 - Corners up more in big smile

In Picture 15 the corners of Dan's mouth begin to rise up even more, turning the small smile into a big smile. As the corners rise more, there is a greater sense of positive emotion. Because of this, the mouth in this picture might be expressing even more *happiness, satisfaction, or contentment* than the small smile in Picture 14.

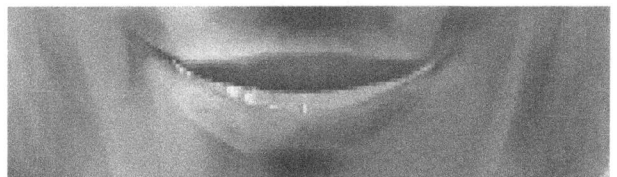

Pic 15a

Picture 15a – Corners up more with teeth in big toothy smile:

Picture 15a is similar to Picture 15, except here we see some pearly whites showing. Notice that when the teeth show in a smile, it tends to amplify the sense of a positive feeling. Pictures 14, 15, and 15a also seem to be expressing positive emotions, such as *happiness, satisfaction, or contentment*. But having some teeth showing can add enthusiasm to the smile and make the sense of the positive stand out even more.

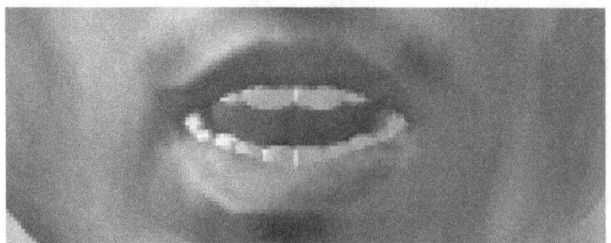

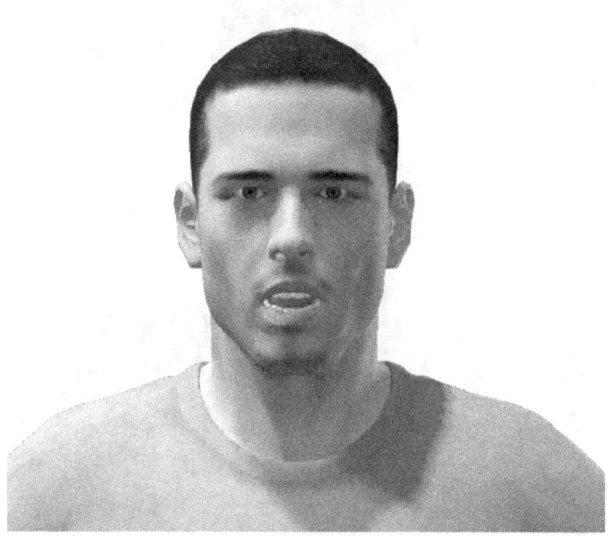

Pic 16

Picture 16 – Mouth open:

In Picture 16 Dan's mouth is open. At first glance, you might think that the person is saying something or about to say something. By itself, a slightly open mouth might not say much, but we will see that it can amplify other facial expressions.

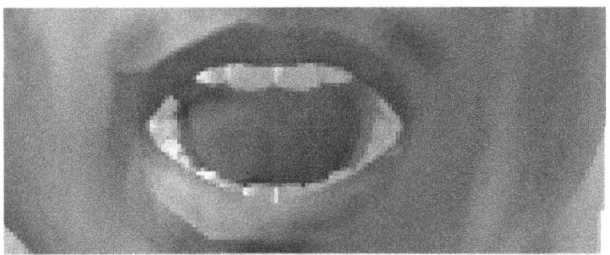

Pic 17

Picture 17 - Mouth open wide:

In Picture 17 the mouth is open wide. Again, just by looking at the picture, you might think that Dan's mouth is open because he is speaking. In this picture, it could even be that he is singing. But as the mouth opens more, it begins to communicate more. Remember, the more that parts of the face move away from their natural, more neutral, resting position, the more likely it is that they are communicating something. A mouth open wide like this might be expressing *shock or surprise or even annoyance*. Again, we want to look at it in combination with other facial expressions, which we will do shortly.

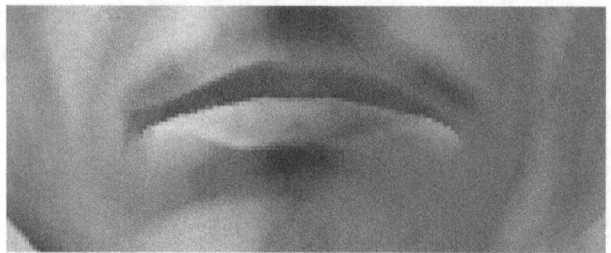

Pic 18

Picture 18 - Corners or mouth down slightly in small frown:

In Picture 18 the corners of Dan's mouth are starting to droop down. This is what happens when people frown, and just as with a smile, a frown can communicate a lot. When the corners of the mouth droop down just a little, we call it a small frown. Frowns are known to be associated with negative emotions such as *sadness, unhappiness, or disappointment*.

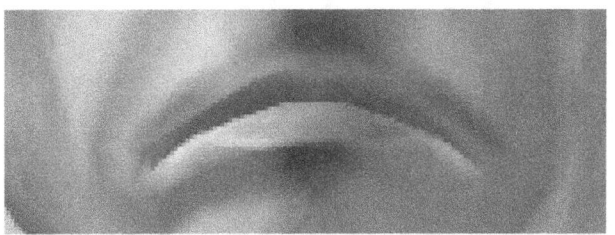

Pic 19

Picture 19 - Corners down a lot in big frown:

In Picture 19 the corners of Dan's mouth move down more, which gives the impression that there is even more negative emotion going on. When the corners go down more like this, we call it a big frown. While Picture 17 suggested some *sadness, unhappiness, or disappointment,* this one does even more because the downward arc of the mouth is greater.

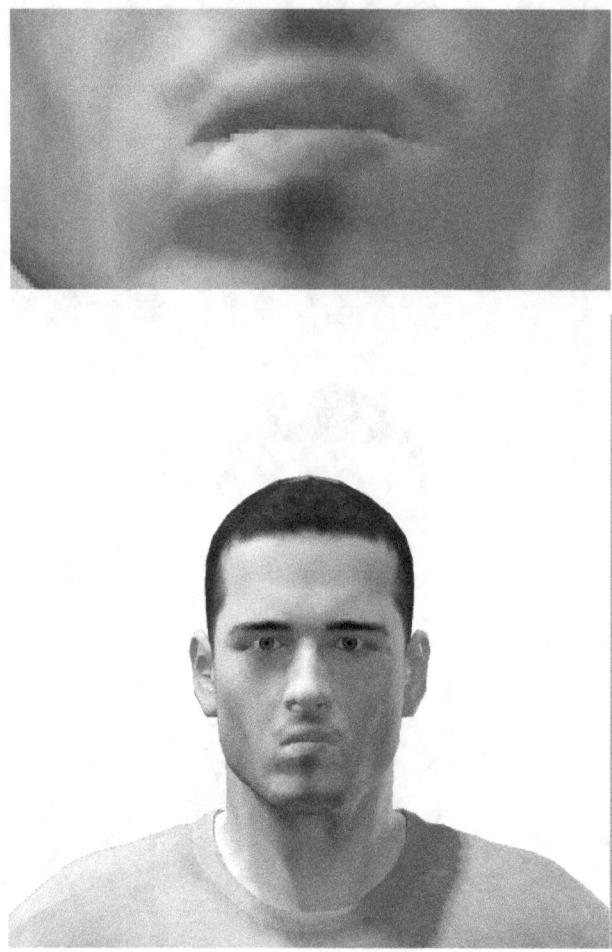

Pic 20

Picture 20 - Lips puckered:

In Picture 20 Dan's lips are pulled together in a pucker. A pucker is often a sign of something sour or unpleasant. A pucker is the classic response to eating something distasteful. But a pucker can also happen when someone is *experiencing* something *sour or unpleasant or distasteful*. A pucker can also be a sign of *anger or annoyance*.

Putting the Pieces Together

Looking at parts of the face in isolation can help us become more aware of the small, subtle things that go into facial expressions. But when it comes to reading the map of the face, the real magic happens when we start putting the parts together. As you can see from the examples above, just noticing what is happening in one part of the face sometimes does not give us enough information to get a good sense of what someone is trying to communicate nonverbally. But when we combine all of the facial clues, things become much clearer. Let me show you some combinations of facial expressions or combos, as I like to call them, so you can see what I mean.

Facial Combos

Facial expressions tell stories. They tell us stories about what might be going on with others. These stories are the product of many different pieces of information that come together as a whole. Below are some faces that contain different combos of brow, eyes, and mouth information. Let's try and read some of the stories these expressions and gestures might be telling.

Pic 21

Picture 21 - *Slightly wide eyelids plus a smile*

Take a look at Picture 21 and notice your first impression. I imagine you might be sensing a clear pleasant feeling being communicated nonverbally by the face. Now go back and take a look at Picture 8. Notice your impression with that picture. You might notice that the eyelids in Picture 8 are slightly wide, just as they are in Picture 21. But in Picture 8, it is much less clear why they are wide.

There are many things those wide eyes might be communicating. But when we add the smile to the eyes, as we do in Picture 21, it suddenly becomes very clear what is being communicated. His face is communicating that he is feeling pretty positive.

Pic 8   Pic 15   Pic 21

Now take a look at Picture 15. Here is a smile all on its own. The smile does seem to communicate a positive feeling all by itself. But can you sense how adding the slightly wide eyes in Picture 21 makes the positive feeling come across even more? Combining the eyes and the smile makes the nonverbal communication clearer, and also stronger in its emotional impact.

You might have to go back and forth between Picture 21 and Picture 15 a few times to get the difference because it is subtle. Part of breaking down the faces into separate parts above was to get better at noticing the small, little differences. These little differences can actually make a big difference, even when we don't realize it.

Pic 21a

Picture 21a - Slightly wide eyelids, a smile, plus smiling eyes

In Picture 21a you can see that the smile and the slightly open eyelids are the same as in Picture 21. But there is something else going on here. Can you see it? It's the eyes. In this picture, we added not only eyes slightly wide open, but also smiling eyes, as you can see in Picture 11a. Let yourself try and sense the difference between Pictures 21 and 21a.

Pic 11a   Pic 21   Pic 21a

The smiling eyes add a lot to the picture and provide important information about how this person might be feeling. Smiling eyes are often a sign of a more full-bodied, sincere smile. To smile with your eyes like this, you have to really put a lot of yourself into the smile, and people can often sense the difference. This type of smiling with your eyes is called a "Duchenne" smile and is seen to be a much stronger indicator of someone really meaning it when they smile.

Think about when you have to pose for a picture and the camera person tells you to "say cheese." When this happens, we usually just smile more with our mouth. We are putting on a happy face, but not necessarily feeling happy. Now imagine someone telling you something really funny. You are likely to smile when this happens. But it is more likely that the smile will be a Duchenne smile, which makes more than just the corners of your lips go up. It makes your whole face smile.

The eye smile conveys a lot. And what is so cool about this is that this often affects people even if they don't realize it. Now that you know about the different kinds of smiles, see if you can notice them on people.

Pic 22

Picture 22 - Slightly wide-eyed plus a frown

Now try this. Look at the eyes in Picture 22. Now look back at the eyes in Picture 21. Do they look different to you? Does it seem to you that the eyes in Picture 21 are happier and the eyes in Picture 22 are more anxious or sad?

Now cover the rest of Dan's face in these two pictures and just look at the eyes. They are the exact same eyes in both pictures. When you cover the mouth, it's easier to see that they are the same. But when we see the mouths in these two pictures, it actually makes us interpret the eyes differently. When the mouth is smiling, we tend to interpret the eyes as happy, and when the mouth is frowning, we interpret the eyes as more anxious or sad. Pretty cool, huh?

Pic 23

Picture 23 - Brow slightly lowered with more on one side and eyebrows slightly pulled together plus a smile:

Picture 23 is interesting because things are being communicated that could be seen as contradicting one another. The lowered forehead with eyebrows pulled together and one brow a little higher than the other is the same as in Picture 5. We discussed how this kind of brow is often associated with being confused or a little annoyed. But when you look at the mouth in this combo picture, it is smiling, and smiling is often associated with more positive emotions.

Take a look at Picture 5 again and notice the sense you get. Can you feel how the brow conveys a lot of emotion? But the mouth does not because it is in a more neutral position. Now look back at Picture 23. Can you sense the difference in what this face is conveying?

Pic 5

Pic 18

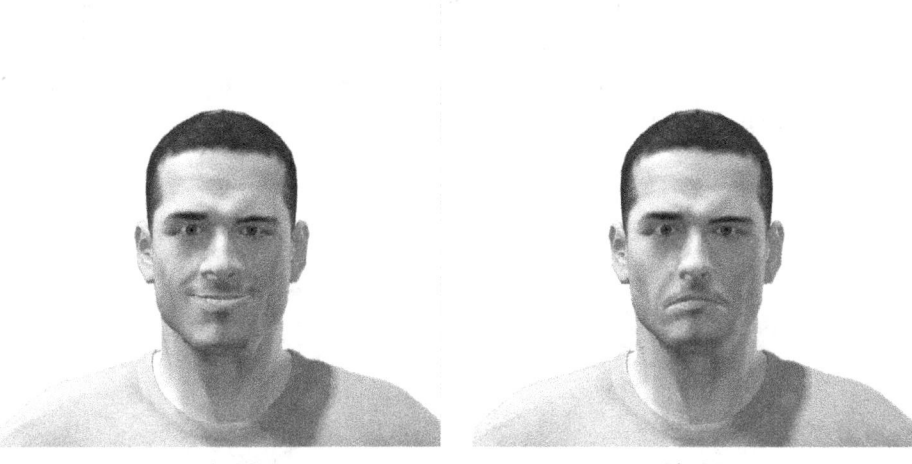

Pic 23   Pic 24

Even if you try to focus just on the brow in Picture 23 and try not to focus on the mouth, you can't help seeing it out of the corner of your eye, and it affects how you read the brow. The feeling that the mouth is communicating is not the same as what the brow is communicating. This has the effect of softening the sense of annoyance or confusion the brow might be communicating on its own.

For me, this makes me think that Dan might be annoyed or confused, but is trying to cope with it and soften it with the smile. The smile seems to communicate that "I'm feeling something negative (which is communicated in my brow) but it's not really that big of a deal and hasn't affected all of me. While part of me is annoyed, part of me is not taking it too seriously." That is what I take from the nonverbal communication in this picture. How about you? How do you explain the differences between the expressions of the brow and the mouth?

You might be noticing that I am making up a story about what I imagine might be going on with this person, based on what his face is communicating. That is something we do all the time, whether we realize it or not. We make up stories about what people might be thinking and feeling based on the information they are communicating to us and on what we know about them to begin with. These stories are part of the maps we make of other people to help us understand them better.

Pic 24

Picture 24 - Brow slightly lowered with more on one side and eyebrows slightly pulled together plus a frown:

Now take a look at Picture 24. You will probably notice that the brow here is the same as the one in Picture 5 and Picture 23. But the feeling in this picture is much different. Take a look at 23 and then at 24, and let yourself sense the difference. As you can probably tell, the main difference is the mouth. Instead of a smile, there is a frown. It is the same frown that is in Picture 18.

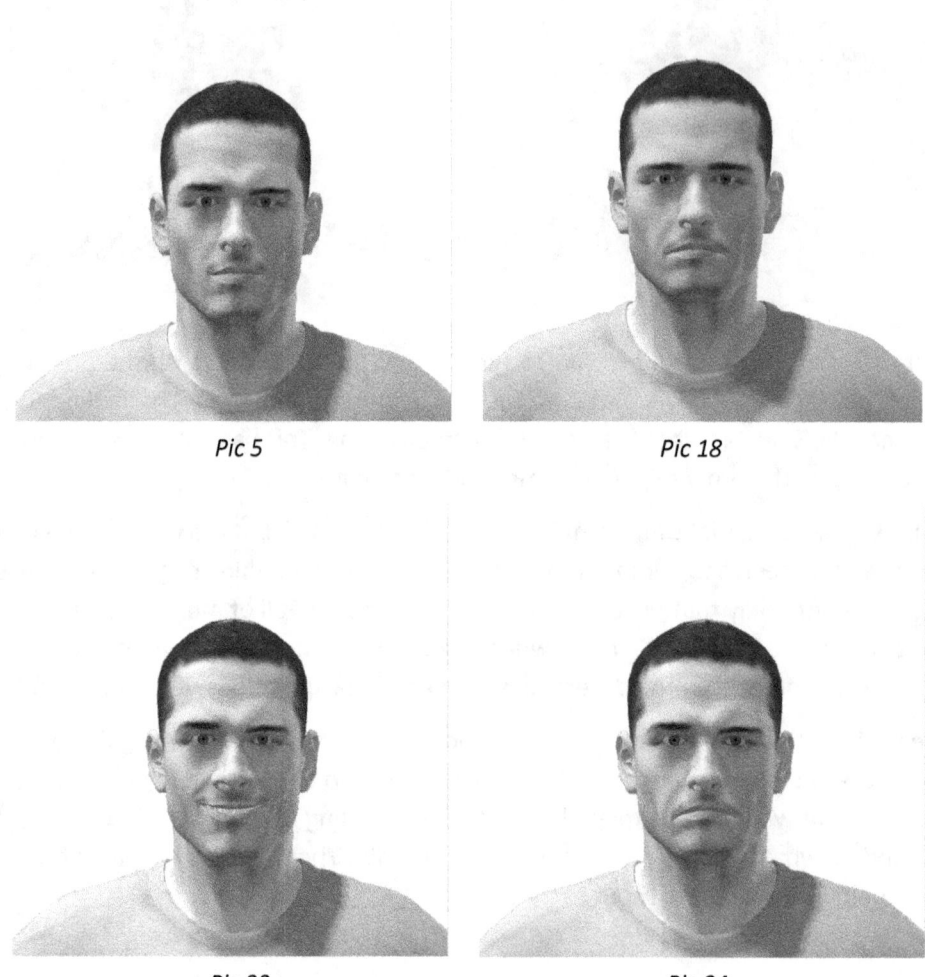

Pic 5

Pic 18

Pic 23

Pic 24

The smile in Picture 23 softens the emotion that the brow is communicating. The frown in Picture 24 does the opposite. Here the frown intensifies the emotion of the brow. Compare Picture 24 to Picture 5. While Picture 5 conveys some possibility of confusion or annoyance, changing the neutral mouth to a frown makes things much clearer.

In Picture 24, the mouth conveys a similar feeling as the brow, giving you two pieces of information for the story you are creating. And the more information we have, the more confident we can be about what is being communicated. It seems much clearer here that Dan is annoyed or angry. While you might have gotten a sense of that from Picture 5 or Picture 18, it is much more pronounced here.

Pic 25

Picture 25 - Brow slightly lowered with more on one side and eyebrows slightly pulled together, plus a pucker:

In Picture 25 we have the same brow as in Pictures 5, 23, and 24, and the pucker from Picture 20. As we said, the brow alone conveys the possibility of confusion or annoyance. The pucker on its own gives the impression of something sour, unpleasant, or distasteful, and maybe even some anger or annoyance. But when the pucker is paired with the lowered brow, it gives us more information and helps us to more confidently come up with a story.

Pic 20   Pic 24   Pic 25

What is your sense when you look at the face in Picture 25? What story do these two pieces of information give you? For me, the pucker makes it much clearer that Dan is pretty annoyed. He definitely seems angry.

Let's take it a step further. Look at Picture 25 compared to 24. Both have the same brow. And both seem to convey anger or annoyance. But do you notice a different feeling when you compare the frown to the pucker? For me, the pucker seems to communicate even more anger and maybe even some aggression. By itself, the pucker in Picture 20 communicates some annoyance. But when it is paired with the lowered brow, it intensifies this and even gives the impression that Dan might be feeling aggressive.

This could be really helpful information to have. Signs of aggression in someone can help us adjust our actions. If someone is just annoyed or somewhat angry, we might act differently towards them than if we feel they are aggressive. If they are angry, we might still try to reason with them or problem solve. We might try to negotiate and engage with them in a certain way. But if they are clearly aggressive, it often might be smarter to walk away or do something to make sure they don't lash out physically and hurt us.

Pic 26

Picture 26 - Brow up with a slight peak and furrow plus a small smile

In Picture 26 we have the brow from Picture 3 and the small smile from Picture 14. As we have discussed, the brow in Picture 3 is possibly suggesting some tension in the form of surprise, anxiety or worry, or maybe even some sadness. The small smile in Picture 14, on the other hand, seems to be communicating more positive emotions, like happiness, satisfaction, or contentment. Many of the other facial combos we have been discussing have had features that seem to support each other and intensify and confirm what is being communicated nonverbally. But here, as was the case in Picture 23, the two different aspects of the face seem to be contradicting each other, with the brow communicating more negative emotion and the mouth more positive emotion. Just as in Picture 23, this has the effect of softening the stress of the brow.

Pic 3 *Pic 14* *Pic 26*

It still seems clear that Dan is stressed. But the smile suggests that the stress might not have completely taken him over. The smile suggests that while part of him is stressed, perhaps part of him is not. It suggests that he is either coping with the stress or that he is not taking the stress too seriously.

Of course, it could also be that he is very stressed but is trying not to show it to others. It may also be that he is smiling to help himself feel better. Did you know that smiling when we are feeling bad can actually help us calm down and feel better? Give it a try sometime and see if it works for you.

There are many stories we can come up with to try and explain these kinds of contradictory facial communications. A good detective keeps gathering facts in order to be sure. But whatever the story may be, it seems clear that the smile softens the stress of the brow.

Pic 27

Picture 27 - Brow up with slight peak and furrow plus an open mouth:

In Picture 27, we once again see the brow from Picture 3. But here it's combined with the mouth from Picture 16.

In Picture 26 the smile softened the tension of the brow. But here the open mouth does the opposite. It supports what the brow is communicating, and even helps to make it clearer. While the brow alone suggests some tension, the open mouth clarifies things and makes it seem as if Dan is experiencing surprise or even shock.

Pic 3   Pic 16   Pic 27

The most interesting part of these combos is seeing how adding an extra piece of information can give us a much different understanding of what someone is communicating nonverbally. We can see that here when we compare Picture 16 to Picture 27.

Take a look back at Picture 16. Dan's mouth is open but it's not clear exactly what he might be trying to communicate. Is he about to say something? Is he holding back a yawn? Did he just let out a big burp? Who knows? It could be lots of things. But when we add the raised brow to the picture, it becomes much clearer. The brow gives us a context in which we can better understand what the open mouth is communicating.

Pic 28

Picture 28 - Brow up, medium slight peak and furrow, and corners of mouth turned down slightly:

Here again, in Picture 28 we have the brow from Picture 3, but instead of a smile or an open mouth, we have a slight frown. Notice the different sense you get looking at this picture. Take a look back at Pictures 26 and 27 and compare the sense you get from each of those to the sense you get from this picture.

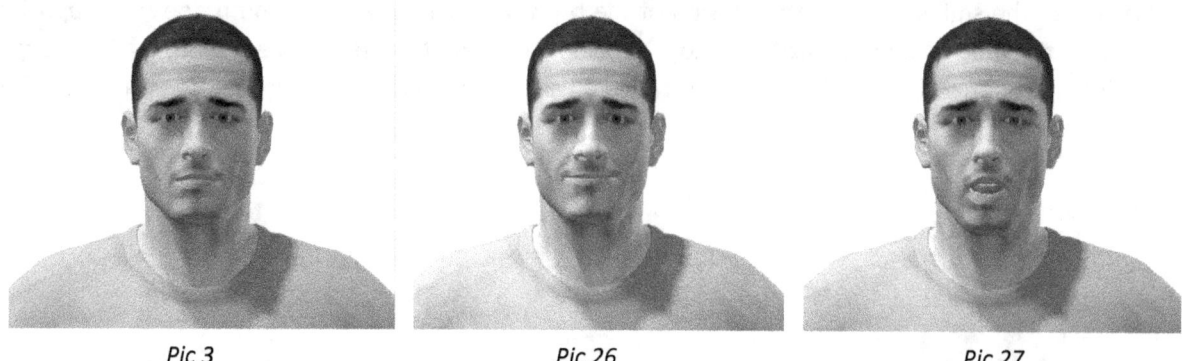

Pic 3   *Pic 26*   *Pic 27*

While Picture 26 suggested someone tense but trying to cope with it, and Picture 27 suggested the feeling of surprise or shock, this picture tells a different story. The slight frown here suggests that this person is sad. The frown supports the feeling the brow is communicating and clarifies it in a slightly different way than Picture 27 did. Here the frown makes it very clear that Dan is communicating sadness.

Crazy Combos

You may have noticed that some facial combos combine different facial communications that help to clarify what is being communicated because the two different parts of the face are communicating similar things. When two parts of the face are communicating the same thing, you can be more confident that the person might be feeling what you are sensing.

There have been a few other combos in which different parts of the face are communicating slightly different things, which can soften an emotion being communicated. This is what happened in Picture 26, where the small smile softened the tension that the brow was communicating.

But when different parts of the face start to express very contradictory things, it can start seeming strange. It can leave you feeling weird because it is really hard to determine what the person is trying to express. When different parts of the face express things that are very contradictory it can look kind of crazy. I call these kinds of contradictions *crazy combos*. Take a look at Pictures 29 and 30 to see what I mean.

Pic 29

Picture 29 - Crazy Combo 1- Brow lowered a lot, eyebrows pulled together with mouth corners up and teeth in smile:

In Picture 29 you have the brow from Picture 6 that is communicating anger or a high level of irritation. But it is paired with a mouth with a big toothy smile, similar to the smile in Picture 15a. As we discussed, the smile expresses a sense of happiness, satisfaction, or contentment, and the teeth amplify this, adding a possible sense of enthusiasm. We have a face that is expressing both a strong sense of anger or irritation, as well as a strong sense of happiness and enthusiasm. It's confusing, to say the least.

Pic 6   *Pic 15a*   *Pic 26*

When communications are contradictory, you don't get the sense that one part of the facial expression is softening the other, as you do in Picture 26. Instead, you get the feeling that something weird is going on. I don't know about you, but when I look at this face, I get a little creeped out. I mean is he enthusiastic because he is going to express his anger by hurting someone? Or is he just so disconnected from his emotions that he does not know what he feels?

Often when people express contradictory emotions it can leave others very unsettled without even knowing why. If this happens to you sometime soon, if you feel weird because of someone's facial expression, you can use your social detective skills to see if you can figure out why. You can see if it seems like the person is expressing different things that contradict one another.

Pic 30

Picture 30 - *Crazy Combo 2 - Very anxious brow and big smile:*

Here is another example of a combo with extreme opposite facial communications. His brow is expressing a lot of anxiety and stress and possibly fear, as the face in Picture 4 does. But he also has a big, overexaggerated, toothy smile. The two facial communications just do not go together naturally, and the combination of them makes Dan look kind of crazed. Don't you think?

Pic 26　　　　　　　　　　Pic 29　　　　　　　　　　Pic 30

In this picture, Dan does not look like he might hurt someone as he does in Picture 29. But he does look like something is about to snap inside of him. He looks like he might be on the verge of a nervous breakdown. This is not the face of someone who is coping well, and there is a sense of unpredictability that would probably make most people want to back away.

Now take a look at Picture 26. In this picture, there are the same kind of contradictory facial expressions as in Picture 30. The face has an anxious brow and a smile. But in Picture 26 Dan does not look crazy. He does not look like he is coping poorly and about to lose it. In fact, it is the opposite.

In Picture 26, Dan does look a bit stressed or anxious, but the small smile makes it seem like he might be coping with the stress and anxiety rather well. As we discussed, the fact that he is smiling here even though his brow is expressing anxiety suggests that he may not be taking the anxiety too seriously. Because he can still smile, it suggests that he is not totally overwhelmed by the anxiety.

Why does Picture 26, which has this kind of contradictory communication, seem less crazy and actually healthier than Picture 30? Can you guess? It's because in Picture 26 the difference between the facial communications is not that extreme. The face in Picture 26 looks a little anxious and has a little smile, so it is easier to see that seeming a little anxious and having a little smile don't have too much distance between them. A little contradiction can convey that someone is coping well and not taking things too seriously. But a very big contradiction is not as realistic and can make it very hard to read the other person, which feels uncomfortable. It also communicates that something may be off with the person.

The Importance of Clear Facial Communication

People usually feel much more comfortable in social situations when they have a good sense of what is going on. This is part of the reason why extreme contradictions in facial expressions can make people feel so uneasy. Extreme contradictions can make us confused about what the other person is really communicating.

It's not just extreme contradictions that make people feel uneasy though. Any extreme, overexaggerated facial expression can seem weird and make people feel uneasy and even scared. While extreme expressions that don't involve any contradictions might be clear in what they are expressing, the intensity can make others feel that the person is not really in control of themselves.

We want to find a happy medium in how much we express to others verbally or nonverbally. Too much and it can be overwhelming. But too little can also be a problem. Sometimes people don't express enough with their faces and this can be difficult. Remember, people feel most at ease when they have a sense of what is going on and when the communication is clear. Just as contradictions make it hard to know what is really going on, so do expressions that don't express enough.

People sometimes use the term "deadpan face" to describe someone who is not expressing emotion with their face. I like to call it "robot face" or "mannequin mug" because it can seem like the other person is a robot or a manikin when they don't communicate anything with their face.

We depend on nonverbal communication a lot, even when we don't realize it. When someone is not giving us any facial communication, we often feel at a loss and don't know how to read them. The moral of the story is that a little works and a lot does not.

A Note on RGF

There is one more thing about facial expressions I want to discuss. It involves a very common suspect in social mysteries named RGF. RGF is a condition most everyone has seen and many of us have without even realizing it. It stands for "Resting Grumpy Face."

For some people, when their face is in a relaxed, resting state, it looks as if they are really grumpy. They might be in a great mood and may be calm but they just naturally look grumpy or even angry. I know lots of really cool, nice, generally happy people who have this. And if I didn't know them better or didn't know about this very common condition, I would think there was something really bad going on inside of them.

Now while RFG is not a life-threatening condition and poses no threat to someone's physical well-being, it can definitely affect someone's social well-being. But the good news is that there are some pretty simple things someone can do to minimize any negative effects of RGF and make sure they don't give others the wrong impression.

RGF has the most powerful effect on people who don't know us very well. Remember, we look for lots of clues when we are figuring out what someone is nonverbally communicating. If we have lots of experiences with someone whose face naturally looks grumpy, we are not going to give their resting facial expression as much weight when trying to figure out what they are communicating. But if we don't know the other person very well, we won't know not to give facial expressions so much weight and will most likely come to the wrong conclusions when trying to figure out what the person with RGF is communicating.

One thing people with RGF can do is to make a point to shift their expression when interacting with others, especially when relationships are new. Even just a hint of a smile can help offset the RGF and keep others from thinking a person is grumpy when they really are not. Another thing that people with RGF can do is emphasize other nonverbal communications to offset what the face may be inadvertently communicating. By using other nonverbal or even verbal communications, they can create a contradiction that will help people to interpret their RGF differently. If others see the person with RGF communicating things that let them know they are not really grumpy it can help others realize that it's just a case of RGF, rather than a case of the other person being upset.

One of the things this once again highlights is that we often need more than one piece of information to tell what is going on inside someone else. A good detective considers all the clues to create a bigger picture of what is going on inside others. We will talk more about this later in the section on context. But it is good to always keep this in mind, especially in a world where it is so common for people to have RGF.

DIY: Building Face Mapping Skills

Here are a few DIY practices to help you sharpen your face mapping skills. Give them a try and see what you think.

1) Mirror mapping

Mirror mapping is pretty straightforward. Basically, you find yourself a nice mirror and make lots of different faces while looking at your reflection. You can look at the pictures of faces in this section and try to imitate them. When you're doing this, see if you can sense what it feels like to make those faces. Remember how we said that smiling can actually help put you in a better mood? It's really true. Making other facial expressions can affect how you feel as well. Frowning or making an angry expression can often increase a sense of anger in your body. The same thing is true with sad or scared facial expressions. Give it a try and see if you notice any change in how you feel when you make different faces.

Mirror mapping can help you become more familiar with all the different things a face can communicate. It can also be very helpful in building your own ability to communicate different feelings with your face. We often communicate a lot with our faces without even being aware of it. While sometimes this can be a good thing, there are other times we might not want to communicate something to someone, but our facial expression gives us away, such as if you are talking to a cute boy or girl and want to come across as confident, but your facial expression is communicating that you are nervous. By practicing different facial expressions in a mirror, you will become more aware of the things your face communicates. And when we are more aware, we can not only communicate with our face better, but we can also be more skilled at not letting our face communicate things we want to keep private.

2) Partner face mapping

This is very similar to mirror mapping but here you do it with a partner. Find someone to practice with and take turns making a variety of facial expressions. See if you can guess what the other person is trying to communicate nonverbally. This can be a great way to test out if the things you do with your face actually express what you're trying to express. I have had a lot of people be really surprised to find out that what they thought they were expressing with their face was not what other people were seeing. Feedback can help you fine-tune your facial expressions and get better at effectively communicating nonverbally.

3) Facial Syncing game

Did you know that when mechanical clocks are in the same room, they start to tick in sync with each other? Their rhythms align just by being near each other. When we are getting along well with others, we often sync with them as well. Sometimes when people are really connected, they might know what the other person is going to say. When we sync together, our conversational dance is more likely to be very smooth, because we are more tuned into the flow and rhythm of the conversational dance. Often when people are in sync with each other, they can even sense each other's mood and respond in ways that match each other's mood more accurately. There are lots of ways we can get better at syncing with others. One great way is the facial syncing game.

In the facial syncing game, we try to mirror or mime what another person is doing. Have you ever seen a mime copy what someone else is doing? When they do, they are basically playing the syncing game. Of course, mimes sometimes do this to someone without getting the other person's permission to do so, and that can feel insulting to people. So, make sure that when you play this game, you get the other person's permission first, and that you do it in a friendly way.

To play the facial syncing game, find a partner and let them know you want to mirror their facial expressions. You can start by having them intentionally make faces and see if you can copy what they are doing. When you are doing this, make note of what you think the other person's face is communicating. Are they making a happy face? Is it a sad, or angry, or scared face? See what your eyes notice. Then see if you can copy the face they are making, and see if you can feel the same feeling in your own body that you think they are expressing with their face. Remember, the face we make can actually affect how we feel. So, see if you can sense that feeling in yourself as you make the face.

Once you have done this, have the other person try to face sync with you. And when they do, see if the face they are making matches what you think your face looks like. This can be a great way to get feedback about how well we are able to communicate with our facial expressions.

Combining Clues to Test Our Hunches

Did you notice in this section on facial expressions that when I talk about what these facial expressions might be communicating, I often used words like "might" and "may?" That is because reading nonverbal clues is sometimes not as clear as reading verbal expressions.

If someone says "I'm mad," it is usually pretty clear what they are communicating. But nonverbal clues often can have a number of different interpretations. They are pieces of a bigger communication pie, and together with other pieces of information, these nonverbal expressions help us to better understand what is going on with other people.

Facial expressions are clues. A good detective takes many different clues and puts them together to build their hunches. Then they test out their hunches. You want to take the clues you get from facial expressions and combine them with the clues you get from other nonverbal and verbal information. When trying to make sense of the facts and solve our social mysteries, there is other information we get from people that we want to take into consideration as well. The more clues you have, the more likely you are to accurately get what is going on with someone.

We will talk more in later chapters about all the different kinds of clues we get from people that can help us to understand them better. But for now, I just want to make the point that we always want to look at all the facts together, and see if they support or contradict each other.

Main Ideas Chapter 7

1. What is facial farsightedness? P - 101
2. What is the first step in dealing with facial farsightedness? P - 101
3. What is face mapping? 101
4. What are some different things the brow does to communicate feelings? P - 101
5. What are some different things the eyelids do to communicate feelings? P - 108
6. What are some different things the mouth does to communicate feelings? P - 115
7. What are crazy combos? P - 135
8. Why is clear facial communication important? P - 137
9. What is RGF? P - 138
10. What is mirror mapping? P - 138
11. What is partner face mapping? P - 139
12. What is the facial syncing game? P - 139

Chapter 8: Listening to the Body

When talking about facial expressions, we worked our way down from the brow to the eyes to the mouth. Let's continue working our way down from the face, and move to our next category of nonverbal listening suspects, which is body listening suspects. There are three prime suspects that are helpful to watch for when considering if body language is playing a role in a social mystery. They are *body posture, body placement,* and *body movement.* Let's take a look at each one of these.

Body Posture

PRIME SUSPECT #13:

BODY POSTURE BLINDNESS

Posture refers to the position in which someone holds their body when standing or sitting. The way we hold our bodies communicates a lot to people. Our bodies can often say much more about how we are feeling than our words. It makes sense if you think about it. After all, it's in the body that we actually feel our emotions. We may use our minds to understand and make stories about what we are feeling. But the actual feelings themselves are experienced in our bodies. Being aware of what we are feeling in our bodies is an amazing tool for a social detective, and missing these important nonverbal cues can be a powerful culprit in many social mysteries.

We will talk more about how to become more skillful at noticing all the things we might be feeling in our bodies in the chapter on the eight senses. But for right now, let's just talk about some feelings the body might express and communicate to others, and the impact that can have on our exchanges with other people.

Just as is the case with facial expressions, body expressions are not always completely clear. As with facial expressions, you want to look at the clues that body expressions offer, and combine them with other information to make sense of the facts and try to figure out what is going on with other people. Let's start from the top and work our way down the body.

Neck Posture

We don't often look at the neck itself for clues about what someone is communicating to us. But the neck can express a lot because of how it positions the head. When the neck is in a neutral position, it does not tilt or turn the head, so the head is level and facing forward. (See the picture of Dan in BP 1).

Dan BP 1

If we are in front of someone, this neutral neck posture gives us nonverbal information that the person is paying attention to us, because of how it is positioning the head in a way that makes it face us. If the neck is twisting to the side and turning the head to the side while we are in front of the person (see Picture BP 2), we will most likely get the message that their attention is elsewhere.

Dan, BP 2

Of course, if we are to the side of Dan, and his neck is turning his head to face us (Picture BP 3), we will most likely get the message that he is paying attention to us. In fact, we may get an even stronger message that he wants to be paying attention to us because turning your head to face someone requires effort. And more effort suggests more motivation.

Dan, BP 3

How about if the neck tilts the head to the side so it is at an angle? What kind of message might this give off? Take a look at Picture BP 4.

Dan, BP 4

What might Dan's tilted head be communicating? Some common things a tilted head might communicate are confusion, annoyance, or even concentration. When people are confused or annoyed, they often tilt their head to the side. They also do this when they are thinking intently about something. From looking at Picture BP 4, it might be difficult to determine what exactly is being communicated. But how about when we add some facial communications?

Dan, BP 5

When we add the facial information in Picture BP 5, does it seem any clearer what might be going on with Dan? The brow here is up in the center and more on one side, and the mouth is scrunched. This makes it seems clearer that the person might be confused.

Dan, BP 6

How about Picture BP 6? Dan's brow here is up a bit, but closer to neutral than in the last picture, and the eyes seem to be looking up. Eyes looking up like this are often a sign that someone is thinking about something. When we put the more neutral face together with the upward eye gaze and the tilted head, it paints a picture of someone who might be concentrating on something they are thinking about.

Dan, BP 7

Now if we furrow the brow just a little and scrunch the mouth (BP 7), the same tilted head and upward gazing eyes start to paint a picture of someone who might be annoyed. We can again see how the context of any specific piece of information affects how we make sense of it, something we will be talking more about in later lessons.

Let's look at another neck posture.

Dan, BP 8

In Picture BP 8 we have the same head tilt and upward eye gaze we had in BP 6. But here the head is also tilted a little bit upward. This gives an even stronger impression that Dan is thinking. Looking up often conveys thinking and concentrating, and when the head is tilted upward, it just adds to what the eyes are already communicating

Of course, there could be a bird about to poop on Dan's head or a UFO passing by. But that would be more information to add to our list of clues when making sense of what Dan is communicating. And if that were the case, he might look more like this...(Picture BP 9).

Dan, BP 9

Let's look at one more neck posture here: Picture BP 10.

Dan, BP 10

In this one, Dan's neck is tilted downward, which makes his head face down. What feeling do you get when you see this picture? What does it seem like the head is communicating? A downward-turned head might be a sign that someone is feeling bad. Of course, if the face also communicates some sadness, it will make it more apparent what the downward-tilted head is communicating (see Picture BP 10a).

Dan, BP 10a

But even without that, the downward-tilted head communicates a lot.

A downward-tilted head might also be a sign that someone wants to avoid eye contact for some reason. Someone might want to avoid eye contact because they feel embarrassed in front of another person and don't want to look at the person because it will make them feel more embarrassed. Or maybe they feel mad at someone or hurt by them and want to avoid closeness by avoiding eye contact. In these situations, the downward-tilted neck turns the head downward to go along with the eyes that are looking downward.

In many species like monkeys and dogs, staring in the eyes can be a sign of challenging, and avoiding eye contact and turning the head downward can be a way to let the other animal know you acknowledge that they are the leader. This can happen with people too. A downward-turned head can sometimes communicate that someone is being obedient, subservient, or submissive towards someone else.

For example, if someone gets in trouble or is intimidated or bullied by someone, they might avoid eye contact and turn their head downward as a way of letting the other person know they are submitting to them in some way. They might submit to the teacher who is scolding them or the bully who is intimidating them. They communicate to the other person with their downward-turned head and eye gaze that they are giving them power and authority. Even if the person is making eye contact, the downward-turned head can communicate giving the other person power. See if you can feel this dynamic when you look at Picture BP 11, where the head is down but the eyes are looking towards you rather than looking down, as they are in Picture BP 10.

Dan, BP 11

DIY: Observing and Sensing Neck Posture

To get a better sense of the effects of neck posture, stand in front of a mirror and try out the neck postures we have been talking about. Notice how your neck moves your head. And as you do, see if you can get a sense of the different feelings that can be communicated when we use our neck to shift our head.

Shoulders and Back Posture

As we continue down the body, we come to the shoulders and back. Our shoulders and back can communicate a lot. Take a look at Picture BP 12 and see if you can get a feeling of what the posture of Dan's shoulders and back might be communicating. In this picture, the shoulders and back are hunched over.

Dan, BP 12

Hunching is often a sign that someone is not feeling confident. Hunching might be a sign of feeling disempowered or even sad or depressed. Again, other surrounding clues like facial expressions or what the person is saying or what just happened to them can give many additional clues as to what the hunching is communicating. But see if you can get a sense of how this kind of hunching might convey a lack of confidence, a sense of personal power, or a feeling of sadness.

Can you sense that from looking at Picture BP 12? Do you get a feeling of what Dan might be feeling when you look at it?

Now, look at Picture BP 13. See if you can sense the difference here.

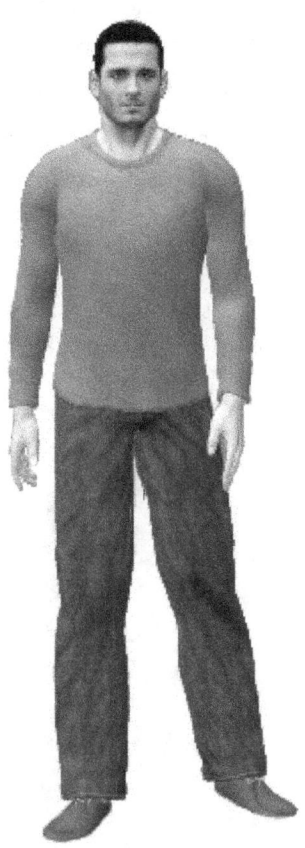

Dan, BP 13

Dan's shoulders and back here are straight and strong looking. This type of posture is often associated with a sense of strength and confidence. Can you pick up more of a sense of confidence in this picture compared to the one above where Dan is hunching?

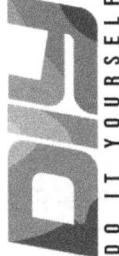

DIY: Sensing Shoulder and Back Posture

Let yourself hunch as in Picture BP 12 and notice how you feel when you do. Often our body response to copying a posture can give us great clues as to what someone else's body posture might be communicating. See if you can notice a sense of being less confident or powerful or even sad when you copy this posture. Then straighten your own back and shoulders and notice what it feels like. Do you feel more powerful and confident when you do this?

Arm Posture

Do you ever wish you could just get your arms out of the way? Do you ever feel like your arms are just dangling there right in front of you and you don't know what to do with them? Well if you do, you're not the only one. Many people often feel a sense of awkwardness about what to do with their arms. Arms often just hang in front of us, doing nothing except making us really self-conscious.

When we are using our arms, it's great. They can be very helpful. But when we are not using them, then what? Maybe we put our hands in our pockets or cross our arms in front of us to try to put them away until we need them again. Or maybe we hold them behind our back hoping no one will notice we even have arms. It can sometimes be stressful trying to figure out what to do with these dangly appendages. And sometimes the more we think about what to do with them, the more awkward they seem. I call this problem *awkward arm syndrome*. Countless people right now all over the world are suffering from it. But fortunately, there is a cure.

While it might make us feel better to think it doesn't really matter what we do with our arms, the truth is it does. The positioning of our arms can communicate a lot. But knowing what our arms can communicate can help us decide what to do with them, which can make us feel less awkward. So, let's talk a little about these strange, useful, but often baffling appendages called arms.

Pictures can often say a thousand words, so let's start with a picture. Take a look at Dan crossing his arms in Picture BP 14. Why do you think he is crossing them? What is his body language communicating?

Dan, BP 14

Arm crossing might be the result of not knowing what on earth we should do with our arms when we are not using them for something specific. There have been many times I've crossed my arms just to get them out of the way. It's actually quite comfortable having them folded up right there in front. But what do you think arm crossing might communicate to others?

Crossed arms can often communicate a sense that someone is not open. It can also communicate that the person may be feeling protective. Maybe they feel scared and are trying to protect themselves by covering their body with their arms.

Turtles and snails go in their shells when they do not feel safe. Snakes coil up and pill bugs roll into a ball. For humans, crossing our arms can be a way we go into our shell and coil, to try and keep ourselves separate and safe from the outside world. I call this *turtling*.

Crossing the arms might also convey irritation, impatience, or anger. Take another look at Picture BP 14 again, and see if you can sense the different things that this arm posture might communicate.

Now let's try a little experiment. Take a look at Picture BP 14A.

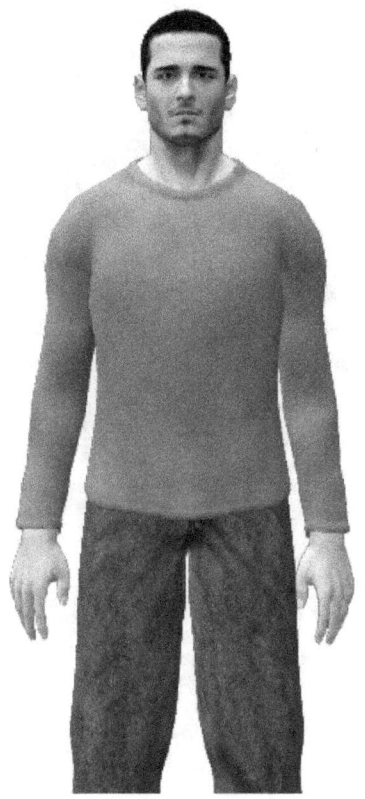

Dan, BP 14A

Notice the different feeling you get when the arms are not crossed. Dan may still seem a little serious in this picture but nowhere near as much as in Picture BP 14.

His face is actually the same in both pictures. But you may get the sense that his face is more serious when his arms are crossed. This is because the crossed arms are giving more information, which makes us have a different interpretation of the neutral face. It's pretty cool to see how adding different information like crossed arms can actually make us see things differently.

The arms in Picture BP 14A are comfortably resting by Dan's sides. The hands are open and the palms are facing inward in a natural resting position. All this suggests more openness on Dan's part. There is a sense of ease because the arms are in a natural resting position. Can you sense the feeling of openness and ease in Picture BP 14A?

In Picture BP 15, Dan's palms are turned outward.

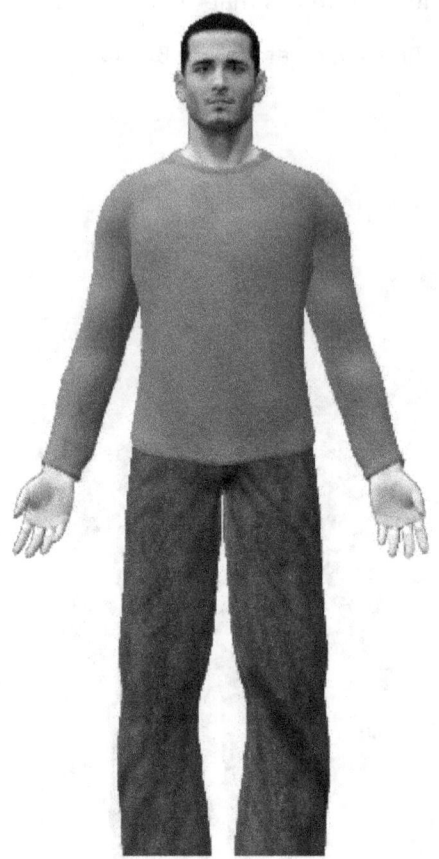
Dan, BP 15

    His shoulders and chest are also a little more open. It's a subtle difference from Picture BP 14A. But sometimes subtle can be significant. Dan's position is not as natural in Picture BP 15 as it is in Picture BP 14A because hands don't naturally rest in an outward-facing position. But even though it is not as natural and at ease, the forward-facing palms and the more open shoulders and chest communicate even more openness.

    You might not stand for a long time in this position. That might feel unnatural. But knowing how being physically open in this way might communicate more openness to others can help you understand this important part of body language a little better. And while you might not stand like this for a long period of time, you might experiment with opening a little like this for just a few seconds and notice how it feels.

    The way Dan's arms are positioned in BP 15 communicates a much different feeling than what he is communicating in Picture BP 14, where his arms are crossed. When his arms were crossed, Dan was closing and protecting. But here Dan is opening and actually making himself sort of vulnerable. This opening shows a sense of trust in the other person because just like other animals, we usually do not open in this physically vulnerable way to people we do not feel safe with. So, if you want to feel more open with someone and communicate more openness with them, try opening a little with your arms and shoulders and chest and see how it feels.

    How about Pictures BP 16 and BP 17? What do you notice here?

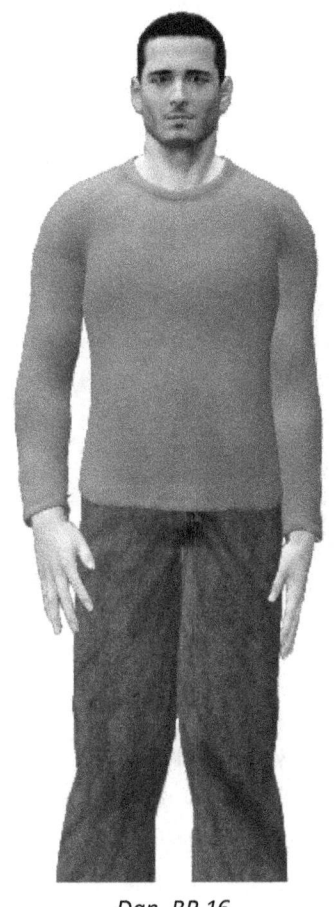 

Dan, BP 16 *Dan, BP 17*

In these pictures, Dan's arms are not closed, but there is some serious awkward arm syndrome going on. These are not the images of someone in a natural comfortable resting posture. It seems like he has no clue what to do with his arms.

When you see someone with arms that are not in a natural position, it can often give the message that the person is not feeling comfortable or relaxed. This brings us back to the age-old question, "What do we do with these dangly appendages when we are not using them?"

Of course, you can try to put them in a natural resting position, but that is often easier said than done. Sometimes when we try to put our arms in a natural resting position, we start to feel more awkward, which makes it even harder to know what to do with them.

In times like this, when my arms seem like strange alien things protruding from my body, I like to have some backup positions I can use so I don't have to stress about my arms, and I can put my attention on more important things instead.

So, let's look at some things you can do with your arms when you might be experiencing awkward arm syndrome. Picture BP 18 shows what I like to call "the thinker."

In this picture, Dan's arms are not really in a resting position as they were when they were by his side. But there is a natural feeling here. His left arm is kind of crossed over his body, but not in a way that makes it seem that he is trying to close and protect. It seems like he is crossing his arm over in order to support his right arm as he holds it up.

Also, his right arm is holding a position that makes it easier for his right hand to rest on his chin. His left arm is supporting his right arm so it can rest. And his right arm is positioned so his right hand can support his chin, so his head can rest on his hand.

There is something else being communicated that is very interesting. Do you notice how having his hand on his chin gives the sense that Dan is paying attention and thinking? There is something about a hand on the chin that can communicate someone is thinking intently about something, just as the head turned to the side and eyes looking up can.

Have you ever seen a picture of this sculpture?

It's by a famous artist named Rodin, and it's actually called "The Thinker." The way the man is resting his chin on his hand gives the impression that he is thinking intently about something. If you are ever having trouble figuring out what to do with your hands, and at the same time want someone to know you are really paying attention to them and thinking about what they are saying, put a hand on your chin and be "The Thinker."

Now check out Picture BP 19.

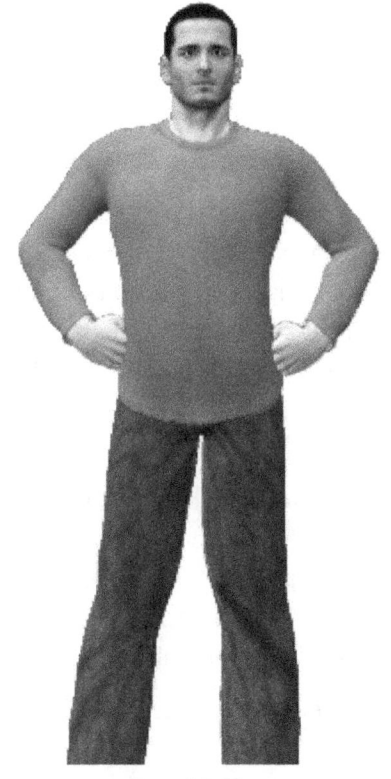

Dan, BP 19

This is what I call *formal superhero pose*. Do you get the superhero vibe looking at this one? OK, how about if we change it up a little (Picture BP 19a)?

Dan, BP 19a

Now can you sense the superhero vibe? Isn't it interesting how a little piece of information like a cape can change how we see things?

Take a look back at Picture 19 and see if you can notice the superhero vibe even when there is no cape. His arms are to the side, with his hands closed in fists and placed right above his waist. It gives a very strong confident feeling, don't you think? Now, it might also seem a little unnatural. If you were talking to someone and they were standing like this for a long time, it might seem a little stiff and awkward. Unless you are wearing a cape and fighting supervillains, you probably want to use the formal superhero pose sparingly.

But we can soften the formal superhero pose a little and still convey strength and confidence while not looking like we just came out of an Avengers movie. Check out Picture BP 20. I call this *casual superhero pose*. Here the hands are still on the hips as in formal superhero pose, but it's different. See if you can notice what the difference is and notice if you sense a different feeling. Here the hands are open rather than in fists. The open hands create much more of a relaxed feeling. This is a position that can help a lot with awkward arm syndrome. When done with a nice straight back, it can also communicate a sense of confidence.

Another strategy that can potentially help with awkward arm syndrome is to comfortably put your arms behind your back. Take a look at Picture BP 21.

Dan, BP 21

What kind of feeling do you get from this? Does it seem like his arms are *comfortably* behind his back? Not really. In this picture, Dan looks like he is straining and forcing his arms behind his back. It seems like he might even be hiding something back there.

In this picture, Dan's shoulders are scrunched up high, which is often a sign of tension. His body is pretty straight as well. Sometimes a straight body can communicate confidence. But here, when taken along with his arms placed awkwardly behind his back and his scrunched shoulders, it makes him look even more tense. These body communications are not going to communicate comfort and ease to others.

In Picture BP 22, Dan has his arms behind his back again.

Dan, BP 22

He still looks like he might be a little strained but it is way better than his positioning in Picture BP 21. He looks way more comfortable here. This is because his shoulders are not up as high. They are more relaxed. His arm positioning also seems less strained and his abdomen area is slightly curved, which makes it seem that he is a bit more relaxed.

Now, just to show how positioning different parts of the body can affect how we interpret the arms, take a look at Picture 23.

Dan, BP 23

In this picture, the arms are behind the back just like they are in Picture BP 21. But here Dan's arms are lower, which brings his shoulders down and makes them more relaxed looking. This has a big effect on how natural and comfortable he looks. With his hands lower it also gives the impression that he might have his hands in his back pockets. Hands in pockets give more a sense of resting and ease, as well. It's similar to what we saw above when Dan had his elbow resting in one hand and his chin resting on the other hand.

When we are feeling a bout of awkward arm syndrome coming on, we can also try putting our thumbs or hands in our front pockets. Picture BP 24 shows Dan with his thumbs in his pockets.

Dan, BP 24

Thumbs are a good alternative if our pockets are small. Otherwise, it can feel very awkward trying to cram our hands into tiny pockets.

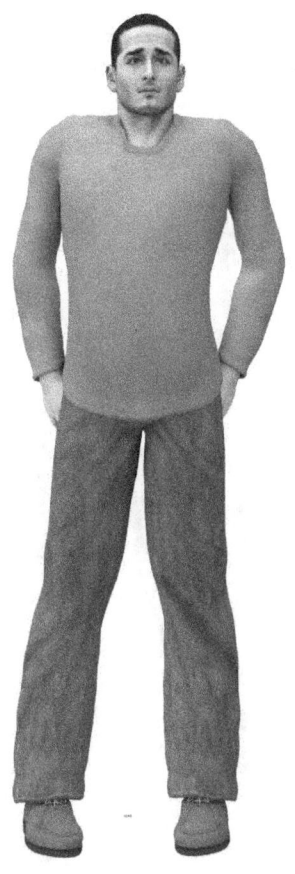

Dan, Tiny Pockets

Personally, I like cargo pants for this. Cargo pants have lots of room for hands. And they look cool too.

We started this section with an example of arms crossed in the front, and we talked about how that can give a message of being closed. There are a few other ways we can have our arms in front without giving such a strong message of being closed off. Take a look at Picture BP 24A.

Dan, BP 24A

Here Dan's arms are in front but they are lower and not completely crossed over his body. This can be a nice balance of closing while still keeping open. And it offers a nice resting place for his arms.

Sometimes when we are feeling nervous in social situations, it helps us to feel more comfortable if we "turtle." But as we mentioned above, too much turtling can give people the message that we are closed off. In Picture BP 24A, the hands in front create a little sense of turtling, which might help Dan feel more at ease in a social situation in which he is not feeling totally comfortable. But it is not so closed off that it would give others a strong message that he is not open to them.

Dan, BP 24B

Picture BP 24B gives another example of arms in front that offers some turtling but does not close Dan off too much. This one is also nice because the interlocking fingers can both contribute to some balanced turtling and also give a sense of ease because the hands are supporting one another.

I like this one because there is room for Dan to move his hands around when talking. He can move both his hands together while keeping his fingers interlocked, giving him a place to put his hands while at the same time keeping a little bit of turtling going on to help him feel more comfortable. Certain body movements, when done right, can also be a great way to communicate positive things to others.

One last example is *the lean* (see Picture BP 25).

Dan, BP 25

The lean can be a great one as long as you have something good to lean on…

Dan, Lean and Fall

If done right, the lean provides a place for one hand to be, while at the same time making it very natural for us to put the other hand on our hip. And the lean gives that natural sense of ease we often get when we are supporting parts of our body, as was the case when our hands were on our hips, or when our elbow was in our hand and our chin was in the other hand.

Another thing you might notice in Picture BP 25 that also communicates a sense of ease is the positioning of the legs. Notice how Dan's left leg is bent a little. This makes his lower body look more comfortable. And this is a nice segue into another body position suspect – leg positioning.

Abdomen and Leg Posture

Let's continue moving down the body, and talk about the abdomen area and the legs. I like putting these two together because they often affect one another.

Abdomen

When the abdomen is in a neutral position, we probably don't pay a lot of attention to it and it will not affect how we interpret someone else's body language a great deal. But when there is some curve or bend in the abdomen, it is capable of communicating either relaxation and ease, or tension and awkwardness.

Let's start with a little awkward abdomen, shall we? Take a look at Picture BP 26 and notice what feeling you get seeing the positioning of Dan's abdomen.

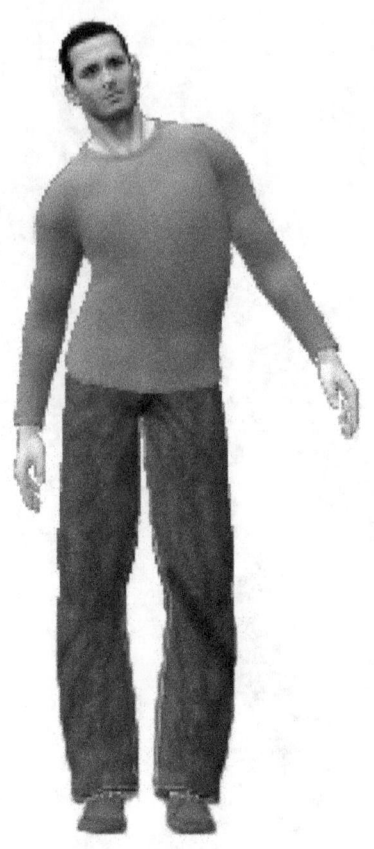

Dan, BP 26

There is some major curving going on there. I don't know about you, but when I see Dan in this position, I get uncomfortable. To be honest, the first thing I'm wondering is if he has to go to the bathroom or has really bad gas.

Take a look at Picture BP 26a and see if you can notice what crossing the legs a little can add to this. Here it seems pretty clear to me that Dan needs to get to a restroom pretty quickly. But whether it's a bathroom issue or not, an abdomen that is curved in an unnatural way communicates that something is not quite right with Dan. It communicates awkwardness and a lack of ease.

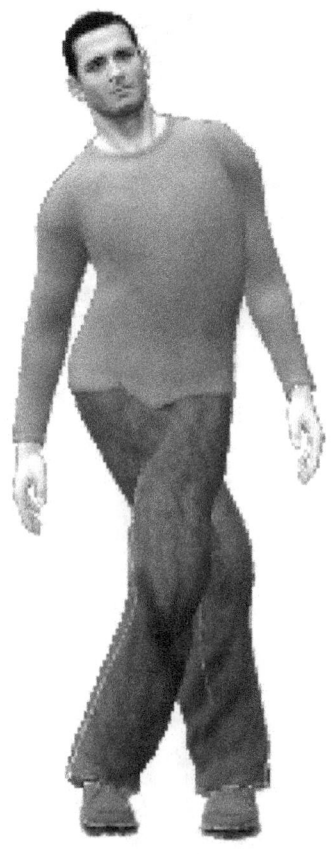

Dan, BP 26A

In Pictures BP 22, BP 23, and BP 25, Dan has some curving going on in his abdomen region as well. But here the curve makes him look more comfortable as opposed to less. In these pictures, the rest of his body looks like it is adjusting to the curve, which makes him seem more relaxed and at ease. This is much different than Picture 26, where the curve makes him look like he is going against gravity and creating a strain rather than a sense of ease.

Sometimes it's difficult to keep track of how all the different parts of the body affect what we are communicating nonverbally. In this chapter, we are just giving some common examples to help you start to think more about this kind of nonverbal communication. Even if you don't understand every single thing the body is communicating, just knowing these common examples can help a lot.

Another thing that can often help us determine what our bodies are communicating is noticing our own body and being aware of how it feels when we are in different positions. Try this awkward abdomen pose and notice how it feels. Does it feel comfortable to you? Would you feel comfortable having a conversation with someone while in this position? See if you can adjust your body while keeping some curve in your abdomen, and notice how you move different parts of your body to make the abdomen curve feel easier and more natural.

Legs

Let's take a look at the legs. Just as with the abdomen, when the legs are in a relatively neutral position they don't communicate much. It's only in unnatural positions when combined with other body positions that they may contribute to a sense of awkwardness.

In Picture BP 27, Dan has his legs crossed as he did in Picture BP 26A.

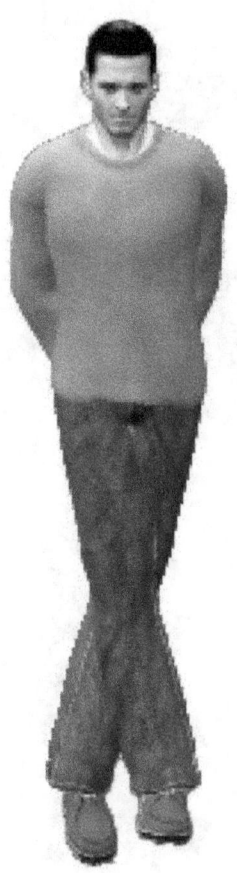

Dan, BP 27

But here the crossing seems natural. This is due to two things. First, his legs are not crossed as dramatically as they were in Picture BP 26a. It's a gentler cross, one that keeps Dan's body centered and at ease. And of course, the second reason that this does not seem awkward is that the rest of his body seems to be at ease.

Pictures BP 28 and BP 29 show a couple of other common leg positions.

Dan, BP 28   *Dan, BP 29*

In BP 28 Dan has his legs in a slightly wide stance, while in BP 29 his legs are together. As you might sense, both of these seem pretty neutral. Both can work in a wide variety of situations. I will add just one little variation that is sometimes nice. It's the gentle knee bend. You can see this in Picture BP 30.

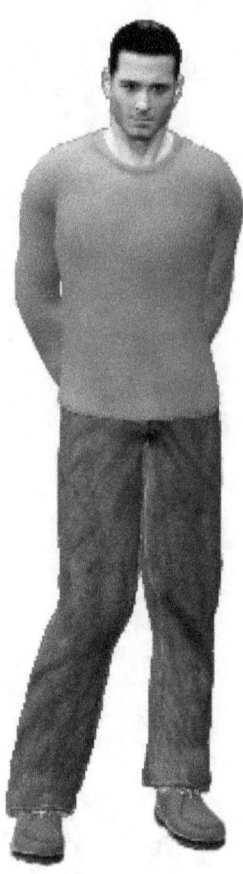

Dan, BP 28

Notice how Dan's right knee is slightly bent. You might not even notice it if you were not looking for it. But it can help to communicate a subtle sense of ease with our bodies. But even more important than what it communicates to others is the fact that it can help us feel at ease. I know that for me a slight bend of the knee can make my whole body feel more relaxed. Give it a try and see what it feels like to you.

Sitting

We could have a whole other long discussion about what to do with our legs, as well as other parts of our body when we are sitting. There are actually many comfortable leg positions we can use when sitting in a chair or on the ground. The one thing to be careful of is trying not to open your legs too much. There is something to be said for being too open.

Take a look at Picture BP 31.

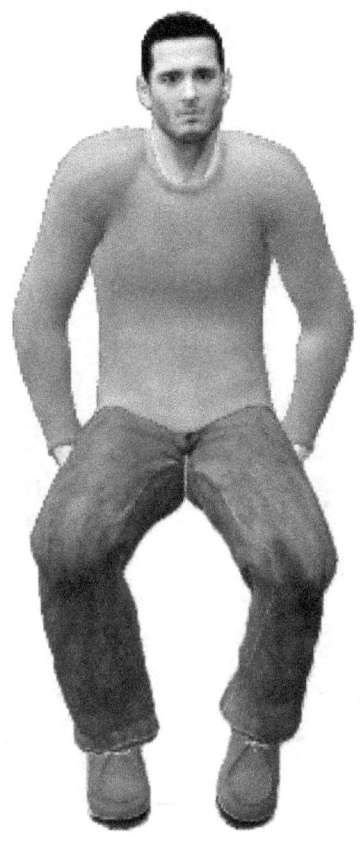

Dan, BP 31

Here Dan's legs are partly open. To me, it seems like just the right amount of open. He looks comfortable in this position and the degree of openness seems comfortable to the viewer. Now compare Picture BP 31 to Picture BP 31A.

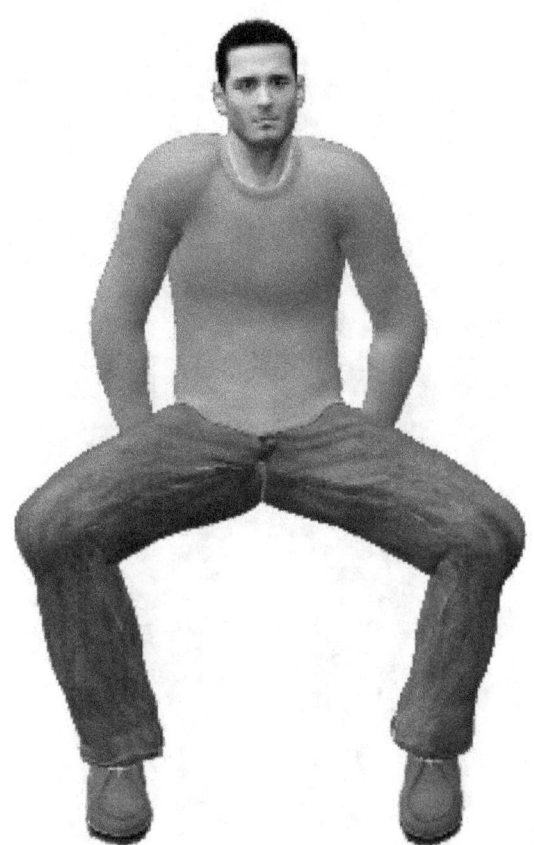

Dan, BP 31A

In addition to it seeming almost uncomfortable and not very natural, there is just way too much crotch right up front and center. Let's just tell it how it is ok? People don't want to see your crotch when you're having a normal social interaction. They just don't. Unless your crotch is the main topic of discussion, you probably want to put it away.

When Dan's legs are open that wide, his crotch becomes the center of attention. You can try to look away but it's right there. Crotches are more personal places and when they are right out there in front, it can make people uncomfortable. In Picture BP 31 you can still see Dan's crotch, but it's not screaming, "hey look at me," like it is in Picture BP 31a. While we want to communicate openness with others, there is such a thing as being too open.

There are many different leg positions when sitting. Here are a few other nice ones to keep in mind if you need suggestions for sitting legs. Picture BP 32 – sitting with ankles crossed, Picture BP 33 – sitting with legs crossed, Picture BP 34 – sitting with legs crossed with arms behind head.

Dan, BP 32   Dan, BP 33   Dan, BP 34

DIY – Feeling into Body Postures

Pair up with someone and copy some of the different body postures in this section, doing the comfortable ones as well as the awkward ones. Notice what it feels like to do the different postures. Does the way you feel change at all when you do different body postures? Next have your partner do it, and notice the sense you get when they do the different poses. Tell each other what your experiences are, both the doing and the watching.

Next, go out in the world and look for what others are communicating with their body postures. Make a note to yourself about what you are sensing in others' body postures.

Body Placement

PRIME SUSPECT #14:

BODY PLACEMENT BLINDNESS

Have you ever heard someone talk about product placement? You might hear this said when you're watching a movie or television show, and they put a name brand item in the scene, like someone drinking an ice-cold Coke in some television show. Basically, what happens with product placement is that companies pay television shows or movie companies big money so they will put their product in an ideal place in a scene of the show. They want to put it in the ideal place (the sweet spot) where people will see it and have a good feeling when they see it. They might want to place the product in the hand of the good-looking hero of the show or in a scene where something good happened so that people get a good feeling at the same time they see the product. They do this to advertise the product so that people like it more and want to buy it.

Well, body placement is kind of similar. The placement of our bodies in social situations can have a powerful effect on what people might think or feel about us. *Body placement blindness* happens when we are having trouble seeing how the placement of our bodies can affect the product we are trying to sell.

Of course, the product we want to help sell as social detectives is the person. We want to help our clients or ourselves have good product placement so that others associate a good feeling with us. When looking for culprits in social mysteries, it can be very helpful to keep body placement in mind.

Basically, when it comes to social situations, we want to place ourselves in the right location. The sweet spot. Placing ourselves in certain ways can help people have more positive thoughts and feelings about us, while other types of positioning might result in people having more negative thoughts and feelings.

Let's go into some important aspects of body placement so we can see more clearly. There are two main categories of body placement that can have a big effect on our social interactions. They are 1) personal, interpersonal, and impersonal space and 2) body direction.

Personal, Intrapersonal, and Impersonal space

Personal, intrapersonal, and impersonal space have to do with how close our bodies are to other people's bodies. *Personal space* is the space we need to feel comfortable with our sense of separateness from others. If others are in our personal space and *too close for comfort,* we might feel a little suffocated or uncomfortable, and in such situations, we might back away to get a little physical distance. For a good example of this, check out the chapter with "Back Away Bobby" in *Diary of a Social Detective*.

Interpersonal space is more about closeness. It is the space we share with another person that helps us to feel close to them. Sharing a space with others helps us feel connected to the people we are interacting with, so it does not feel like they are *too far for friendship*.

Impersonal space is that place outside of interpersonal space where someone is so far away that it makes it hard to feel connected to them. Figure 7.1 illustrates what personal, interpersonal, and impersonal space might look like for someone.

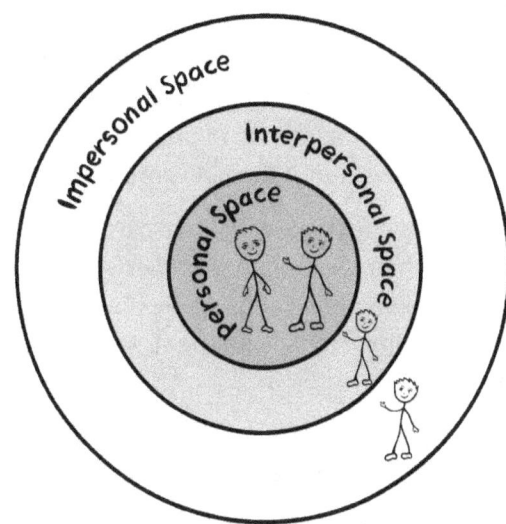

Figure 7.1, Personal, Interpersonal, and Impersonal Space

We want to try our best not to be too close or too far away in social situations because either of these things can be powerful culprits in social mysteries. If we are too close to others, it can make people feel uncomfortable. People need some personal space and we want to respect that. But if we are too far away, it can make it hard to connect with them. When we are too far away, we move outside of the interpersonal space we share with others, which makes it harder to connect or feel close to them. You want to find *the sweet spot* where you place yourself close enough but not too close. This way you're not too close for comfort or too far for friendship.

There are some situations in which we might want someone in our personal space. In those situations, the line between personal and interpersonal space is fuzzy. But understanding some of the factors that affect our personal space needs can help make this less fuzzy.

There are four main factors that affect how we determine our needs for personal space. They are: 1) how well you know someone; 2) how you are getting along with the other person; 3) your mood or the other person's mood at the moment; 4) both people's general comfort with physical closeness. Let's take a closer look at each of these.

1) How well you know someone

When we know people well, we tend to need less personal space in order to feel comfortable. If you think about this you will probably see how it's true. Imagine yourself with your dad or mom or sister or brother. You might feel very comfortable being physically close to them. You will probably even feel comfortable being so close that you have physical contact, maybe by sitting on the couch next to each other, side-by-side touching, or with your arms around each other. You might not even notice having physical contact with them for long periods of time while you are together because you are so comfortable with them. But if it were some stranger on a bench, you might feel much less comfortable having physical contact with them.

With family members, you might get really close when talking. But with strangers, you would probably feel uncomfortable talking with them if there was not enough personal space. And your friends are probably somewhere in the middle. You might feel more comfortable with less personal space than you would a stranger, but not as much as you would with a family member. So how well we know someone affects how comfortable we feel being physically close with them.

2) How you are getting along with the other person

How well we are getting along with the other person also affects our comfort with physical closeness. When we are feeling positive about the other person, we usually tend to need less personal space in order to feel comfortable. We might even want to be closer to them physically when we are feeling good feelings between us. But when we are not feeling positive about them, we often want more space.

I imagine that when you are feeling good feelings with your parents, you will be much more comfortable being physically close to them. But when there is some tension between all of you, you will want more space. It's the same with friends. It makes sense if you think about it. Feeling more positive things in our relationship with others makes us feel safer and more comfortable with them. And feeling safer and more comfortable lets us feel more at ease being physically close.

3) Your mood or the other person's mood at the moment

The way we feel in ourselves also affects how close we want to be to others. When we are calm and at ease, we are often receptive to physical closeness with others. But when we are agitated or stressed or annoyed, we often want more space from others. Sometimes the opposite is true. Sometimes when we are really upset, we might want more closeness. We might want a hug or hand on the back for some physical comfort. That has the potential to help us feel better. But we usually only want that with people we know well and feel positive about at the moment. Even if we know someone well, and even if we usually get along well with them, if we are not feeling positive with them at the time, or we are feeling upset, we probably will not want to turn to them for physical comfort.

This is helpful to remember when we are with someone that we know is upset. Even if we are very close to them, they may not want physical comfort like a hug or a pat on the back if they are upset, especially if their being upset has anything to do with us. If you are in a situation like that, it's always good to ask first before offering physical comfort or getting too close into their personal space.

4) General comfort with closeness

The fourth factor in determining the right amount of personal space is the overall comfort level of a person. Some people are just less comfortable with physical closeness than others. It's not because they don't feel close to others or are not feeling positive towards them. And it's not because they are particularly grumpy or upset at the moment. Some people do not feel comfortable with physical closeness or displays of affection even in the best of circumstances. It's helpful to know that people are different like this. It can help us to make good calls about how close to be with others. It can also help us not to take it personally if someone does not want to be too close to us physically. It may just be that they are not comfortable with physical closeness with anyone.

DIY: Discovering Your Own Personal and Interpersonal Space Needs

As we mentioned above, different people have different definitions of what is too close for comfort, as well as what is too far for friendship. Some people don't ever like anyone near them, while others don't seem to get uncomfortable even if strangers are really close to them. Some people feel connected to others even when they are pretty far away, while others need people to be fairly close to feel connected to them.

I call the space you need between you and others to feel comfortable your *personal space bubble*. And the closeness you need between you and others to feel connected is your *interpersonal space bubble*.

Now while the size of both of these bubbles can change depending on the people we are with, how we are feeling about them, and what our own mood is, there is usually a general personal and interpersonal space bubble that most people have.

Getting a better idea of our own personal and interpersonal space bubbles can help us a lot in social situations. It gives us a starting point when trying to determine other people's comfort with closeness. Let's play a little game to get a sense of what our own personal and interpersonal space bubbles look like.

Find a partner. Make it someone you know and don't have negative feelings with at the moment, but not someone you are so close with that your personal space bubble will be extra small. Friends are good for this.

Let's call the two people Person A and Person B. First, we will get a sense of person A's personal and interpersonal space bubbles. Have person B stand about 10 feet away from person A. While looking at each other, have Person B take slow steps towards Person A, one step at a time, pausing between each step. Now Person A, it's your job to notice what it feels like in your own body as Person B gets closer and closer. Our bodies help us understand where our personal and interpersonal space bubbles are.

You will probably notice that when someone is ten feet away, it is hard to feel really connected to them. I don't imagine that if you were hanging out with a friend and having a nice conversation you would be this far away. At ten feet, Person B is most likely outside of your interpersonal space bubble. As Person B takes one step at a time closer, pause after each step to notice how it feels. See if you can notice when they enter your interpersonal bubble, where they are close enough for you to feel more connected to them.

Once Person B gets to that place where they are now in your interpersonal space bubble, ask them to stop taking steps for a minute. Notice what it feels like in your body when they are in your interpersonal space bubble. Now have them take a step back and see if you can sense them leaving your interpersonal space bubble. Notice if it feels good when they enter your interpersonal space like this and notice what it feels like when they leave that space. Usually, when we are in a decent mood and with people that we like, it feels good when they enter our interpersonal space. And if we are paying attention, we will notice when they leave that space.

After taking a moment to notice this edge of your interpersonal space, have Person B continue stepping forward towards you, one slow step at a time. As they do, continue to notice what it feels like in your body as they get closer. Notice how it feels to have them deeper in your interpersonal space with each step.

As Person B continues moving towards you, see if you can notice when it starts to feel uncomfortable. Notice what it feels like when they are too close. This is a sign that they have entered your personal space bubble. As this happens, pay attention to what it feels like in your body. Just notice the discomfort. Notice if you feel an urge to back away. Have Person B hold there on the edge for a moment, so you can get a feel for the discomfort of having your personal space invaded.

Next, have Person B take one step backward. Does that one step get them out of your personal space? Does it help you feel more relaxed when they step back? If one step back is not enough, ask them to take another step back.

After you have done this, switch roles and have Person A take ten steps back. Try the whole thing again with Person B being the one to notice where his or her personal, interpersonal, and impersonal space boundaries are. After you have both done the exercises, compare your experiences. As you are talking about what it was like for you, see if you can notice how close the other person is. See if you can get them right in the sweet spot of interpersonal space so that you have a nice amount of connection without it being too close for comfort.

The Effects of Being Too Close for Comfort or Too Far for Friendship

Being in people's personal space is often a central suspect in social mysteries. I call this *personal space missing*. This can have powerful negative effects on friendships. When we miss where people's personal space boundary is, it can make them feel uncomfortable, overwhelmed, and suffocated. This can lead to them backing away or checking out, as well as leading to them not feeling as positive about their relationship with the person who is invading their personal space.

But being too far away and outside of the interpersonal space we share with others can also be an influential culprit in social mysteries. It can give people the message that we are not interested or involved in our interactions with them. It might also give them the impression that we don't feel safe or don't want closeness with them. I call this *interpersonal space missing* because we are missing the mark when it comes to placing ourselves at just the right distance physically in social situations.

Space in Group Settings

Interpersonal space missing can happen when we are interacting one-on-one with others. But it can also happen in group settings. Just as people have personal, interpersonal, and impersonal spaces, so do groups. It can get a little trickier in groups because each person in a group has their personal space bubble, but the group itself has its own group space bubble, which is an interpersonal space. And then there is the impersonal space outside the group space. That can be a lot of different spaces to keep track of. But once you get a sense of that, it's not too hard to keep track of.

Sometimes in group situations, it can be hard to find the sweet spot in which we are not too close for comfort or too far for friendship. We want to respect each individual's personal space, while also being in a good place within the group's interpersonal space. This can be tricky at times. If we jump right in the center of a group, it might seem like too much, especially if it's a new group or one where people have already been connecting with each other before we got there.

We want to be graceful with how we enter a group so that we don't jump in too abruptly and get too close into people's personal space too quickly. Getting physically closer to others needs to be a gradual process for it to feel comfortable and natural. It is very important to remember this in group settings, since we may be joining an interaction that has already begun.

But at the same time, we don't want to be too far away from the action in group settings. If we are too far from the people in a group we want to be a part of and outside the shared interpersonal space, it will seem like we are not really in the group at all. We need to be fairly close to a group of people for everyone to perceive that we are a part of the group too.

Sometimes it's ok to be right in the center of the group, but you don't want to just barge into the middle right away. Being in the center in a natural, comfortable way usually involves a gradual process. Otherwise, it can feel intrusive and uncomfortable to others. And of course, even if we are in the center of the group's interpersonal space, we want to still be respectful of others' individual personal space.

Sometimes we may be timid about joining a group, and this might make us stand farther from the other group members than is ideal. We may not want to be intrusive or may be nervous that the other group members don't want us there, so we don't get too close. Other times we may try to join the group but not be sure how to gradually work our way in, and we may jump in too deep, too quick. Being aware of individual and group interpersonal space and the need to enter groups gradually can help us to find just the right sweet spot in group situations, as well as when we are interacting one-on-one with others.

Body Direction

How we directionally position our bodies can have a big impact on our interactions with others. Basically, directional positioning is about which way we are facing. When we position our heads and bodies so that we are facing others, it communicates more interest and openness. And when we face away, it can give others the impression we are not as into our interactions with them.

How we position our head is even more important than how we position our bodies. If you recall, we touched on this when we talked about neck posture. When our head is facing the other person, we can look at them, which not only helps us pay attention to them better but also lets them know that we see them and are with them. Of course, it's nice to have our body facing the other person, too. This creates a sense of body openness that helps the other person feel us with them even more.

But if you can't turn your whole body, turning the head will do. And as we mentioned in the neck position section, turning our head towards someone when our body is facing a different direction can sometimes give them an even stronger sense that we are interested, because the act of turning our head takes effort, and effort suggests we are motivated to face them and be connected with them.

Body direction is a pretty "straightforward" topic when you "face it head-on." Get it? "Straightforward." "Head-on." Haha, I crack myself up!

DIY: Sensing the Effect of Body Direction

Let's do a little exercise to understand just how much body direction can affect us in social interactions. Once again, we are going to pair up with someone for this one. Pick a Person A and a Person B. Start up a nice conversation with your partner. It can be about anything you like.

While you are talking, have Person A slowly start to turn away from Person B. Turn both your head and your body. Now as Person A turns more and more away, notice how it feels to both of you. How does it feel to turn away? And how does it feel to be turned away from? Do you notice a shift in your sense of connection with the other person? If you are Person A, do you notice not being as attentive to Person B? Do you notice not feeling as connected with them? And Person B, do you notice this shift too? Do you have a sense that Person A is not with you as much? Does it feel like they are not as interested in you?

After sensing this for a while, have Person A start to slowly turn their head back towards Person B. Just the head. Not the whole body. Do either or both of you notice a shift in how your interaction is feeling when Person A starts to move back to facing you? Can you notice how the direction of the head plays a role in your sense of connection with each other?

Now Person A, gradually turn your body back towards Person B. Do you notice any shift here as the body starts to come back to facing Person B? Person B, do you notice any shifts in your sense of the interaction? See if you can feel into the little shifts in your sense of connection with the other person as you go through these different body direction positions. Once you have done this shift, have Person B do the moving and repeat the same procedure in reverse.

PRIME SUSPECT #15:

BODY MOVEMENT BLINDNESS

Another important way we communicate nonverbally is with the movements of our body. Dance is one of the many ways that people use their bodies to communicate feelings. When people dance, they express so much. The movements can express joy and sorrow, pain, and pleasure. They can let you know that someone is angry or fearful, happy, or sad. And the body movements of dance can communicate all these feelings without any words.

Body movement blindness happens when we are unable to see the important ways body movement can affect what we are communicating to others. By seeing and understanding some of the basic ways body movements communicate, we can become much better social detectives, as well as better social beings ourselves. So, let's take a look at some of the ways that body movement can communicate.

The Basics of Body Movement: Speed, Smoothness and Flow

Some of the most basic ways we communicate with body movements are with things like speed, smoothness, and flow. Let's take a look at each of these.

The speed at which we move different parts of our bodies communicates a lot. Quick movements tend to communicate energy. It takes a lot of energy to move fast, so when we see people moving fast, we will likely interpret that speed as a sign that they have a lot of energy. Having a lot of energy can be interpreted in many ways. It might be a sign that someone is very excited and enthusiastic about something. Or it might be a sign that they are stressed and nervous. It might even be a sign that they are angry.

Just as with other nonverbal communications, making sense of what body movements are communicating often involves us being able to look at other clues for additional information. For example, how do we know if someone moving their arms fast while they are talking is a sign of them being excited, stressed, or angry? Of course, we can look at other clues, such as what they are talking about, to help us make sense of what their fast movements are communicating. But two of the other things that can help us make sense of what fast movements are communicating is the smoothness and flow of the movements.

When people are relaxed or expressing positive feelings, their body movements are often smooth and flowy. And when they are more stressed or anxious, their movements are more likely to be jerky and stiff. For example, when someone is excited, they will probably move fast but their movements will be relatively smooth and flowy, unless they are super crazy overexcited, in which case there may be stress along with their excitement, which will make their excited movements jerkier and stiffer.

Smooth, flowy movements tend to change directions very gently and have very gradual stops and starts. The movements are looser and tend to blend into one another, and it's often hard to know where one movement ends and another one begins. It's kind of like when a car goes around a corner or comes to a stop so smoothly that you barely notice it. You don't notice it because the turns are looser and wider, and it comes to a stop smoothly.

Stiff, jerky movements, on the other hand, are often very abrupt and very noticeable. Movement in one direction does not gently flow into movement in another direction, and the shifts are shorter and tighter. When this kind of movement comes to a stop, it happens in a very abrupt way. This is more like a car making tight turns and lurching around a corner or screeching on its brakes, making everyone in the car jerk from side to side or forward as it changes directions or comes to a stop.

I like to call the more stiff, jerky movements *robot movement* and the more smooth, flowy moments *rag doll movements*. Robots are very stiff and don't move in a smooth, natural way. They seem awkward and even stressed when they move. Rag dolls, on the other hand, seem very loose and relaxed, and you can imagine them moving in a much more smooth, flowy way.

When someone is moving very fast, and also has more robot movements, we will likely see them as tense or stressed. They will probably seem more awkward to us. But if they are moving fast while having smooth, flowy rag doll motions, we will probably be more likely to interpret their fast movements as a sign of them being energetic or enthusiastic. Again, there are lots of other things that will help us make sense of the facts. But speed and smoothness often work together to nonverbally communicate a lot.

To get a better sense of how speed, smoothness, and flow can communicate nonverbally, take a look at the first section of the bonus video. You can find the video online at https://www.socialdetectiveacademy.com/bookbonus/.

DIY: Robot Versus Rag Doll

After taking a look at this part of the bonus video and getting a good sense of the difference between stiff, jerky movements and smooth and flowy movements, let's see what these different ways of moving our bodies can feel like. Ideally, you want to do this in front of a mirror, so that you can not only feel what it feels like to make these movements but can also see what you look like when you're making them. If you are doing this with a partner, let each person take a turn, so that one person can do it and the other can watch and notice what it feels like seeing their partner doing it.

Let's start with rigid, jerky, robot movements. Let yourself move like a robot. Really get into it. Make lots of short jerky moments, abruptly shifting directions and starting and stopping, then walk around a little, making lots of short jerky motions with your body. As you are moving like this, notice what it feels like. If you are near a mirror, watch yourself as you make these robotic movements. Can you feel the stressful feeling when moving your body like that? Does it feel awkward? See if you can get a sense from your own experience of what those movements might be communicating.

Then let's try moving like a rag doll. Get your body very loose. Bend over and sway your arms from side to side. Shake your arms and legs. Shake out any tension in them so your body can be extra flowy and relaxed. Let your whole body flow from side to side and notice what this feels like, then straighten back up and walk around a little. Let your body sway from step to step. Notice the sense of relaxation and ease in your body as you do your rag doll walk.

After you and your partner both take turns with these different ways of moving, think about what it felt like and discuss. Did you notice a difference in your body when you did robot and rag doll movements? Think about if you usually move more like a robot or a rag doll. Or do you move differently? Which felt better to you, robot or rag doll? Discuss how you think you would respond to others who were moving in these two different ways.

DIY: Movement Syncing Game

After you finish the *Robot Rag Doll DIY* give the *Movement Syncing Game* a try. This is similar to the facial syncing game we did earlier, but here we are matching each other's body movements instead. In this game, we try to mirror or mime how the other person is moving their body.

To play this game, find a partner and let them know you want to mirror their body movements. You can start by having them intentionally move in both robot and rag doll ways and see if you can copy them. When you are doing this, make note of what you think the other person's body movement is communicating. Are they moving slow or quick, smooth or stiff, flowy, or jerky? See what your eyes notice. Then see if you can copy the movements they are making. When you do, see if you can actually feel the same feeling in your own body that you think they are expressing with their body movements. Remember, the way we move our body can actually affect how we feel. See if you can sense the feelings in yourself as you move.

Once you have done this, have the other person try to move and sync with you. And when they do, see if the movements they are making match what you think your movements look like. This can be a great way to get feedback about how well we are able to communicate with our body movements.

As we have discussed, when done right, syncing with others can help us feel closer to them. Notice if you feel any closer to your partner after doing this exercise.

Some Specific Body Movements

Speed, smoothness, and flow help us get an idea of some of the general ways in which body movement can communicate. But there are some specific body movements that can communicate a lot. Let's check out a few of these.

How Walking Does the Talking

One specific way we might notice robot versus rag doll movements is in the way people walk. If we walk in a jerky and stiff way like a robot, it can give people the message that we are uncomfortable and not really at ease in our own bodies. A more smooth, flowy walk, on the other hand, can communicate ease and comfort.

The speed at which we walk can also be important. If we walk too fast, it can give people the message that we are not relaxed and at ease. Of course, if we are late for something, we will probably want to walk fast. But in that situation, there is other information, other facts to help make sense of the fast walking. You might even acknowledge to the other person that you are walking fast because you are late, which makes it clear to them what your motivation is.

If both people are walking fast, it might be just fine. But if we are walking fast and it is hard for others to keep up with us, it might give them the impression that we are trying to get away from them.

Remember, one of the key things that contributes to many social mysteries is problems in syncing with or matching others. Walking can be a really powerful way to sync with others. In fact, when people are feeling connected to one another, they often sync their steps when walking without even noticing it.

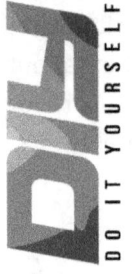

DIY: Noticing Walking

Experiment with robot walking versus more flowy rag doll-like walking and see how it feels. Try each one while walking somewhere. Can you sense the difference in your body when walking in these two different ways? After trying it yourself, see if you can notice others walking in different ways. Notice if people are walking more robot-like or in a more flowy way. Notice if you get a different feeling from people based on the way their body moves when they walk.

DIY: Walking In Sync

Another great DIY you can do is to try and sync up while walking with someone. First, try it discreetly. Don't make it obvious to the other person. Just casually match their steps and notice what it feels like. If you have a friend or partner that you are doing DIY experiments with, you can both try to sync up when you walk together, then talk with each other about what it feels like to walk in sync like that. Try to deliberately walk out of sync and notice what that feels like. Do you feel less connected with the other person?

Statue Versus Sway

Statues can be beautiful, inspiring works of art. When you look at a well-made statue, it can give you a great feeling. Being stiff and not moving works well for statues. In fact, if they started to move it would probably freak most people out. But for real-life people, stiff and not moving is not usually seen as a valuable characteristic unless you are posing for a picture.

Most people tend to move their bodies even when standing relatively still. When our bodies are relaxed and comfortable, they tend to gently sway and shift. It may be a subtle, gentle movement, like the gentle sway of a palm tree. It's something you might not think about when it's happening. But if it is not happening, if there is no movement at all, others will probably pick it up. When people are not moving at all, we often feel uncomfortable because we sense that their statue-like stance may be a sign of them not being comfortable.

There are a few main ways the body shifts and sways to let people know we are not statues. We might shift and sway our whole bodies. If we are standing up, we might shift back and forth on our feet. Or we may sway from the waist, while our feet are more firmly planted on the ground. Waist shifting can happen when we are sitting, as well. Sometimes the arms can do the moving or even the neck. It is often a combination of a few of these that gives us a more flowy palm tree-like motion instead of a stiff, uncomfortable statue-like stillness.

A little shift and sway can make a big difference in what we are communicating with others. When interacting with others, you might want to put a little palm tree sway and shift into your body communications. Of course, you don't want to overdo it. Too much swaying and shifting can come across as just as uncomfortable as none at all.

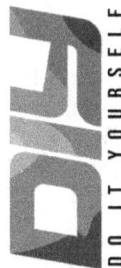

DIY: Statue Versus Palm Tree

Pair up with a partner and play around with body sway. Take turns with statue stillness and palm tree sway and notice what it feels like in yourself when you do it and what it feels like in your relating with the other person when they do it.

Hand and Arm Dancing

Have you ever seen someone speaking in sign language? It's the language used by people who can't hear, and all the words are communicated with movements of the hands and arms. It is such a beautiful thing to watch. But what makes it so beautiful to watch is not really about the specific movements that make up the words. It's the way that the people signing make the movements. It's the way their hands and arms sway and flow and jerk and shake. It's as if their hands and arms are dancing. You don't have to know sign language to sense the feeling their hand and arm dancing is communicating.

It's common that when we speak, we move our hands and arms. Just as with those who speak sign language, the way we move our arms when talking can add a lot to what we are saying.

We might make big, long flowy movements when talking about something beautiful or exciting. Or we may make short robot-like movements when talking about something that makes us stressed or scared. We might touch our hearts with our hands when we are talking about something emotional. Or maybe we make a fist to express anger about what we are saying. There are lots of ways we dance with our hands and arms to add feeling to what we are saying.

Just as the soundtrack to a movie adds so much to the story, our hand and arm movements add loads to what our words are communicating. All nonverbal communication adds to our verbal communication. But hand

and arm movements are often more closely connected to the words we are speaking than some of the other types of nonverbal communication.

PRIME SUSPECT #16:

EYE MOVEMENT BLINDNESS

It is often said that eyes are the windows to the soul. Eyes are most definitely a window into ourselves. They can communicate so much and can help us to really connect with others. Eyes can help us to pay better attention to others and can help others know we are paying attention to them. They can help others feel more comfortable and connected with us. But the same power that the eyes have to help people feel comfortable, attended to, and connected can also make others feel intruded upon, uncomfortable, and not as close to us.

Eye movement blindness happens when we are unable to see the important ways eye movement can affect what we are communicating to others. By seeing and understanding some of the basic ways eye movements communicate, we can become much better social detectives, as well as better social beings ourselves. So, let's take a look at some of the ways eye movement can communicate

Laser Gazing and Attentional Personal Space

We talked before about how eyes show people that we are paying attention. When we look at others, they know we are with them, which can be a good thing. But there is something to be said for too much of a good thing. When we look at people too much or too intensely it can actually be kind of creepy. Not enough eye contact and they might think we are not interested in them, but too much and they might feel uncomfortable.

Looking at others too much or too intensely can feel like an invasion of personal space. We may not be getting into people's personal space physically when we look too long or too hard, but we are getting into their personal space attentionally. Sometimes too much attention can feel *too close for comfort*.

Just as with physical space, we can have personal, interpersonal, and impersonal attentional space. And just as is the case with physical space, we will probably feel more or less comfortable with different levels of attentional closeness for a variety of reasons.

We might feel much more comfortable with our family when they give us lots of focused attention and are in our attentional personal space than we would a stranger. And we might feel less comfortable even with someone we are really close to if we are in a fight with them or feel criticized by them or if we are in a bad mood. And some people just have a different sense of comfort with attentional closeness than others, to begin with.

Problems with attentional space can be an important culprit in social mysteries, so it's helpful for any social detective to keep in mind. Let's give a little attention to attentional space, shall we?

We have talked about many ways we can show people that we are paying attention to them—staying on topic, not interrupting, matching moods, turning our bodies towards them, etc. There are many ways we can show people we are interested and paying attention. But none of these ways of showing attention gets to the heart of attention as much as simply looking at each other does.

It's true that things like asking lots of questions or focusing too much on people's mood might make them feel uncomfortable at times. But it is not as likely that giving too much attention in these ways will make others feel like their attentional space is being encroached on in the same way that looking at them too much or too intensely might. Eyes are powerful things.

One of the main things that determines how hard or intensely we are looking at someone is the *movement of the eyes*. When we are engaging with someone, we often look at them a bit, then shift our eyes away a little, then look back.

Sometimes when we are thinking about something someone said or about how we are going to respond, we look away from the other person to think. We may look up or to the side. We might even close our eyes for a second if we are trying to concentrate. This gives a break in the gaze, which can create a little more attentional space for a moment.

These little breaks for attentional space can often feel good to people, especially if we are keeping our attention with them in other ways, like by staying on topic and keeping up with the conversation.

Moving our eyes like this also makes our gaze less intense. People don't like to be stared at intensely unless they feel very close and comfortable with someone. And one of the main things that makes looking at someone more intense is the amount of time we look at them without moving or blinking our eyes. Moving and blinking the eyes creates a break and keeps the intensity from building too much.

I call this kind of intense gazing where someone does not shift their gaze or even blink much *laser gazing*. I call it that because when someone looks at us like that it can often feel like they are burning a laser into us.

Laser gazing is different than laser focusing, which we talked about in Chapter 2. If you recall, laser focusing is when we imagine a laser beam coming out of our forehead and focusing on the thing we want to pay attention to. This can be a great way of helping us stay focused. But paying good attention does not mean we have to stare too long or too intensely at someone. You can pay really good attention to someone without burning a hole in them with your laser gaze.

So, when we are being sensitive to attentional personal space with others, it's very helpful to be aware of our eye movements and how much time we rest our gaze on others when interacting with them.

Shifty Eye Syndrome

There is another eye movement culprit that can cause problems in our social interactions. It's what I call *shifty eye syndrome*. When someone has shifty eye syndrome, they are moving their eyes. They are not fixing their gaze on the other person, as with laser gazing. But the problem here is that they are moving their eyes in quick, stiff, jerky, robot-like ways, rather than moving them slower with more rag doll smooth and flowy movements. Often with shifty eye syndrome, the person is moving their eyes back and forth, looking all over the place too much while they are interacting with others.

This can give off a strong sense that the person is nervous and uncomfortable. When people are not comfortable in their surroundings or even when they feel like they are in danger, they tend to shift their eyes around. This is what animals who are in fear do when they are afraid of predators. They shift their gaze all around, making sure there is no danger.

When we see others doing this, it gives us a strong sense that they are fearful or distrustful. But we often take that a step further, and when we see someone being shifty like that, we start to think they are not safe or trustworthy. We might get a sense that they are up to something fishy, which is why they may be looking around in that shifty way.

As we mentioned above, shifting your gaze is not necessarily a bad thing. In fact, it can help create the appropriate amount of attentional space with others. But we want to find a balance. We want to find that sweet spot where we are shifting enough so we are not *too close for comfort,* while also not so much that we are *too far for friendship*. And we also want to make sure the shifting is not too quick and robot-like so that it seems like a more comfortable shifting rather than a nervous, fearful, untrustworthy shifting. I think about the way we move our eyes as *eye dancing*.

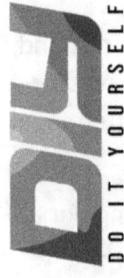

DIY: Graceful Eye Dancing

We can help keep laser gazing and shifty eye syndrome from sabotaging social interactions by doing a few simple things. Basically, we want to make sure we have the right amount of eye movements, and that those movements are slow, smooth, and flowy rather than quick, stiff, and jerky. We want our eyes to dance in a graceful way when we are with other people, rather than either not moving at all or moving in awkward ways that make other people feel uncomfortable.

Let's practice this so we know firsthand what graceful eye dancing feels like. Find a partner and strike up a nice neutral or positive conversation. Start by doing some serious laser gazing with each other while you talk. Really play it up. Laser gaze hard. And while you are doing it, tell each other what it feels like.

Next, have Person A start to do some shifty eye movements while Person B continues to keep their eyes fixed on Person A. Make sure your shifty eye movements are quick, stiff, and jerky to get the whole effect of it. Remember, it's ok to exaggerate here to really get a feel for it. Discuss this while it's happening. What does it feel like to both of you to have this kind of exchange? Now switch and have Person A focus on Person B while Person B does some shifty eye movements.

Once you have both had a turn with laser gazing and shifty eye movements, see if you can shift into slower, smoother, more flowy eye dancing with each other. As you continue talking, allow your eyes to slowly flow away from the other person and then back again, using gentle, smooth motions as you talk. Then discuss what this feels like to both of you.

Nose Gazing

There can be many reasons why people might laser gaze or have shifty eye syndrome. But one common reason people have these problems is that they feel uncomfortable looking in other people's eyes. Eyes can say a lot and looking in each other's eyes can feel very intimate, even when we are trying to keep a good amount of attentional space. This can often feel uncomfortable for people, especially if we are looking into the eyes of someone we don't know very well.

When people feel uncomfortable looking in others' eyes, they often deal with it by laser gazing or shifting their gaze too much. They might laser gaze in order to push through their uncomfortable feelings. They know they should look into the other person's eyes, so they try really hard, even when they feel an urge to look away. The intention is good. But the result can be laser gazing, which makes things more uncomfortable for everyone.

Or maybe they know they should look into the other person's eyes but feel so uncomfortable that they keep shifting their gaze around with robot-like movements because it's hard for them to keep eye contact. This happens a lot when people are feeling awkward with others.

But there is a very simple hack for this, a simple solution that can ease the discomfort that can come from looking into other's eyes. It's what I call *nose gazing*. Basically, nose gazing is just that. It's gazing at the nose. If you are feeling uncomfortable looking right into someone's eyes, try looking at their nose instead. And the brilliance of this simple hack is that people can't even tell!

I have tested this out countless times with tons of people and people cannot tell whether you are looking at their nose or their eyes. But it can make a big difference to the person who is feeling uncomfortable looking at others. Looking at someone's nose does not have the same pressure. This can make it much easier not to laser gaze or shift our eyes too much.

DIY: Practicing Nose Gazing

Let's try a little do-it-yourself experiment with nose gazing. Find a partner and take turns nose gazing. First, look at the other person's nose and see if they can tell where you are looking. Then look into their eyes and see if they notice the difference. Unless you are super close up into the other person's physical personal space, you probably won't even notice when there is a shift from the nose to the eyes and back again. And while you're doing this shifting back and forth, see if you can notice the difference in how it feels looking at the other person's nose compared to looking into their eyes. Have the other person do the same thing and compare your experiences with each other.

Soft Focus

With laser gazing there is an intensity of the gaze, which makes it feel like there is a lot of attentional energy being put on the person. When someone laser gazes, you can imagine they are seeing you clearly, as if everything is in focus, as if they are seeing you in high definition.

A soft focus happens when we unfocus our gaze a little. We still see the other person, but we are not putting as much effort into focusing our eyes. Things might even get a little blurry when we are soft focusing. We often do this naturally when we are thinking about things or are tired. Our eyes unfocus and things get a little blurry. It can actually feel very relaxing. And when with others, it can decrease the sense that we are focusing all of our attention on them.

Nose gazing naturally creates a softer focus. While people will probably not get that we are not looking in their eyes when we nose gaze, they might pick up that our gaze is a little softer. Nose gazing is not the only way to make our focus softer, but it is an effective way. And if our gaze is softer, we can look at the other person longer without them feeling like we are getting too close into their personal, attentional space.

But we want to be careful not to go too soft in our focus because then people might think we are not paying attention to them or are about to fall asleep. That would be *eye glazing,* in which the eyes are glazed over and we seem checked out. That is much different than a healthy balanced amount of eye gazing. Again, we want to find the sweet spot.

DIY: Practicing Soft Focus

We can still look in someone's eyes and soften our focus. Let's try a little soft-focus gazing to get a sense of what it feels like. Find a partner and have Person A do their best laser gazing into Person B's eyes. Notice what it feels like for both people. Then have Person A try and soften their focus. You can do this by relaxing your eyes and not focusing hard on a particular spot. You can also let your eyes cross a little. Don't cross your eyes too much. Just let them relax and get a little blurry. Notice what this feels like for both people. Switch and have Person B practice soft focus by going from laser focus to soft focus. Then discuss your experience with one another.

Using the Eyebrows to Create Eye Contact Comfort

Another thing that can affect people's comfort with eye contact is what the area around the eyes and eyebrows are communicating. If you remember, we discussed how these areas can communicate a lot. When the brow is relaxed and at ease, it can make eye contact much more comfortable. But when the brow is communicating tension or negative feelings, it can make it uncomfortable to hold eye contact with someone.

Take a look at Picture BP 36.

Dan, BP 36

These eyes and brow are in a neutral position. You can probably imagine that looking in these eyes would be relatively ok. Now take a look at Picture BP 37.

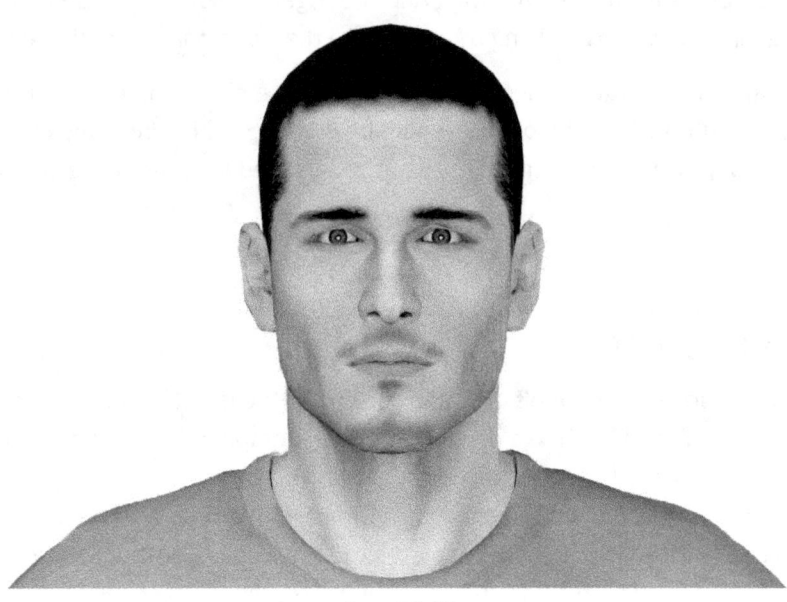

Dan, BP 37

These eyes have the eye smile we were discussing in the facial expression section. And the brow is up just slightly, giving off a more positive feeling. Again, looking in these eyes would probably be okay. They might even be a little easier to look into since a positive feeling is being communicated.

Now take a look at Pictures BP 38:

Dan, BP 38

...and BP 39.

Dan, BP 39

In these, the eyes and brow are communicating more negative feelings. In Picture BP 38 there is an anxious sense in the eyes, and in BP 39 there is a menacing, intimidating feeling being communicated. Can you imagine holding eye contact with someone whose eyes and brow are like this? It would probably not be the most comfortable thing, and we would be more likely not to want to look too long into that person's eyes.

DIY: Noticing How the Brow and Eyes Affect Eye Contact

So, let's experiment a little with eye and brow communications and see firsthand how these things affect our comfort with eye contact. Pick a partner and while you are talking, share some eye contact. You can chat about anything as long as it is not too emotional. Pick a topic with a positive or neutral mood. Let both people start with neutral eyes and brow. Then have Person A try to shift their eyes and brow to match the ones in Pictures BP 37, BP 38, and BP 39. As you are talking with your partner, give at least ten seconds with each eye/brow expression before you switch to the next.

While this is happening, both Person A and Person B should notice what it feels like when Person A is making different expressions. For Person A, what does it feel like to look at Person B while your eyes and brow are making these different expressions? Does your gaze feel different? Person B, notice what it feels like for you. Do you notice a change in your comfort level when Person A makes different expressions? Does it feel more like Person A is laser gazing when making expressions like the ones in Pictures BP 38 and BP 39? After Person A makes the different expressions, have Person B do the same and then discuss.

Conversation and Eye Contact Comfort

Another thing that can really affect our comfort with eye contact is conversation. If we are having a nice conversation with someone about something positive or neutral, we will be more likely to feel comfortable with eye contact. And we may look into the other person's eyes for longer periods of time. If the conversation is more negative, especially if it involves some criticism or anger towards us, we may start to feel less comfortable with eye contact.

If a conversation gets too personal or goes into a topic that is uncomfortable for someone to talk about, they may decrease eye contact or engage in laser gazing or shifty eye behavior. As a good social detective, you always want to think about whether something in your conversation is affecting the quality and quantity of eye contact you are having with someone else.

In general, conversation can make eye contact more comfortable. When we are talking with someone, a good amount of the attention we are giving each other is on the topic of conversation. We might still be placing some of our attention on the other person's eyes but a good amount of our attention is on the conversation.

When the conversation stops or is filled with lots of awkward silences, the eye contact starts to take up more of the attentional space. There is no more conversation to act as a buffer and our connection with the other person becomes all about eye contact. This can feel very uncomfortable unless we know someone very well.

The most awkward part of an awkward silence is that nervous stare--looking at the other person and not knowing what to say. Awkward silences often trigger laser gazing or shifty eyes. And the worst part is that if we are trying to keep eye contact during an awkward moment like this, it can distract us from thinking about what might be a good thing to say next.

If this happens, you might want to try looking away for a minute. Remember we said that people often look away when they are thinking. So, it would be very normal when an awkward silence happens to look away for a moment to think about what to say next. This can also take some pressure off the other person and allow them to think about what they can say next, too.

The main point here is that conversation is often a buffer that can make us more comfortable holding eye contact for longer periods of time. Keep this in mind when deciding how long to hold eye contact with others before throwing in some nice flowy shifting away from their eyes.

DIY: Graceful Eye Dancing and Noticing the Comfort in Conversation

Let's do another DIY here to get more of a feeling about how our comfort shifts around holding eye contact, when we are in conversation and when we are not. We will need partners for this one. Ideally, it should be someone you know and feel some comfort with, but not too much comfort, like a parent or family member.

Strike up a nice conversation about something neutral or positive. While you are talking, practice some nice flowy eye movements back and forth, making eye contact for a bit, then smoothly looking away and then coming back to eye contact. I call this *graceful eye dancing,* as opposed to *the awkward eye dancing* that happens when we have shifty eye syndrome. As you are talking and gracefully eye dancing, notice your comfort level with the amount of eye contact you are having.

After talking for a few minutes, stop talking and just look at each other. Keep a good amount of eye contact in the silence. You can glance away a bit and then come back as you did when you were talking. But no words. Notice what it feels like. Notice your comfort with eye contact in the silence. Does it feel less comfortable to you? Is it harder to hold eye contact for longer periods of time?

Then let yourselves resume the conversation and notice how that feels. Did it all of a sudden get more comfortable when the conversation started back up? Try this again going from talking, to silence and then back to talking again. Really try to notice the difference as you do this. After you have done this a few times start talking with your partner about what you noticed when you stopped talking and then when you started talking again.

Gaze Avoiders

There are some people that just never feel comfortable making eye contact, no matter hard they try. While a chronic lack of eye contact can often mean someone is upset with us or not able to connect well, that is not always the case. Some people just want way less eye contact than others.

For some people, it can be hard for them to pay attention to what others are saying when they look at them so they look away to keep their attention on what is being said. You can easily recognize people like this. These are the people who seem like they are totally checked out. They look as if they have not heard a word you have said, because they were looking somewhere else and maybe even fidgeting with something while they were looking away. But this kind of person will come back and respond to what you were saying and be right on topic. They will demonstrate to you with what they say, that they have been paying attention to you even though they have not been looking at you.

If you come across someone like this and find out that they really are listening, you can cut them some slack. And if you are someone like this, you can cut yourself some slack. You now know how eye contact can help people feel close and connected. Knowing how helpful eye contact can be can help gaze avoiders try and make more eye contact. But if someone can't, there are other ways to help make up for it like being really good at listening and responding verbally.

The Power of Eyes in Hellos and Goodbyes

One last note on the eyes. We have talked about how eyes let others know we are paying attention to them. But they do much more than that. They let others know that we recognize that they exist. Looking at someone acknowledges that we see them and recognize that they are there with us. Acknowledging others and letting them know that we recognize that they are there with us is especially important when we first greet them and when we are saying goodbye.

It feels really good to others when we greet them with eye contact, and when we don't, it can feel really bad. It can feel as if we don't have much interest in them and that they are not important to us. That can start a social interaction off on a bad note.

Making eye contact when saying goodbye is also very important. Goodbyes mark the end of a time we have spent with someone. We want to acknowledge this shift away from being together. Acknowledging the shifting away from being together actually highlights the time we spent together and can help to give the people we were with a nice feeling about our interaction. If we don't look at them when saying goodbye, it can give others the feeling that our time together was not that important.

Not looking in the eyes when saying hello or goodbye is often a culprit in social mysteries. As you are building your social detective skills, it's helpful to keep this one in mind and always make an extra effort to make good eye contact at these times.

Take a look at the second section of the bonus video for examples of the eye movement and focus issues we have been discussing here: https://www.socialdetectiveacademy.com/bookbonus/

Section 2 starts at 11 minutes 11 seconds.

Main Ideas Chapter 8

1. What is body posture? P - 141
2. What is body posture blindness? P - 141
3. What are some of the things neck posture can help to communicate? P - 141
4. What are some of the things shoulder and back posture can help to communicate? P - 153
5. What is awkward arm syndrome? P - 156
6. What are some of the things arm posture can help to communicate? P - 156
7. What are some of the things abdomen and leg posture can help to communicate? P - 171

Chapter 9: Listening to the Voice

While we tend to think of music as something that comes from instruments, there is a very important kind of music that happens when we speak. This kind of vocal music has a powerful effect on our interactions with others, and when we are having trouble hearing or understanding this voice music, it can create a lot of problems in our relationships with others.

Even though we use our voices to communicate verbal information, voice music is a type of nonverbal communication. Of course, the words we use to communicate have a big effect on people, but so do the nonverbal communications that go along with the words.

Remember, nonverbal communications such as voice music are like the soundtrack of a movie. While words communicate important parts of the story in a movie, the soundtrack also communicates a lot, sometimes even more than the actual words. The way we say what we say is very important. This will become clearer when we look at our voice music video examples.

PRIME SUSPECT #17:

VOICE MUSIC DEAFNESS

There are several culprits that can cause difficulty hearing all the important things that can be communicated in the music of the voice. I call them *voice **music deafness suspects***. These suspects are Decibel Deafness, Melody Missing, Rhythm Missing, Phrase Missing, Tempo Missing, and Timbre Deafness.

Decibel, melody, rhythm, phrasing, tempo, and timbre are all important parts of music. When you hear a song, it is these things that bring the song to life. They create and communicate the feeling and mood of the music. And they also create and communicate the feeling and mood of the music of our voice when we are talking. So, let's go over these prime suspects one by one.

Decibel Deafness

A decibel is a unit of measurement. Basically, the decibel level of something refers to how loud it is. Things with low decibels are quiet, and things with high decibels are loud. When someone whispers, it's usually at around 30 decibels. A normal conversation is at around 60 decibels and an ambulance siren is about 115 decibels.

The loudness of a voice communicates a lot, as most people who have had someone get mad and yell at them know. A loud voice often goes with more intense and often negative feelings, while a softer voice is often associated with more calm, relaxed, and often even tender, warm, and positive feelings.

A voice that is a little loud, but not too loud, can sometimes give the impression of strength. And a soft voice, while often having positive qualities, can sometimes come across as not powerful or assertive.

While there are lots of possibilities, one thing is clear. The decibel of our voices communicates a lot.

DIY: Getting to Know the Louds and Softs

Take a look at the bonus video at 17 minutes 58 seconds for examples of different decibels. Notice the different feelings you get when the speaker says things at different decibels. Bonus video: https://www.socialdetectiveacademy.com/bookbonus/.

Example: What do you mean you didn't do your homework? (Loud and soft)

Example: Give me back my banana. (Loud and soft)

Then listen to the person saying different things and make a note of the decibel the person is speaking at. Then see if you can guess the decibel in the following section.

DIY: Decibel Guessing Game

To play this game you need a smartphone and a decibel measuring App. There are many out there on the App store on a smartphone.

It's best to play this game with two or more people. To start, turn on the decibel monitor (DM) on your phone and just start talking in your regular voice. Have a nice conversation with each other. Notice the measurements on the DM. Try to keep the DM in the middle of everyone, so you can get accurate readings. Do you notice that different people naturally speak at different decibel levels? And if so, do you notice a difference in the feeling you get when they talk, based on how loud or soft their voice is? When doing this, make a note of everyone's normal decibel level.

Next, have everyone whisper as you all talk. Make a note of the decibel levels of your whispers as well. Then have someone sneeze, cough, sing, and whistle and note the decibel levels of those things. Next, start to talk in an intentionally loud voice and make a note of what decibel levels people's loud voices are. Are different people's loud voices similar in decibel or do you notice some people being much louder and others being much softer? And do you notice a difference in the feeling you get when people are talking loudly?

After you have played with some specific louds and softs, just let the DM do its thing while you all are having a nice conversation. See if you can position the DM so that everyone can see it. Casually glance at it at different points of the conversation to notice the decibel levels.

If you are really motivated, you can get a decibel meter and go around measuring how loud different things are so you can increase your ability to estimate what decibels things are at.

Melody Missing

When you arrange a series of notes in music in an organized way, they make a melody. Different notes have different pitches. The pitch of a note is how high or low the note is. But it's not just musical instruments that have different pitches. People's voices often have different pitches, as well. People whose voice is high have a high pitch, while people with low voices have a low pitch.

If you think about people you know and what their voices sound like, you will probably recall how different people's voices have different pitches. There is a general range of pitch that someone's voice usually has. Your mom and dad probably have different pitch ranges. Men often have a lower pitch range than women, so your dad's is probably lower than your mom's.

While melodies involve other things, like rhythm and phrasing, pitch is the central part of what makes up melodies. The melody expresses a lot and is often what stands out the most in music. There are happy melodies and sad melodies. There are melodies that express anger and some that can create a sense of stress and nervousness. Other melodies can make you feel warm and fuzzy inside.

Just as in regular music, the music of our voice almost always has melodies. In fact, when people don't have melody in their voice it usually seems strange. So, let's take a look at Video Melody (Voice Melody Video) where we can listen to some of the different types of melodies our voices might have and what those melodies might be expressing.

Take a look at the bonus video at 19 minutes 23 seconds for examples of melody in the voice:

https://www.socialdetectiveacademy.com/bookbonus/

DIY: Playing with Voice Melody

You want to have a partner or group of people for this DIY. Start with one person using the music in their voice to communicate to the other people. First do this without words, just as they did in the video. See if others can guess the feeling you are trying to communicate, based just on the voice melody you are using.

Next, do the same thing but start using words along with the melody. Start with words that match the feeling in your voice. Try using a happy melody while talking about something you are happy about or while just saying "I'm happy." See if others can sense the matching of the words and the melody.

Next, try using words and melodies that don't match. For example, talk about something that makes you happy, while using sad melodies in your voice. Then discuss what this is like for everyone. What is it like when the mood of the words and melody match? What is it like when the mood of the words and the melody don't match?

Rhythm Missing

In music, rhythm refers to patterns of long or short notes. In melodies, there is often a combination of notes that have a variety of different lengths. Along with changing the pitch, changing the lengths of the notes helps to create the feeling in the melody.

But rhythm can communicate a lot when there is no shifting in the pitch of a note. Drums are a good example of this. Many drums keep the same pitch when they are played, but still communicate a lot through the combination of notes that have different lengths. The same is true when we are talking. The rhythm of our speech can have a big effect on our communication to others.

Take a look at the bonus video at 23 minutes 15 seconds to see how rhythm can communicate different feeling flavors just by changing the length of the notes: https://www.socialdetectiveacademy.com/bookbonus/.

Phrase Missing

Phrasing is also important in the feeling that music communicates. Just like rhythm, phrasing can affect the feeling of melodies. Phrasing involves little changes in the rhythm and decibel of notes. These little changes in the rhythm and decibel make a huge difference in what both the instruments and our voices communicate.

It's actually difficult to have natural sounding music without some changes in the rhythm and decibel level. Phrasing helps things not sound mechanical and robotic. This is also true for our voices as much as it is for musical instruments. Phrasing is one of the main things that help keep us from having robot voice. We will talk more about robot voice below. But as you might imagine, just as we don't want to move like a robot, we also don't want to talk like one.

Take a look and listen to the bonus video section on phrasing at 26 minutes: https://www.socialdetectiveacademy.com/bookbonus/. In this video, we can hear firsthand how rhythm and decibel level help to create phrasing, and how the way we phrase things can have a big effect on our communications with others.

Phrasing can express a lot. When you use your good social detective skills to tune into this, you will be surprised at how many awesome social clues you will get to help you solve social mysteries and better understand the social world.

DIY: Noticing Phrasing in the World

Listen to some different kinds of music and see if you can notice the changes in rhythm and decibel in the phrasing. You can do this by yourself, but it's nice to do it with a partner and compare what you heard.

After doing this with music, see if you can notice phrasing when you are interacting with people. This is a good opportunity to practice your social detective skills. Just listen with awareness when you are with people and see what you can notice.

DIY: Fun with Phrasing

For this one, you want to find a partner. Pick a Person A and a Person B. Take turns saying the sentences below while emphasizing the different words by shifting your rhythm and decibel level slightly, just as you saw in the video on phrasing. See if you can get the feel for the different ways you can phrase the same sentence.

As you are doing this, notice if it feels any different to you to say the sentence with different phrasing. If you are the listener, see if you notice your partner shifting the rhythm and decibel and emphasizing different words. After Person A has taken their turn doing the speaking, switch and have Person B do the talking and Person A do the listening.

Next, let yourselves both improvise. Have a nice conversation and practice phrasing. You can go wild and exaggerate. Be a little silly and have fun with it. Practice emphasizing different things in what you are saying with each other.

When you both have had a turn, and have had time to play and have fun with phrasing, discuss what this was like, both as the speaker and as the listener.

<u>Sample sentences</u>

Can you please say something?

I don't want to go with you.

That's my banana.

You better not do that.

Think up your own, too.

Tempo Missing

Another thing that communicates a lot in conversations is the tempo at which we talk. Tempo usually refers to how fast music is. Slow songs have slow tempos and fast songs have fast tempos. As you might imagine, tempo affects the feel of music.

Slow songs are often gentler and more relaxing. They often express more heartfelt, tender feelings like love, kindness, or peacefulness. Slow tempos can also express feelings like sadness. Faster tempo songs, on the other hand, are often more energizing. They might express more enthusiasm or excitement. They can also express less positive feelings like anger or stress.

Talking tempo can express other things, too. For example, talking at a slower tempo can communicate that we are really thinking about what we are saying. But it can also communicate things like boredom, sadness, disappointment, and sleepiness.

When we speed up our talking tempo, it might suggest we are interested and enthusiastic about the conversation. But when we start talking too fast, it can seem like we are in a rush or stressed, or you know that maybe we drank too much coffee. People often talk at a medium tempo, which can communicate that they are calm, yet alert and interested.

Just as is the case in music, we want to try and match tempos with the person we are talking to. If we are playing music with someone and our tempos don't match, it will probably not sound good. It's the same with conversations. Remember when we talked about mood matching? One way we can help to match others' moods is to be aware of whether our own talk tempos are matching.

We also talked in the verbal dancing section about some of the potential problems with fast talk. Fast talk is talking with a fast tempo. So, if you are seeing tempo missing as a possible problem in a social mystery you are trying to solve, you can take a look back at the verbal dancing section, as well as the mood missing sections, to help you crack the case.

Take a look and listen to the bonus video section on tempo at 29 minutes and 30 seconds to see a few examples of how tempo can affect the feel of music and conversations: https://www.socialdetectiveacademy.com/bookbonus/

Timbre Deafness

The final quality of voice music we are going to explore is timbre. Timbre refers to the texture or color of sound. Timbre is what lets you tell the difference between a guitar and a piano, even when they are playing the exact same note at the exact same decibel. It's also a big part of what helps you tell the difference in people's voices. If your mom and dad and friend all said "hello" at the same pitch and decibel, you could most likely tell who was talking because of the timbre or texture of their individual voices.

Timbre does more than that, though. It does more than just help us tell the difference between people or instruments. Timbre can communicate feelings and moods. For example, have you ever heard an electric guitar playing hard rock? Rock music uses distortion, which gives the sound a hard, edgy feeling. But if you take the same guitar and play the same thing with a different timbre, the feeling of the music is much different, even when the pitch, rhythm, decibel, phrasing, and speed are the same.

People's voices are the same. Have you ever heard your mom or dad or teacher say something when they are in a good mood and then say the same thing when they are upset? Do you notice a difference in the timbre of their voice? If not, I'll bet you will after today. And I'll bet you do notice it, even if you are not aware of it. People use different timbre to communicate without words.

Take a look and listen to the bonus video section on timber at 31 minutes 53 seconds to get a better idea of how timbre can affect the feeling flavor of the music in people's voices: https://www.socialdetectiveacademy.com/bookbonus/

Robot Talkers

If you have ever heard a robot talk in the movies or real life, you probably can tell the difference between the way they talk and the way most humans talk. The main difference is that robots tend not to have good music in their voice. Robot talk is mainly missing melody and phrasing, which are key ingredients in communicating feeling.

People often say actions speak louder than words. Well, nonverbal communications are important actions, and they often do speak much louder than words. They are often better at convincing us about other people's feelings than their words are.

For example, if someone says "Hi, it's nice to see you," we usually listen to the music in their voice for confirmation that what they are saying is sincere. If their voice music is happy, it will match the words and we will be more likely to believe them.

But imagine someone saying "Hi, it's nice to see you" in robot voice. Imagine them saying that in a voice that is flat and monotone and conveys no emotion. It will probably make it difficult for us to trust the words they are saying because their actions and their voice music are not in line with their words.

We tend to have a natural desire to be understood and to understand what others are experiencing. We feel safer and more comfortable when others get us and when we get them. While words help us to know each other's inside world, nonverbal communications add a lot to our understanding of each other. So, when people talk without music in their voice, it makes it much harder to get a good sense of what is going on inside them. As a result, we are likely to feel less comfortable with them.

To make this worse, when we don't have enough information about what is going on with others, we often go to the worst possibility and imagine that the other person is upset, annoyed, or just not interested. But the irony is that for many people who tend to speak in robot voice, their lack of voice music has nothing to do with how they are feeling. It is true that some people might talk more like a robot when they are nervous or in a negative inside place. But for those people who don't naturally have a lot of music in their voice, their robot-like talking has nothing to do with their mood.

I have known quite a few robot talkers over the years and most of them have the same feelings as everyone else. For some reason, they just don't have that natural voice music that most people do. So, while robot talking might not directly be a problem for them, it creates problems in these people's interactions with others. The good news is that many people who talk in a robot voice can learn to bring a little music into their speaking, which can make their social worlds better. By following the DIYs in this voice music section, robot talkers can learn how to add more color and feeling to their conversations, which is guaranteed to make their social lives livelier and more comfortable for all.

DIY: Robot Voice vs. Human Voice

Let's play around a little with the robot voice and see if we can notice the different impact that robot voice has, compared to our regular human voice. I call a voice with the regular characteristics of voice music, *human voice*. I call it this because it is these characteristics of voice music that give our voice a sense of humanness, with all the feeling and expressiveness that go along with that.

Get a partner for this one. Pick one person to go first. We will call the first person, Person A. Let Person A tell Person B about something they feel happy and excited about. But as you are talking, try to use your best robot voice. Next, tell them something you are angry about, then something you're sad and nervous about. Talk about all of these things with no music in your voice.

After you have finished talking, discuss with Person B what it was like on both ends of this. What did it feel like to talk in robot voice? What was it like to hear someone talk with no feeling about things they had feelings about? Then have Person A go back and talk about the same things, but with good voice music. Try to recall the things we talked about in this chapter on voice music. Try to let the music in your own voice express the feelings you are sharing with your words. After you have done this, discuss the differences you noticed when there was feeling in the voice compared to when there was not. Then switch and have Person B be the speaker and Person A be the listener, and follow all the same steps.

PRIME SUSPECT #18:

HYGIENE

One last category of nonverbal communications that is a major culprit in social mysteries is *body hygiene*. When I talk about body hygiene, I'm mainly referring to how clean we keep our bodies. This might seem superficial and not as important as some of the other culprits that can cause social problems. But problems with hygiene can communicate a lot to others. So, let's take a quick look at hygiene.

Some of the main hygiene problems I've come across that can cause social problems are things like messy hair, dirty clothes, strong body odor, bad breath, and things like nose picking or farting loud or in confined spaces. These are important things for a social detective to keep in mind when trying to solve cases.

People who are having hygiene issues often don't notice it in themselves. We can easily get used to our own smells, and might not look in the mirror enough to notice our messy hair. And some people fart and pick their noses without even thinking about it. But these things can be noticed by others and can affect how people feel about us.

We communicate a lot with how we care for ourselves. When someone is clean and smells good, it gives the message that they care enough about themselves to take care of themselves. We tend to see clean people as more confident and more capable. And we tend to see people who don't have good hygiene in a more negative light.

Besides, it's often not as pleasant to look at someone who is really messy or picking their nose, and it is definitely not pleasant to smell bad smells like body odor, bad breath, or farts. If people see or smell things that are unpleasant when they are with us, they will likely develop a negative association with us. They will develop a bad feeling about us because of the bad sights and smells that accompany being with us.

This is an easy fix once we are aware of it. Awareness of how hygiene can affect our social relationships can help us remember to take a little time to clean up. So, keep this one in mind when exploring social mysteries.

DIY: Spotting Nonverbal Communications in the World

Increasing our awareness about some of the nonverbal things that are communicated can help us be better nonverbal listeners, as well as better nonverbal communicators. See if you can go out into the world and look and listen for all the nonverbal communications that are going on all around you.

See if you can notice what people are communicating without words. Notice the facial expressions, body postures, and movements. Notice what the eyes are saying and what the voice is saying with its music. Notice their hygiene and the feeling you get when you encounter good hygiene, as well as poor hygiene. See if you can be aware of your own nonverbal communications, and use the things you learned in this section to communicate exactly what you want to communicate to others.

There is a whole world of communication just below the surface. Becoming more aware of these types of communications can provide you with greater social understanding, which can help you to be a better social detective, as well as a better friend to people in your own life.

Main Ideas Chapter 9

1. What is voice music deafness? P - 199
2. What is decibel deafness? P - 199
3. What is melody missing? P - 200
4. What is rhythm missing? P - 201
5. What is phrase missing? P - 201
6. What is tempo missing? P - 203
7. What is timbre deafness? P - 203
8. What are robot talkers? P - 204
9. What can poor hygiene communicate nonverbally to others? P - 205

PART FOUR

Getting to Know the Senses

Chapter 10: The Eight Senses

In this chapter we are going to talk about some of the most powerful tools a social detective has access to--tools that allow us to really understand our social world, not just with our minds, but with our whole being. These are tools that will help us transform all the information we have discussed into firsthand experience, from something we have read about to something we experience directly.

Reading about something can help us understand that thing better, but it's not the same as experiencing something firsthand. For example, you can read all about skiing. You can read about how to hold the poles and how to stand on the skis. You can read about how to turn when going downhill and how to stop. A good book on skiing might even describe the feeling of flowing down the slope and the feeling of the wind on your face as you are moving.

But all the words in the world could not equal the actual experience of skiing. No words on their own could give you the feeling of exhilaration you might have if you were actually skiing yourself. You could read a whole book about what it's like to ski but that would not be as powerful or informative as actually getting on the skis and going down the hill.

Similarly, while reading about how different things affect us socially can be very helpful, it is still not as powerful as actually experiencing the effects of those things firsthand. The tools in this chapter can help you turn what we have been talking about in this book into real, direct experiences. They can help you ski down the beautiful mountain of social relationships and experience firsthand all the things that can make your interactions with others better and more satisfying.

The tools I am talking about are actually very basic. They are tools you are very familiar with and use in many ways every day. They are your natural eight senses. Yes, eight senses! We often think of our senses in terms of our first five senses of **seeing, hearing, smelling, tasting, and touching**. But there are three other senses we will talk about in just a minute. Let's jump into getting to know our senses better.

Getting to Know Our Eight Senses

We use our senses all the time. We often use them without even realizing we are using them, and we automatically respond and react to the information our senses are giving us. If there is a loud sound, we may startle and jump without thinking about what we sensed with our hearing. If we get cold, we might put on a jacket without thinking much about how our skin touching the cold air made us feel. We may see something interesting in our field of vision and turn towards it, and maybe even get distracted by it without thinking a lot about how our sense of sight affected us. The information we pick up with our senses constantly affects us and we often don't even register how what we are sensing is impacting us.

This is very true in our social world as well. We automatically sense things going on between us and others. Our senses take in the information. The things we sense can affect the quality of our relationship with the other person without us even realizing it.

In this chapter, we are going to talk about and practice ways of becoming more aware of the information our senses are giving us about our social world. By doing this, we will be better able to use this information in ways that can help make our social relationships the best they can be.

So, let's start by talking about the eight senses and how we can become more aware of the information they give us in our everyday lives. Then we can talk about how to use this information to understand and navi-gate the social world better. The first five senses help us gather the facts. The 6th through 8th senses help us make sense of the facts.

How the First Five Senses Help Us Gather the Facts

Most of us are pretty familiar with our first five senses. These senses are incredibly important. They help us to form relationships with everything outside of us. They are bridges to the outside world and to other people. They help us take in information and get to know other people. They are how we gather facts about the outside world.

We see people's nonverbal body language with our eyes and get to know them better through doing so. We hear their verbal communications and the music in their voice with our ears. Sometimes when they have poor hygiene or use lots of perfume, we get information from our sense of smell. When we are close to people, we often touch, which can bring us closer and be a way we exchange affection and care.

We might not use taste very often in social situations. I can honestly say I do not know how any of my friends taste, and I hope to keep it that way. Taste definitely helps us get to know pizza much better, though. But you get the idea. Without our first five senses, we would not be able to gather any information about any-thing outside of our own bodies, which

I think might feel very lonely.

The 6th, 7th, and 8th Senses

In addition to our first five senses, there are three other very important senses that we have and use all the time. And they also help us to form connections with others, as well as with ourselves. While the first five sens-es help us form relationships with the world outside of us, the 6th and 7th senses help us get to know ourselves better and in doing so, help us to form deeper relationships within ourselves. And by knowing ourselves better, we become better at making sense of the information we get from our first five senses. We become better at making sense of the facts, which can help us make better decisions about how we interact with others. This can improve the quality of our relationships.

The 8th sense brings it all together, as we will see. It helps us to deepen our relationship with ourselves, as well as have better, more satisfying relationships with others. So, let's take a closer look at our 6th, 7th, and 8th senses.

The 6th Sense

The 6th sense is our sense of what is going on inside our bodies. It's about what we feel inside. We might feel emotions in our bodies. We might feel comfort or discomfort. Maybe our head hurts, or we feel butterflies in our stomach because we are nervous. There are lots of things that might be going on inside us. When we can sense those things inside, we are using our 6th sense. For any of you that like science terms, this 6th sense, the sense of our bodies, is called our interoceptive sense.

When we notice we are feeling happy or sad or angry or scared, it is often because we are sensing these feelings in our bodies. We may have a tingly feeling in our chest when we are happy and excited, or a heavy, sinking feeling in our stomach when we are sad. Maybe our muscles tighten and we get a hot feeling in our neck and head when we are mad, or perhaps we get a tight, electric-current type feeling and the hairs on the back of our neck stand up when we are scared.

When you feel emotion, it is often in your body. You might have thoughts or images that go along with the feeling that you sense with your 6th sense. But with emotions, there is usually a physical sensation that is felt somewhere in the body. Our bodies also react to other people, and the interactions we have with others can greatly affect how we feel in our bodies.

We don't just feel emotions in our body. We might also feel sleepiness or energy. We might feel our empty stomach and have a sense of hunger in our bodies. If we have not had enough water, we will feel thirst in our bodies, and when we drink water and quench our thirst, it can feel really good.

Our 6th sense gives us a lot of important information about how we are feeling and how things affect us. It not only gives us invaluable clues, but it can also help us make sense of the information we are getting from our other senses by letting us know how others' actions affect us.

In Chapter Two we did the body scan to help us get a better sense of how our bodies help us make choices. Let's take another look at this awesome exercise and see how it can help us become more aware of all the important information our 6th sense is giving us.

DIY: The Body Scan—Take Two!

So, as we discussed in Chapter Two, it's helpful to first do the body scan in a quiet place with your eyes closed, so you can focus on what is going on inside your body without getting distracted by what you hear or see. As you get the hang of it, though, you can do it almost anywhere, even with your eyes open, as a way of checking in with yourself.

Start by getting in a comfortable position. You can sit or even lay down if you like. Close your eyes and imagine your spotlight of attention. Shine that spotlight on your feet so that all your attention focuses on your feet. Let everything else go dark except the place where your spotlight is going. And as you do this, allow yourself to notice what it feels like in your feet. Are they hot or cold? Do they feel heavy or light? Is there a comfortable feeling in them, or do they feel uncomfortable? Or maybe there is just a neutral feeling. Be poetic in how you describe the feelings in your feet to yourself. Maybe they feel bubbly or tingly like there is a little river of energy running through them. Maybe they feel as if they are tightening or releasing. It might feel like static in your feet, like when the radio is not tuned in properly. Or it might feel like water flowing or feathers tickling, or little rubber balls bouncing up and down in there. Let your words and your imagination find ways to describe what it might feel like in your feet.

As you shine your spotlight of attention, you may also find that the feeling seems to have a shape or color to it. It may seem like the feeling is moving in a certain direction or as if it is very still. It may seem as hard as steel or as soft as tapioca pudding. It may even feel as if it is stronger in one spot and weaker in other parts of your foot, or as if there is one specific spot at which the feeling is starting and then radiating out to other places.

For some people, it may be hard at first to sense what it feels like in your feet. If this happens, you can wiggle your toes and see what that feels like. Our bodies can feel things in lots of ways. Our bodies can physically feel things, like when we wiggle our toes and sense them rubbing against our shoes. We can also feel things in deeper, subtler ways, like when we feel emotions or more quiet sensations. Sometimes sensing these more subtle, quieter feelings takes practice. Doing things like wiggling our toes can help us to better focus our spotlight of attention on our bodies so that we get better and better at sensing subtler feelings and sensations.

It is important to remember that there is no right or wrong way to do the body scan. If we are focusing our spotlight on our body, we may feel many different things. Success is not about what you feel or how much you feel. It's about how well you can build your ability to shine your spotlight on your body so that you can get to know yourself better.

Once you have spent a little time shining your attention on your feet, let your spotlight move up to your lower legs. Do the same thing here that you did with your feet. Notice if there are comfortable, uncomfortable, or neutral feelings. Notice temperature and tension. Be poetic in your description of what you are feeling in the same way you did with your feet above.

After spending some time with your lower legs, move your spotlight to your upper legs, then to your waist, and then to your stomach and chest. People feel a lot of the more subtle sensations, like emotions and tensions, in their chest, so make sure to give some special attention to this area.

Keep slowly moving the spotlight to cover all the places in your body. From your stomach and chest, you can move up to your throat, then to your shoulders and arms. Next move to your back and up the back of your neck, all the way to the top of your head. Then come to the front again and let your spotlight shine on your face and eyes and mouth. Notice all the different flavors of sensation you might be feeling in your body in different places.

When you are done scanning your whole body with your spotlight of attention, slowly open your eyes. As you do, see if you can keep some of your attention with the sensations in your body. The sensations are always there and are always affecting us, even when we are not aware of them.

Building Awareness of the 6th Sense

Many people have trouble with the 6th sense. They may not have spent much time trying to notice it, so they might feel kind of disconnected from it. In addition to the body scan, here are some other things you can do to become more aware of your 6th sense. The key is to put your spotlight of attention on your body while you are doing these things.

1) *Feel the music:* Music often evokes feelings in our bodies. Feeling the music in your body is one of the things that makes it enjoyable. See if you can feel the rhythm or the melody of it in your body.

2) *Dance:* Once you are feeling the music in your body, see if you can move your body with the rhythm or the melody. You can start with a tap of the finger or a little drumming to the beat on your leg. Then let more and more of your body move to the rhythm and melodies of the music. You don't even need music to dance. Sometimes you can let yourself just dance in silence, too. Both ways can be fun.

3) *Physical exercise:* The more you move your body and pay attention to it, the more aware of it you will be. Exercise is a great way to do this. You can do things like skateboarding, sports, dance, yoga, gymnastics, or martial arts and notice what your body feels like when you do these things. Or you can do things like running or bike riding. Even going for a walk can help you connect more with your body.

4) *Massage:* Getting a massage can be a great way to connect to your body. And it is fun and relaxing. You can get a massage from someone else or give yourself one. I often rub my own hands or feet or neck as a way of relaxing. It feels good to do this and when our body is feeling something good it can make it easier for us to put our spotlight of attention on it.

5) *Take a bath or shower:* Just like a massage, a bath or shower can feel really good. It's like a water mas-sage. Next time you take one, see if you can notice the sensations in your body that come with the experience.

6) *Pay attention to your first five senses:* Things we sense often evoke sensations in our body. And some of our first five senses, like taste and touch, are directly connected to our body sensations. You can do things like noticing the flavor or texture of foods. Notice if your mouth waters when you are about to eat something tasty or if you get tense when you eat something sour. Notice what the cold feels like on your skin or how the sound of screeching car brakes or music you don't like makes you feel. How about the smell of stinky garbage, or fresh-baked chocolate chip cookies, or the sight of a big A on a test you get back from your teacher? How do those things make your body feel? See if you can notice how things like this that you experience with your other senses make your body feel.

And it's not just the first five senses that can affect how your body feels. Things occurring in your seventh and 8th senses can also evoke feelings in your body. We are going to do a few DIYs for the other senses, and you can try to be aware of your sixth sense while doing them as a way to get more connected to your body.

https://www.socialdetectiveacademy.com/body-awareness-practice/

The 7th Sense

The seventh sense is not ESP, but you could say it is a kind of mind-reading. It actually is how we sense our own minds, so in a way, that is mind reading. It's just that you are reading your own mind rather than other people's. The seventh sense involves sensing what and how we think. Thinking usually involves talk in our mind, as well as images in our mind.

For example, if I ask you to think about your summer vacation, you may have words and images that come into your mind about what you did last summer. You may have memories come into your head, like being on a beach in Hawaii or being at home playing your favorite video game. These memories may involve words, as well as images. But how do you *know* you are thinking these thoughts? You know because you are sensing yourself thinking them.

If I ask you what you are thinking about, you will put your attention on your mind and maybe say "I'm think-ing about what I am going to have for lunch." The reason you know you are thinking about lunch is that you are sensing your thoughts. This is the seventh sense, sensing what is happening in your mind.

You might also sense the quality of your thoughts. You might notice your mind being clear and sharp, or fuzzy and distracted. Or you might notice thinking lots of negative or fearful thoughts, or maybe you will notice thinking more positive thoughts. The reason you can tell the quality of your thoughts is that you are sensing them and are aware of what you are sensing.

Sometimes we may be unaware of what thoughts we are having, or of the quality of our thinking. Usually, when someone is unaware of what's going on in their mind, it's not because they are unable to sense their own mind. It's because they are not paying attention to what they are sensing with the seventh sense.

We may be daydreaming on automatic pilot and not even realize what we are thinking about. Or we may be thinking of something stressful and feel our whole body tense up, and not even realize that the thoughts we are having are responsible for our stress. Or we may be fuzzy-headed and easily distracted without even realizing it.

But the reason we don't realize these things is not because we can't sense them. It's because we are not putting our attention on them. And because we are not putting attention on them, we will not really be able to observe them. Giving something attention helps us be more aware. And the more we are aware of things like our own mental activity, the more power we have to understand ourselves and make our minds do what we want them to do.

In Chapter 2 we talked about using our *spotlight of attention* as a way to help us be the master of our minds rather than our minds being our master. What we were really talking about was how being able to sense our own mind can help us be more in control of our thoughts and attention. Let's do a little review of the spotlight of attention and mind mastering as a way of practicing how to better sense our own minds.

DIY: Sensing the Talk in the Mind

In the following four DIY detective training exercises, we are going to practice some things that can help us master our mind through increasing our awareness of the seventh sense, or specifically, our ability to sense the talk in our mind.

The four DIYs we are going to practice here are: 1) Finding our talk; 2) Labeling our talk; 3) Noticing the flavor of our talk; 4) Having conversations with our mind. Let's do a little practice for each of these four things.

1) Finding the talk

In this DIY detective training exercise, we are going to locate a very important part of our mind. We are going to locate the part of our mind responsible for our verbal thinking. I call this verbal thinking, "mental talk." This place inside our minds is where we talk to ourselves. So, let's locate this place inside of us.

Get in a comfortable sitting position and close your eyes. Take your spotlight of attention and shine it right into your mind. You want to look for the place inside of you where you talk to yourself. For many people, this is right in the center of their head between their ears.

You can test out where your talk is by doing a simple experiment. Start saying the alphabet to yourself. Don't say it with your voice. Just say it inside. Think it. A,B,C,D.... Where do you notice yourself thinking the alphabet? Is it in the middle of your head? Is it to the side? Or is it somewhere else? Just let yourself notice where you are thinking it or hearing it inside.

When you locate the place where your mental talk is, shine your spotlight of attention right there. Wherever the spotlight goes, that is where your attention goes. For now, we want that spotlight right on the place where you are reciting the alphabet.

Once you have your spotlight of attention shining on your mind, you can stop reciting the alphabet. Don't stop shining your spotlight there. Just stop reciting the alphabet. Now just watch and wait to see what comes up next in your mind. All you need to do is keep your spotlight of attention on your mind and watch. Something is bound to come up in that space.

If nothing comes up in your mind, you are either a master at quieting your mind or you have fallen asleep. Minds are seldom completely quiet. It might also be that you have gotten distracted and are not noticing anything in your mind because your spotlight of attention is completely off and you are not even thinking about noticing what's going on in your mind. I know this one well. I can't tell you how many times I have started off trying to notice what's going on in my mind and ended up thinking about some cool video game or something like that for a long time before I realized I was supposed to be noticing what was going on in my mind.

But if this happens, have no fear. It happens to everyone. The trick is to just come back if you get distracted. Remember what we said before. If you get distracted ten times but come back to what you are trying to pay attention to eleven times, you win.

So just keep coming back to your mind. Keep bringing your spotlight of attention back to that space in your mind where you think things, and see if you can notice when thoughts arise. Notice when thoughts come into your mind. You can also notice if a particular thought carries you away, and you forget to notice when other thoughts come up.

But if you get distracted, just remember, it happens to all of us. And when it does, just bring that shiny old spotlight back to your mind and let your mind know who is boss.

2) Labeling your talk

A great strategy to become more aware of our mental talk is *talk labeling*. For this, all you need to do is say the word "talk," either out loud or to yourself, every time you notice yourself thinking in words. You don't have to say what the thought is or how it makes you feel. All you have to do is say the word "talk" as a way of making a note to yourself. This can help keep us from getting lost in the stream of thoughts that we often get lost in. So, while keeping your spotlight of attention on the place where verbal thoughts are in your mind, let yourself say the word "talk" every time you notice a verbal thought come up.

3) Noticing the flavor of our talk

Another thing you can try and notice is what I like to call the *flavor* of your verbal thoughts. Do your thoughts have a happy flavor or a sad flavor? Are they stressful thoughts, or calm, peaceful thoughts? Are they thoughts that make you feel more confident or less confident? There can be many different flavors to our verbal thoughts, and getting a sense of the different qualities of our thoughts can be very helpful.

4) Having conversations with our mind

Once we are more aware of where our verbal thoughts are, when they arise, and what flavor they have, it becomes easier to have good conversations with our mind. And having conversations with our mind helps us be even more aware of what we are sensing with the 7th sense. So, after you have tried the first three of these DIY practices, see if you can start talking with your mind.

First, you can say "hi" to your mind, just as you would to a friend. You can ask it how it's doing. You can ask it if it is clear and focused, or fuzzy and distracted. You can ask it if it is awake and alert, or sleepy. If there is no one else around, you can even do this out loud. But you can do it silently, as well.

After saying hi and starting up your mental conversation by asking your mind some questions, you can tell your mind what you need from it. You can tell it when you need it to pay attention to something. You can tell it to stop daydreaming when you need it to be clear and focused. You can even tell it to think more positive thoughts if it is being negative.

See if you can start to have some conversations with your mind. Say hi. Ask some questions. Tell it what you want from it. You can do this when you wake up, or before you go to sleep. Any time you think of it, you can strike up a nice conversation.

It may seem a little strange to ask your mind questions. But it can really help you to develop an awareness of your 7th sense and all that is going on in your mind.

DIY: Sensing the Images in the Mind

Now we are going to do a similar DIY, but here we are going to focus on sensing the images we might have in our minds. Images are another type of thought. They are our nonverbal thoughts.

The four DIYs we are going to practice here are: 1) Finding the images; 2) Labeling the images; 3) Noticing the flavor of the images; 4) Shifting the images. So, let's do a little practice for each of these four things

1) Finding the images

In the last few DIYs we started by noticing the place inside where our talk is located. Here we are going to do the same thing but with our nonverbal thoughts, with our mental images. Some people think in images and others don't. Don't feel bad if it's hard for you to find clear images in your mind. Just do the best you can and know that different people's minds work differently.

Let's start by thinking of an apple. Imagine in your mind a nice shiny, juicy, delicious apple. Notice the place in your mind where you mentally see this apple. For some people, they sense their nonverbal thoughts in the same place they sense their verbal thoughts – right in the middle of their heads between their ears. Other people tend to sense their mental imagery closer to their forehead in between their eyes and some actually sense their mental imagery as if it were outside of them just above their forehead. You might even experience it somewhere else. Where it is not important. The goal is to just notice where your mental imagery happens.

When you locate the place where your mental talk is let yourself shine your spotlight of attention right there. Wherever the spotlight goes that is where your attention goes. For now, we want that spotlight right on the place where you are sensing the image of the apple.

Once you have your spotlight of attention on this place you can stop trying to imagine the apple. Don't stop shining your spotlight there. Just stop trying to picture the apple. Now just watch and wait. Just wait to see what comes up next in your mind. All you need to do now is keep your spotlight of attention on your mind and watch. Something is bound to come up in that space.

If no images come up in your mind, that's fine. This might be because you are getting distracted and not aware of all the images that are coming up in your mind. But it also might be because you don't usually think in images. It's ok if you get distracted. It happens to everyone. If you do get distracted just remember what we said before. If you get distracted ten times but come back to what you are trying to pay attention to eleven times you win.

So just keep coming back to your mind. Keep bringing your spotlight of attention back to that space in your mind where your mental images are and see if you can notice when images arise. Notice when images come into your mind. You can also notice if a particular image carries you away with it and you forget to notice when other images come up.

2) Labeling your images

As we mentioned with talk, a great strategy to help become more aware of our thoughts is thought labeling. With nonverbal thoughts, all you need to do is say out loud or to yourself the word "image" every time you notice an image arising in your mind. You don't have to say what the image is or how it makes you feel. All you have to do is say the word "image" as a way of making a note to yourself. This can help keep you from getting distracted by your mental images. So, while keeping your spotlight of attention on the place where your images are in your mind, let yourself say out loud the word "image" every time you notice an image come up.

3) Noticing the flavor of our images

Just as we did with mental talk, it can be helpful to try and notice the flavor of our mental imagery. Do your images have a happy flavor or a sad flavor? Are they stressful images or calm, peaceful thoughts? Are they nice to look at or not so nice? Are they images that make you feel more confident or less confident? There can be many different flavors to our images, and getting a sense of the different qualities of our images can be very helpful.

4) Shifting the images

When we become more aware of where our nonverbal thoughts are, when they arise, and what flavor they have, it becomes easier to shift them in the ways that we want. It also becomes easier to create new mental images of our own choosing. So, after you have tried the first three of these DIY practices, see if you can start shifting the images in your mind and creating new ones.

For example, let's say you have an image in your mind that is not so good. Let's say it's an image of someone bullying you. Let's say that in the image the bully looks really big and you look much smaller. Once you notice the image and label it you become more aware of it. And with more awareness, there is more ability to shift the image.

If you had an image like this and became aware of it, you could try and shift it. You could make the bully shrink and make yourself get bigger. You could even imagine a giant soundproof bubble come down and surround the bully, making it so you can't hear him talk anymore. You could imagine him pounding on the bubble trying to get out. Then you could imagine yourself blowing really hard and launching the bubble up into the air and watching it get smaller and smaller until it disappears completely.

Or maybe you get home from school, but when you go to start working on your homework, you notice in your mind the image of a huge pile of homework on your desk. All the papers are scattered and falling on the floor and taking over your whole room. Images often describe things we are feeling or thinking. This one might be describing you feeling overwhelmed with all the homework you have that day. And thinking about the image will probably make you feel even more overwhelmed.

But if you are aware you are having this kind of imagery, you can shift the image and imagine all the papers organizing themselves in a nice neat pile. You might imagine the pile getting smaller and you just standing there with a smile on your face, hard at work going through the papers and filling them all out quickly and easily. Then you could imagine yourself finishing all the work and going outside to play before dinner.

Or maybe you are stressed about giving a speech in school the next day. You might imagine standing awkwardly in front of the class and all the kids looking bored or laughing at you while you talk. You could shift this image and imagine everyone listening and showing you with their nonverbal communications that they are really interested in what you are saying. You might imagine the teacher with a proud look on her face as she listens to you talk. You could even imagine yourself as a rock star up on stage in front of the whole classroom and picture all the students cheering you on as you go up in front of the class to talk.

Observing the Observer

So, here is a question for you. In the last few DIYs, I asked you to try to get to know your own mind better. But if your mind is part of you, who is it that is trying to get to know your mind better? Who noticed where the thoughts are in the exercise above? Who labeled the thoughts and who noticed the flavor of the thoughts and had a conversation with your thoughts? Who is it that notices when you get distracted or when your mind is clear or fuzzy?

Of course, the person who noticed all these things is YOU. You did all these things. You used your mind to observe different parts and qualities of your own mind. I call this part of your mind that can be aware of the things going on in your mind *the observer*. The observer is a powerful thing. I think of it as the bigger YOU. It is the bigger mind that all the thoughts and qualities of mind are a part of. It is the bigger self in which all the senses are just parts. The observer is the bigger you that is capable of being aware of all the little parts of you.

The observer is very important. It is the part that shines the spotlight of attention. It is the part of us that helps us be aware of things. And it is the part that helps us notice relationships. As we go on to other exercises, we will see more of how this observer part of our mind helps us in many ways. Let's do a DIY to help us better experience our observer.

DIY: Observing the Observer

Let's come back to looking inside with your spotlight of attention. Sit in a comfortable position and close your eyes. Let yourself turn on your spotlight of attention and allow it to rest on the place where you experience talk in your mind. Let it light up that space and come back to noticing if any thoughts arise in that talk space. If they do, just label what you are experiencing by saying the word "talk" to yourself or out loud.

After doing this for a minute, shift your attention just a little. Keep watching the place where talk arises. But as you do this, see if you can notice the part of you that is labeling the talk, the part that is shining the spotlight and noticing the talk. The part that is noticing is your observer. This is the bigger YOU. Just let yourself become aware of the part of you that is observing the talk. Let yourself notice yourself observing.

If you really want to trip yourself out, see if you can shine your spotlight of attention on the part of you that is observing and observe yourself observing your thoughts. And while you are doing this ask yourself this question— "Who am I?" Ask yourself "Am I my thoughts?" Then ask yourself, "Am I the observer of my thoughts?" Then if you really want to play with this, ask yourself "Am I the observer of the part of me that observes my thoughts?" It can become like one of those halls of mirrors. You know the ones where you see a reflection of another reflection of yourself and it seems like there are reflections of you going on into infinity.

But we don't have to make it that confusing. The main point here is that you are not your thoughts. You are not any of the sensations you sense or are aware of. You are the observer of your thoughts and sensations. You are the one who shines the spotlight of attention. You are the one who makes sense of all the facts and information your senses give you.

That is a big part of the observer's job—of *your* job: To organize and make sense of all the information your senses give you and to look for patterns in the information and tie the pieces of information together into a bigger story about what is happening. We will talk more about this in the section on context.

For now, just try to notice what it feels like to see yourself as the observer. After doing this for a few minutes, let yourself open your eyes. But as you do, see if you can keep the feeling of being the observer. Let yourself open your eyes and sense what you see. See if you can observe yourself seeing things with your eyes. See if you can observe yourself hearing things with your ears and using all your senses. Observe yourself noticing your senses. It is guaranteed to help you become more aware of all the things around you, as well as all the things inside of you.

The 8th Sense

We build a good relationship with people by exchanging information—by showing interest in getting to know the other person, and by listening and responding and all the other things we have been talking about. The same is true for our relationships with our minds and bodies and other senses. By paying attention and listening to our minds and bodies and other senses, these parts of us become our friends. I call this having a good relationship with ourselves.

But how do we know if our relationship with ourselves or with others are getting better or worse? How do we measure? Of course, with other people, we can measure things like how often we get together with them, how much they tease us or compliment us, how much we give each other attention, or stay on topic or mood match. We can use all the things we have been talking about to help measure how well a relationship is going. But that really does not fully do it. Those things can give us some information, but the real test of how well a relationship is going is how we feel. And this is where the 8th sense comes in. When we are connected to our 8th sense and aware of the information it is giving us, we can determine very easily how well a relationship is going because we can feel it.

If someone is being really nice and attentive and engaging, we can notice all those things with our first five senses. But we will feel the quality of the relationship inside of ourselves. We will feel good in our bodies when we think about the relationship, which we will sense with our 6th sense. And we will have more positive thoughts about the relationship and sense that with our 7th sense.

Our 6th and 7th senses will be giving us information along with the information from the outside world. And all this information comes together to give us an experience of the quality of the relationship, which we sense with our 8th sense. The 8th sense is sensing the combination of all the other senses and how they come together to create relationships.

It's kind of like how you make cookies. You take eggs, flour, sugar, and butter and put them all together. Then you mix and swirl them into one big sticky gooey lump of goodness. Then you cook the batter and end up with cookies. You are taking lots of things and putting them together to make the final thing.

A raw egg, or a cup of sugar or some flour or butter will not taste good on their own. But when you put them all together and cook them, they create something completely new from all the separate parts. All the ingredients that might not be particularly exciting on their own come together to create a delicious treat. It's the same socially. All the parts we have been talking about in this book come together to form our relationship cookie. And we sense that with our 8th sense. Our 8th sense is what lets us know how that relational cookie tastes.

So, our 8th sense senses relationships. It can sense the quality of our relationship with our own mind and body. When we are aware and connected to our thoughts or our bodies, our 8th sense can feel it. And when we are not aware or connected to these parts of ourselves, our 8th sense can feel that too.

Our 8th sense also senses our relationships with other people. It can sense when there is closeness, comfort, and connection between us and others. And it can sense when there is distance, discomfort, and disconnection. It can sense if there are strengths as well as problems between us and others, which can be very helpful information.

Many clients who come to me with social mysteries are shocked when they first realize that there is a problem in their friendships with others. There may have been lots of clues that problems were building in the friendships. But if they were not sensing the quality of their relationships, they may have missed lots of important information that could have kept their friendship from getting bad.

The 8th sense takes information from the other senses to help determine how our relationships are doing. While the first five senses give us a lot of information about how our relationships are doing, the 8th sense tends to draw a lot from the 6th and 7th senses. Let's look at how we might experience the quality of relationships with both of these two senses.

Sensing Relationships in the Body

The body can give us a lot of information about the quality of our relationship with ourselves. A good relationship with ourselves often comes with a sense of knowing ourselves and feeling more in control and comfortable with our body. We might have a sense of wholeness or fullness or a sense of warmth. A good relationship with our body often comes with feeling more flexible and fluid. We might also feel more confident and coordinated.

But a good relationship with our bodies does not always mean we are feeling good. It's more about being well connected, which might mean we are actually more aware of how we are not feeling good. Maybe we are more aware of some pain in our body or of feeling stressed or anxious. Or maybe our good relationship with ourselves puts us in touch with feeling awkward or uncomfortable. But when we are well connected to our bodies, there is often a feeling of comfort with ourselves and a sense of smoothness and flow like we might feel when we are having more rag doll movements.

When we are not in a good relationship with our bodies, there is often a sense of not knowing. It can feel like our body is some alien that we don't understand, which can make us feel out of control and uncomfortable in our bodies. When we don't have a good relationship with our bodies, we might feel fragmented or empty or cold inside. There is often more of a solid, unmovable quality instead of a more flexible, flowy quality. When we are tuned into our 8th sense, we will be better able to notice differences in the quality of our relationship to our own body.

If our relationship with others is good, we might experience a sense of ease and comfortableness with other people. Our bodies will probably be more relaxed around them. We might feel a warmth, fullness, wholeness, or a sense of connection in our chest. We might feel positive feelings like care, kindness, enjoyment, happiness, or love inside when we are with that other person or thinking about them. When we are in good relationships with others, there is often a sense of attraction and a feeling in our body of being pulled closer to them in some way. And usually, there is a sense of openness towards the other person. When we are open, we are more receptive to the exchange of information with the other person.

On the other hand, if things are not going well in our relationship with someone, we might feel awkwardness and discomfort with that person or when thinking about them. Our bodies will probably feel more stressed around them. There might be a sense of cold or emptiness or disconnection around the other person. We might also experience negative feelings like irritation, anger, distrust, hurt, rejection, or loneliness. Instead of attraction and pull towards, we might have a sense of repulsion or pushing away from the other person when we are with them or thinking about them. Usually, there is also a sense of being closed off and protective, which makes us less receptive to a nice exchange of information with the other person.

There is a particular sense in the body when we are relationally closed to another person. There is a tightness and sense of contraction I call *making a fist with your body.* When we make a fist, we close our hand and tighten it up. We do this to protect and defend. In addition, a closed fist does not allow new things in and actively keeps things out. You can't put anything into a closed fist, and you also can't let things out. When our body gets "fisty," closing and protecting, it makes it hard for new things to come in or to let parts of ourselves out to be shared, which makes an exchange of information difficult.

When we are feeling relationally positive, our bodies are more like an *open hand*. Open hands tend to be more relaxed and receptive. They are not protective and they are able to let new things in. They can pick things up and hold them. When we feel comfortable and good around others, our bodies are like open hands. They are relaxed and receptive to letting others in, as well as to let parts of ourselves out to be shared. And with this, there is more opportunity to exchange information with others.

Whether our relationships with ourselves or others are good or bad, we will be able to sense it if we are in touch with our 8th sense. And being able to sense the quality of our relationships is a powerful thing. Most relationships we have will have times where they are not going great. But if we can sense this early on, we can take that feedback and use it to try and make the relationship better. And that is really the main thing we do as social detectives. We try to make relationships better.

Sensing Relationships in the Mind

We have talked a lot about how exchanging information is a way we connect. Being connected might be experienced in our minds as information moving back and forth between us and others. If it is a connection with ourselves that we are sensing, it might be experienced as information moving back and forth between different parts of ourselves.

With others, we might sense this kind of connection by really getting what they are saying or how they see things, or maybe by taking in what their body language is communicating. We might also get from their verbal or nonverbal responses that they are really understanding us. This sense of understanding or being understood might cause us to have certain feelings in our bodies, as we have talked about. But in the mind, it is often the awareness of understanding or of the flow of information back and forth that helps us to sense the quality of our connection.

We might have the sense of an exchange of information within ourselves between our mental thoughts and the observing part of ourselves. Our observer might perceive our mind thinking different thoughts. We might even say things to ourselves like "I'm thinking about X." Our observing part might also notice the state of our mind. If our mind is focused and clear, the observer will be aware of that. And if our mind is fuzzy, our observer will be aware of that, as well. It will be aware because there is a good exchange of information between the mind and the part of us that is observing the mind. And that good exchange of information will give us the sense of a good relationship with our own mind.

When there is a good relationship between us and others or between us and ourselves, there are often other clues we might notice. We might have more positive thoughts about the other person or even about ourselves. We might have a sense of familiarity in our mind, like we really know this other person or this part of ourselves. We might also have positive images like us being physically close with another person or images of them smiling and of us in a positive exchange. These are all things that can help us assess that the relationship is going well.

On the flip side, our relational sense might perceive problems between us and others that might show up as negative thoughts about the other person. Maybe we think they don't really like us or are judgmental of us. We might think they don't really know us or that they are not a nice, caring person. We might have judgmental thoughts like "they are a jerk" or "they are mean." We might have images of them making mean faces or of them walking away from us or laughing at us or leaving us out of a conversation they are having with others.

Just as we sense positive things between us and others when we are tuned into our 8th sense, we will also be more able to sense problems between us and others. This is good because it can help us catch problems early on so we can fix them and not let them damage our relationships.

So, let's do some DIYs to help us get more in touch with our 8th sense.

DIY: Noticing Relationships with Your First Five Senses

Let's start by measuring how connected we are to our first five senses. We can use a scale of 1-10 to measure, with 1 meaning you do not feel at all connected to a particular sense. It means you are totally unaware of any information that sense is giving you. This might happen if you are playing a video game and you are really into it and your mom tells you it's time for dinner. She may begin by saying it really loud but you are so into your game that you genuinely do not register a word she is saying. She may say "How could you not hear me?" And you might say "Honest, Mom, I really did not notice you talking at all." I know from personal experience it may be totally true. If you are really into your game you might be unaware that she is even talking to you, even though your ears are working fine.

In a situation like this, you could honestly say you scored a 1 on how aware you were of your hearing. A 10 on this scale would mean you are totally connected to your sense of hearing. It would mean that you are noticing every tiny little thing that sense is telling you. If you scored a ten on hearing your mom calling you for dinner you would be fully aware of everything she said. You would probably also notice the quality of her voice and how loud or fast she was talking. You might even hear other sounds around you, like your brother or sister in the other room pulling the chair out to sit down at the dinner table.

Keeping this scale in mind, get in a comfortable position and let yourself close your eyes. Let your observer take your spotlight of attention and shine it on your vision. With your eyes closed, notice what you are seeing. Ask yourself, "Am I aware of what I am seeing? Am I noticing everything that is in my field of view?"

With your eyes closed, you might just be seeing dark. It doesn't matter what you are seeing. What is important is how aware you are of what you are seeing. Are you in a good relationship with your sense of vision? Are you fully paying attention to your sight or are you distracted and not really taking in the visual information around you? Just to get another point of view, open your eyes for a minute and notice what you are seeing now. Ask yourself again "How aware am I of what I am seeing?" Choose a number on the scale.

Now try this. With your eyes still open, shift your spotlight of attention and let your mind wander. Think about something else other than what you are seeing with your eyes. Think about what you're going to do later today or maybe even what your ears are hearing right now. Then see if you notice your relationship with your eyesight changing at all. Do you notice being any less aware of your visual sense when you put your attention other places?

Give yourself a number for this one too. Then close your eyes again and see if you can bring your spotlight of attention back to your vision. Notice how the quality of your relationship to what you are seeing changes as you shift your attention back to it.

Let's do the same thing with the rest of our first five senses. With your eyes closed, let your spotlight of attention come to your sense of hearing. On a scale of 1-10, notice how aware and connected you are to what your ears are hearing. Then let your spotlight roam as we did with our sight, and see if you notice being less aware of your hearing when you do this. Give this a number too. Then come back to hearing and see if your number goes up.

Try this with all your senses. Let your attention go to touch and see if you can notice what your skin is sensing. Are your clothes touching your body? What's the temperature like? Notice if your score changes when you shine your spotlight of attention elsewhere. Then notice if your score comes back up as you intentionally bring your attention back to your sense of touch.

Notice if you are smelling anything or tasting anything. You might not be experiencing much with these senses if you are not smelling something or eating something. But you can still notice those senses. You can notice that there is not much information coming to you through those senses.

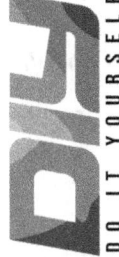

DIY: Noticing Relationships with Your 6th Sense

Let's do this again with our 6th sense. Without thinking too much, bring your attention to your body and give yourself a number on a scale of 1-10 for how aware and connected you are to your 6th sense right at that moment. Then give your body a little more attention. Turn up the spotlight of attention and shine it in a more focused way on what you are sensing inside. Do a quick body scan, starting with your feet and working your way up and all around your body, noticing sensations in it.

Notice if doing this changes the number you give. Does your number go up when you give more intentional attention to your body? Do you feel more connected to yourself when you make an effort to shine your spotlight of attention on your body?

DIY: Noticing Relationships with Your 7th Sense

Now let's do the same thing with our 7th sense. Without thinking too much, bring your attention to the places where talk and images happen and give yourself a number on a scale of 1-10 for how aware and connected you are to your 7th sense right at that moment. As we did with the body, give your mind a little more attention. Turn up the spotlight of attention and shine it in a more focused way on your mind. See what comes up in your talk space and image space. Then notice if that changes the number you give. Does your number go up when you give more intentional attention to your mind? Do you feel more connected to your thoughts when you make an effort to shine your spotlight of attention on your mind?

DIY: Noticing Relationships with Others

Practice One – *Sensing Positive or Neutral Relationships*

For this one, pick someone you know, someone you have a positive or neutral relationship with. It can be a kid or an adult. Close your eyes and let yourself imagine this person. While you are imagining them in your mind, start feeling into the quality of your relationship with them. Let's start here by putting some attention on our 7th sense. Notice the thoughts you might have about them. You can ask yourself the questions below to get a better sense of the quality of your relationship with this person.

- Do you have positive thoughts about them?
- Do you have a sense like you know them and they know you? If so, is it a sense that you know them a little like you would an acquaintance, or do you have a deeper sense of knowing as you might with a close friend or family member?
- Do you feel like you understand this person and they understand you?
- In general, is there a nice, easy flow of information that goes back and forth between you and them when you interact or is it difficult to exchange ideas and information?
- When you think about them do you think they like you or you like them?
- Do you notice yourself liking qualities they have or do you have a sense of things they might like about you?
- Do you have judgments about them or feel they have judgments about you?
- In your mind, do you believe they accept you or reject you?
- See if you notice any images that might go along with this person. When you think about them, what images come to mind?

- Are there images of you doing nice things together?

- Are they smiling In your mental pictures of them? Does their face look happy or kind, or sad or angry?

- Now let your mind go to past interactions you have had with this person. Do positive thoughts and images come up when you reminisce about your past experiences with this person? Or are the thoughts not so positive? Or perhaps some of both?

- When you let yourself think about your history with this person and all the different interactions you have had, can you recall any times your interactions had elements of the suspects we have been talking about in this book? For example, how has their attention been with you? How have they been at staying on topic or mood matching? Are they verbal crowders or do they give lots of space in conversations? What has their nonverbal communication been like with you? Ask yourselves the same questions about how you have been with them. And then think about how those positive or negative things in your interactions might have affected how you feel about this other person. For a full list of all the suspects we have been talking about, take a look at Appendix X.

With all these things floating around in your mind, let's turn attention to your 6th sense and start to notice how you might sense the quality of this relationship in your body. Let yourself do a quick body scan as you keep this person in mind. Do you have a general overall sense of the feeling of this relationship in your body? When you think about this person, what they look like, how you have exchanged information with each other, the things you have done together in the past, what does your body feel like?

Recall the things we discussed above about how we might experience the quality of a relationship in our bodies. If your relationship with someone is good, you might feel things like ease and comfortableness, relaxation, warmth, fullness, wholeness, or a sense of connection in your chest. You might experience positive feelings like care, kindness, enjoyment, happiness, or love, or a sense of attraction and a feeling in your body of being pulled closer to that person. Overall you might have a sense of openness in which your body as well as your mind is receptive to the exchange of information with the other person.

On the other hand, if your relationship with the other person is not so good, you might feel awkwardness, discomfort, stress, coldness, emptiness, or disconnection. You might also have negative feelings like irritation, anger, distrust, hurt, rejection, or loneliness, and a sense of repulsion or a pushing away. If things are not going well, you are not likely to feel as safe and might feel more closed off and protective and not as open to the exchange of information, especially around things that are vulnerable for you. You might experience this as making a fist with your body, as opposed to a sense of your body as an open hand that is receptive to others.

Even in good relationships, you might have some of both. You might feel some good feelings in your body as well as some not so good ones. A good friendship does not mean everything is good all the time. But hopefully, the good outweighs the bad. And with good relational sensing, you can notice the things that are not going as well and try to fix them early on.

Practice Two – *Sensing Poor Relationships*

For this one pick someone you have had some troubles with, someone you have not gotten along with or had a fight with, or even someone you would like to be closer to.

Repeat all the steps from the DIY above on sensing positive or neutral relationships. We can often get a lot of insight by tuning into our 8th senses and really feeling into the quality of our relationship with someone we are having trouble with. Doing this can give us clues as to where the difficulties might be between us and the other person, and this can help us come up with social remedies to make that relationship better. So, as you do this DIY with someone you don't have a great relationship with, see if you get any ideas on how to make the relationship better.

Practice Three – *Sensing Relationships in the Moment*

In the last two DIYs we did, we explored the quality of relationships with people based on our past experiences with them. We were not sensing what was happening in present interactions with them. We were sensing our history with them. We were feeling into the *context* of our relationship with them. What we are going to do in this DIY is practice sensing the quality of relationships with others in the present moment based on what is going on right now as opposed to what has gone on before.

In reality, the quality of our relationship with others can shift from moment to moment based on a lot of different factors. It might shift based on the mood we are in at the moment or because of circumstances happening to us or around us. Or the shifts might happen because of things going on between us and the other person, or because of things we notice or find out about the other person in the moment.

Maybe you have a friend over and you want to play video games, but they want to talk and ride skateboards. You might have been feeling great about the relationship before, but now your different wants and needs along with how you negotiate those differences might affect your feeling in the moment. Having information about the shifts that happen in the moment can help us make better choices and keep the quality of our relationships with others positive.

DIY: Practice Sensing the Quality

So, let's do a DIY to help practice sensing the quality of relationships with others in the moment. You can do this throughout the day when you have interactions with others.

Start by noticing the information you are getting from your five senses when you are with someone. Let your observer notice the topic of conversation and how your verbal dance is going. Let yourself think about the suspects we have been discussing in this book and see if you notice any of those suspects at play in your interactions with this other person. Are you both staying on topic? Are you mood matching or mood missing? How are your verbal dance and nonverbal communication? Again, you can refer to Appendix X for a list of all the suspects we have discussed.

Once you have made note of the information you are getting with your five senses, let yourself bring *some* of your attention to your 7th sense. Notice I said *some* of your attention, not *all* of it. You don't want to close your eyes and take all your attention away from the other person. That would definitely change the quality of your relationship with them in that moment. So just bring some attention to your mental space and get a sense of it.

Do you notice anything in your thoughts and images that might give you clues about the quality of your relationship with this person at that moment? Are you having nice thoughts about them when you let yourself think about them? Or are you having more negative thoughts? Or are your thoughts neutral?

Then let yourself put some attention on your 6th sense and notice how being with them feels in your body. Do you notice positive feelings in your body when you are with this person? Does your body feel a sense of ease or comfort? Is it relaxed? Do you feel warmth, fullness, wholeness, or a sense of connection in your chest? Are there positive emotions like kindness, enjoyment, happiness, or love? Is there a sense of attraction and a feeling in your body of being pulled closer to them in some way? Are you open and receptive to the exchange of information with the other person?

Or are the feelings more negative? Is there a sense of awkwardness and discomfort? Do you feel stressed with them? Do you have a sense of cold or emptiness or disconnection in your body? Are there more negative feelings like irritation, anger, distrust, hurt, rejection, or loneliness? Instead of the kind of attraction and pull we often feel when things are good with others, is there a sense of repulsion or a pushing away from the other person? Does your body feel a sense of being closed off and protective that might make you less receptive to a nice exchange of information with the other person? Does your body feel more like it is making a fist instead of being open?

Once you have noticed all these things, give the quality of relationship you are sensing with your 8th sense a number on a scale of 1-10, as we did in the last few DIYs. If you are sensing a good quality of relationship with this person, just enjoy it. Maybe even let yourself savor the good thoughts and feelings that go along with it. And if the quality is not great, see if you can use some of the things that we have discussed in this book to make the quality better. Let yourself think about all the suspects that might lead to problems in relationships, and see if any prime suspects jump out at you. If they do, see if you can use some of the remedies we have discussed for those suspects.

Noticing the quality of our relationships with others in the moment can be an incredibly powerful tool for any social detective. Give it a try and see how it works for you.

Main Ideas Chapter 10

1. What are our first five senses? P - 207
2. How do the first five senses help us gather facts? P - 208
3. What is the 6th sense? P - 209
4. What is the 8th sense? P - 217
5. How can we use the body scan to build awareness of our 6th sense? P - 210
6. What are some other things we can do to build our awareness of our 6th sense? P - 210
7. What is the 7th sense? P - 211
8. How can we use the body scan to build awareness of our 7th sense? P - 214
9. What are some other things we can do to build our awareness of our 6^{7h} sense? P - 210
10. How can we better sense images in our mind? P - 214
11. What is the observer? P - 216
12. How can we become more aware of the observer? P - 216
13. How does the 8th sense use information from the other seven senses? P - 218
14. What are some ways we might sense the quality of our relationships in our bodies? P - 221
15. What do we mean when we say "making a fist with our bodies? P - 222
16. What are some ways we might sense the quality of our relationships in our minds? P - 221

PART FIVE

CONTEXT AND PERSPECTIVE TAKING

Chapter 11: Context

We have been talking a lot in the previous chapters about how exchanging information is a big part of social relationships. Exchanging information with others is an important way we gather facts as a social detective. We have talked about the many verbal and nonverbal ways we exchange information with others and how gathering information helps us to know people better and have deeper relationships with them. But all that information can be a bit overwhelming and hard to manage at times. How do you remember and make sense of all the information being exchanged? That's where context comes in.

Context has to do with the things that surround something. The things that come before and after, as well as other things that might be happening right then, help to form a context. For example, if someone is singing a song with their band, all the other instruments that surround the person's singing create a context for their singing. The guitar, bass, keyboards, and drums all surround the vocals to create something bigger.

When you go to a restaurant for dinner, all the people and things and situations in the restaurant create a context for your dinner. All of those things will affect your experience of dinner. For example, being there with your friends instead of your family will affect your restaurant experience. The type of restaurant will have an effect too. If it's a formal restaurant, you might act differently than if you go out for burgers at a fast food restaurant. The people you are with, the type of restaurant, the reason you are there, all the other people in the restaurant, along with many other things, all come together to create a context for your restaurant experience.

Context and Making Sense of the Facts

At the beginning of this book, we talked about how you need to gather the facts and then make sense of them in order to solve a social mystery. In that discussion we talked about how when we are trying to solve a social mystery, it's very helpful to look for clues surrounding the situation that is a mystery to us. The facts or information before or after an event help us to make sense of the event. Those things that surround the event are the context.

In the nonverbal communication section, we talked about how things like facial expressions, body language, or voice music may not give us enough information to know what a person is communicating nonverbally. For example, someone may make a facial expression that could be either sad or angry. It might be hard to tell what they are expressing with their face based just on that information.

But if we know the information about the situation in which they made that facial expression—the context—it can help us make sense of what they are communicating. For example, let's say you find out that right before the person made that face, they got the news that their best friend was moving across the country. This information would help to create a context for making sense of their facial expression. In that situation, it would be clearer that their face was expressing sadness rather than anger.

Another example of how context helps us make sense of things can be seen with trying to understand the meaning of words. If I ask you what the word "bark" means, what would you say? You might say it's the sound a dog makes. But you might also say it is what trees have on them.

The word can mean different things. But if we know the words that surround the word "bark," it becomes much easier to make sense of the facts. If I say "I heard the dog bark all night long," it would be clear that we were talking about the sound a dog makes. And if I said "that tree has really rough bark on it," the words surrounding "bark" would create a context to help us get what the meaning of the word is.

How Context Helps Us Organize and Remember Things

So, context can help us make sense of information, of the facts we gather. But it can also help us to organize the information we gather so it is easier to remember and not be as overwhelming. Let me give you an example of how context can help us organize and remember information. I'm going to say some words and I want you to remember them. Here you go – "John, fish, spot, pond, bucket, dinner, run, squirrel, tree, bark, pee, laugh. If I ask you in an hour to pick those words out of a list of one hundred words it might be hard for you to remember them.

But now let me tell you the story about John and his dog Spot. One day John took his dog Spot down to the pond. John went fishing and caught a big fish. He was really happy with his catch. He liked fish and was planning to eat it for dinner. He put the fish in a bucket and started fishing some more. Spot seemed to like the fish too and while John was not looking Spot took the fish and started running off with it. John chased him but Spot was too fast. Then Spot saw a squirrel in a tree and dropped the fish to bark at it. The squirrel ran off pretty quickly but dogs don't always have the best memory, and Spot seemed to forget about the fish. He left the fish where it was and started peeing on the tree. When John caught up and saw the fish laying on the ground and Spot peeing, he started to laugh.

Now after hearing that story, if I asked you an hour later to pick those same words from a list of one hundred other words, it would probably be much easier. In fact, I bet you could tell me the story an hour later without any clues to remind you. That is because the story provided a context, and the context helped to organize the words and make them easier to remember. Stories themselves often can be easier to remember than separate pieces of information.

Stories can create relationships between separate pieces of information and give them meaning. And these relationships between pieces of information and the meaning the relationships create make it much easier for us to remember things. It's much easier to remember one story and all its connected pieces than to just remember a bunch of random unconnected pieces of information.

Context Helps Us Understand Others Better

When it comes to social relationships, context can help us better remember all the information we exchange with others. And it can help us make better sense of the information, so we can better know the other person.

Let me give you another example to help make this clear. I'm going to tell you about Susan and Donna. Susan has black hair, brown eyes, and is in 12th grade in high school. She got C's in all her classes this semester. She is applying for college for next year.

Donna has long, flowy black hair and big, kind-looking brown eyes. She loves science and wants to go to college to study biology. She wants to become a doctor someday, so she can help people. Up until this last semester Donna got straight As in all her classes. But this last semester was rough for her. She got really sick and missed three weeks of school. Then just as she was getting better, her grandmother got sick and her whole family had to go to New York for a week to help her. Her grandmother is a little better but still sick and Donna worries about her a lot. She really loves her grandma.

Donna asked all her teachers for her homework when she was absent and tried really hard to catch up, but with all that was going on it was hard for her. She ended up getting Cs in all her classes. Donna was really upset because she wants to go to a good college next year, and she was afraid that her drop in grades might make it harder for her to get into college. She knew she was capable of doing well, but was afraid that the people at the college might not know that and might not accept her.

After reading about Susan and Donna, who do you feel like you know better? Who do you feel like you have a nicer feeling about? Do you have a clearer image in your mind of one of these two girls? And if you were the person at college who decides who gets in, do you think that you might be more likely to accept one of these two girls than the other even though they both had the same grades?

I imagine you might have a better sense of Donna and might even have a nicer feeling about her and a clearer image in your mind of her. And I imagine you might be more likely to accept her into your college even though her grades this last semester were not the best.

The reason for this has to do with context. There is more information about Donna. We have information about her *personal context*. Things like what kind of person she is. For example, her kind eyes, love of science, desire to go to college and be a doctor, being capable and being very motivated about school. And we have information about her *situational context*. This situational information would be that she was an A student before, that she got really sick, and that her grandmother was sick.

Knowing these things about Donna personally and knowing more about the situation she has been in helps us make better sense of things and helps us to better understand why she got poor grades this last semester. If you did not know about her being sick and about her grandmother and about how she is usually a great student and a hard worker, you might think her low grades were because she was not smart or did not really care about school. But with this other information, you can make sense of the facts in a much different way.

Here is another example of how context can help us to get to know someone better and more accurately make sense of the things they do. Peter and Ralph are sitting together at a table in the cafeteria at school. It's lunchtime and they are playing a card game as they nibble at the remaining bits of their sandwiches. There are lots of other kids at the table as well, and they all seem to be watching them play. All of a sudden Peter laughs a maniacal laugh and throws his cards down exclaiming "I win! You suck, loser!" Then he punches Ralph in the arm, grabs the bag of chocolate chip cookies out of Ralph's lunch box, gets up, and walks away. All the other kids are laughing and taunting Ralph and calling him a loser.

Now just from hearing that, what impression do you get? If you are like me, you might get the impression that Peter is a bully, and that Ralph has a huge bully bullseye target on him. You might think that all the kids pick on him. You might be wondering how Peter can get away with calling him names, hitting him, and stealing his cookies.

But now let me add some context to the story to help make sense of the facts more accurately. First, let me give you some *interpersonal information* about the relationship between Ralph and Peter. These two are actually best friends. They have known each other for years. All the other kids at the table are part of their friend group. And here is some *situational information* - Peter has been trying to win at this card game with Ralph for months and he loses every time. In fact, all the guys in their group play this card game with each other all the time and for the last few months, Ralph has been on fire, beating everyone. He has been the reigning champion that no one can beat.

But Peter has been practicing a new strategy and was feeling pretty confident he would be able to beat Ralph today. So, Peter decided to make the game more interesting and made a bet with Ralph that whoever won got the other person's dessert from lunch. In addition, all the boys have a ritual when playing the game that the winner punches the loser in the shoulder. Not a hard punch, but a punch.

The boys also often tease each other playfully when doing competitive things, calling each other names like "loser," etc. They all know they don't really mean it, that it's just playful joking, and none of them take it as being mean.

Today the game went on for a long time, and the bell to go back to class had rung. But the boys were close to finishing and decided to finish even though everyone else in the lunchroom was already heading back to class.

In light of this information and the bigger context it offers, you probably have a different interpretation of the events that went on. Knowing all this, the punch probably does not seem as violent, the insult "loser" probably does not seem as critical, and the taking the cookies does not seem like a bully move. There is also information that helps explain that Peter got up so abruptly and left because he was late for class.

Types of Context

There are many types of information that help create context for us to better understand others and our interactions with them. Because there are so many different types of information that help to create contexts, I like to organize them into three categories to help remember and make better sense of them. You could say I am making contexts for the different types of contextual information.

The three main types of contextual information we are going to be talking about are *personal information*, *interpersonal information,* and *situational information*. You may have noticed I used these terms in the examples above. Let's go a little deeper into them.

Personal Information

This is information we gather about other people with whom we are interacting. This information helps us to get a better sense of the inside world of the other person, which can be incredibly helpful in understanding others and our interactions with them. Here are some of the important types of personal information.

Personality Traits

Personality traits are things that make someone who they are. Our personality traits affect how we make sense of things, respond to things, and interact with others. Here are some questions you can ask yourself about others as well as yourself that can help identify important personality traits:

1. Are they playful or serious?
2. Do they joke a lot, or do they not have a sense of humor?
3. Are they sensitive to criticism?
4. Do they tend to blame others for things, or are they good at taking responsibility for their actions?

5. Are they kind, thoughtful, and sensitive to other people's feelings and needs, or not so much?
6. Are they easygoing and flexible, or do they get upset when things are difficult and when things change?
7. Are they generally nervous or relaxed?
8. Are they more introverted or extroverted?
9. Are they more insecure or more on the confident side?
10. Are they more talkative or more on the quiet side?
11. Are they comfortable with feelings and affection, or not so much?
12. Are they good at talking about how they feel, or not so much?
13. Do they see that most people have good qualities and bad ones, or do they tend to see things in all-or-nothing terms, as if people are either all good or all bad?

Example: Personality Traits of Humor vs. Sensitivity to Criticism

Let me give you an example of how personality traits might increase our understanding of others and our interactions with them in ways that can help us in our relationships with them. Let's say you are with your friend Dan, and that you like to joke and be funny with your friends. Let's say that for you it is a way of being close to them. You tell Dan when he sneezes that he sounds like a walrus. You are just being playful and trying to connect to Dan through humor. But when you say that, Dan frowns, furrows his brow, and leaves.

Without having a good sense of some of Dan's important personality traits and how they contribute to the context of your interactions with him, you might be totally confused and see this as a huge social mystery. But if you have a clearer picture of some of Dan's personal information, you would know that Dan does not like to joke a whole lot and is sensitive to criticism. Knowing this, you would understand why he reacted the way he did. You might be careful about making jokes with him, because he would not make sense of your joking in the same way that you did. While in the context of your personal world, it was playful and a sign of friendship, while in his personal context it was serious and a sign of criticism.

Personal History

The experiences we have had in our lives can affect how we make sense of things and respond to things in the present. They also affect the kind of person we are and how we treat others. Many things in our personal history can be important to context. Below are a few examples.

1) Was the person ever bullied or taken advantage of, or were they generally treated kindly by others?
2) In the past, did they have relationships with others in which they playfully teased each other but also let each other know they really accepted and cared about one another? Or did they have relationships that were not very good, where they were often criticized and rejected?
3) Have they had a lot of kind, trustworthy friends in the past, or were their friends unkind and untrustworthy?
4) Have they had lots of cooperative relationships with people, or did they have more unfriendly competitive relationships with others?
5) Did they have friendships with others who had to be right all the time, or were other people mature enough to admit when they were wrong?

6) Were their parents loving and emotionally sensitive, or cold and emotionally insensitive?

7) Were they raised to value expressing feelings, or did they get the message that feelings are weak and should be kept to oneself?

8) Were they taught that strong people are independent and don't need others, or that real strength comes from needing others?

9) Were they raised in an honest family, or not so much?

10) Did they spend a lot of time in the past around other people, or were they on their own much of the time?

11) Are there things in their cultural background that might affect how they make sense of   things and respond to things in the present?

These are just a few of the many things in someone's personal history that might affect how they make sense of and respond to things and interact with others. Let's go a little deeper into a few examples to show how aspects of personal history might affect how someone makes sense, reacts, and responds.

Example 1: Personal History of Criticism and Rejection

Let's revisit the card game between Peter and Ralph above. Take a look back to page 227 if you would like a refresher on the card game between Peter and Ralph. This time I want to add a little more context by looking at more historical contextual information. Let's say Ralph has a history of relationships with others in which they playfully teased each other but at the same time let each other know that they really accepted and cared about one another. If this were the case, we can expect that Ralph's personal history will result in him not taking Peter's playful teasing personally.

But what if Peter was playing with a different friend Ben who he was close and friendly with but who had a different personal history with people. Instead of having a positive, playful history of friendly teasing let's say that Ben had a history in which he was often criticized and made fun of by people. Let's say that for Ben there was nothing friendly or playful about this.

Do you imagine that Ben and Ralph with their different pasts might make sense of Peter's name-calling in different ways? Ralph will most likely not take Peter's teasing to heart, given that he is used to being playful like that with people he feels close to and accepted by. Ben, on the other hand, might make sense of Peter's playful teasing much differently. Even though Peter meant nothing bad, because of his historical context he might take this as Peter being critical and rejecting him. And if Peter happened to be aware of Ben's personal historical context, he might realize that teasing would feel bad to him and decide not to tease him, which would of course be better for Ben as well as for their friendship.

Example 2: Personal history - Culture

You may have noticed that most of the things I listed in the personal history section were about relationships people had with significant people in their lives. Our relationships affect us a lot. You also might have noticed that many of the things on the personal history list seem similar to things in the personality trait section.

For example, someone might have a personality trait of being sensitive to criticism and also have a personal history in which they were criticized a lot. This may have been the case in the example with Dan above. We know he was sensitive to criticism because of his response. It may be that he is sensitive in this way naturally. But it may also be that he is sensitive in this way because he has a personal history of being criticized. If we knew about him having a history of being criticized a lot, it might have helped us be more careful when joking with him. But the point is that our relationships with other people actually help to form our personalities for better and sometimes for worse.

Our relationship with the culture we were brought up in also affects us. The beliefs, rules, and values of a culture affect how the people from that culture make sense of things and respond to things in the world. Culture affects our context in pretty powerful ways. Because of this, a good social detective will try to get a sense of cultural differences between people as a way of trying to understand others even better. Let's look at an example of how cultural differences can play out in people's interactions with one another.

Let's say that someone comes from a culture where talking fast and loudly and using a certain kind of music in the voice is a way of showing interest. Let's also say that the music they use in their voice to show interest is similar to the voice music others use to show anger. This is actually true. Some cultures use a certain kind of music in the voice to show interest while the same voice music is used in other cultures to express anger.

In our culture, if this kind of voice music is used to show anger, we might get offended when the other person talks to us in that kind of voice, even though for them it's actually a compliment, and a sign that they are interested in the conversation they are having with us. Without this important piece of personal, cultural information to help us form the context, we might easily miss where the other person is coming from and take offense.

Current Mood

What we are feeling at the moment can have a big effect on how we make sense of things, respond to things, and interact with others. By getting a sense of someone's mood, we can have a much better sense of their context, which can help us to understand and interact with them better. Below are some common types of feelings we might have that can affect our personal context in significant ways. You can also take a look at Appendix Y (Feeling List) for a longer list of words for describing moods more specifically.

<u>**Pleasant Feelings**</u>

Open Feelings

Happy Feelings

Alive Feelings

Loving/Caring Feelings

Interested Feelings

<u>**Difficult/Unpleasant Feelings**</u>

Angry Feelings

Depressed Feelings

Unsure feelings

Indifferent feelings

Afraid feelings

Hurt feelings

Example: Current Mood

Let's say you are hanging with your friend Ben from the example above. And let's say you know that he is the type of person that likes to be playful and tease a little. You know from your history with him that he actually likes to relate like that. And let's say that this time Ben sneezes and you tell him in a playful way that he sounds like a walrus. You might expect Ben to laugh and maybe joke back with you some. But instead, Ben makes an annoyed face and in an irritated voice says "Is that supposed to be funny?"

That kind of reaction might seem totally out of character to you. Without any other information, it might seem like a big social mystery and you might feel bad that your friend is being mean to you. But suppose you could peek into Ben's inner world and see more of his personal context at the moment, and when you did, you could see that he was already in a bad mood even before you saw him. Let's say he was really annoyed because his parents told him he lost his video games for a week because Ben's brother told them he hit him. But Ben did not hit his brother and was upset not only because he lost his video games, but also because his parents believed his brother and not him.

Knowing this, it might make more sense why Ben acted differently than he normally might and got a little snappy with you. Knowing what his current mood was even before he saw you might make it easier to not take his snappiness personally. And if you had had some clue about his mood before, you might not have joked with him like that. Sensing the moods of others can be a powerful tool for a social detective. It can give you important information about the personal context of others. You can take a look back at Chapter 3 about mood missing for some suggestions for how to be more tuned into how others might be feeling.

Mental Styles and Abilities

Often people's minds work much differently. For example, a two-year old's mind works considerably differently than a grownup's mind. The two-year-old is not going to understand a lot of what someone older might, and they are going to make sense of things in much simpler ways. A farmer's mind is going to work differently than an artist's mind because they tend to use their minds in different ways which makes them see and make sense of things differently. A farmer might see a vase of flowers and think about what kind of soil was used to plant them and what he would need to do to grow them. The artist might see the same vase and think about how beautiful the colors are and how nicely the light is hitting them and how they could paint them. Minds that work differently are going to naturally respond, react, and make sense of the world differently.

Here are some questions you can ask yourself to help get a better sense of some of the different ways that minds might work:

1) Is the person good with language and able to express themselves well, or do they have trouble with language and verbal expression? People who are not great with language might not understand you as well if you use complicated language when you talk. And they may not say much in conversations, not because they are disinterested, but because it's hard for them to express themselves verbally.

2) Does the person process information fast or slow? Information processing speed is about how fast we think and solve problems and formulate sentences and ideas and things like that. Some people can think quickly, so you can talk fast with them and they get it. Conversations between fast information processors tend to be very lively and fast-moving. But other people take more time to process information, so when we are exchanging information with them, we need to talk slower and be more patient if they respond to us in a slower way.

3) Are they naturally focused and organized, or not so much? This can affect the way someone likes to exchange information. Some people say things clearly and get to the point quickly. Others talk around

things, going off on tangents before getting to the point. Different people might like different ways of communicating and have trouble when others are communicating in a different style.

4) Is the person able to see things from other people's point of view, or do they usually only see things from their own point of view? Some people have trouble seeing things from other people's perspectives, which can have a big effect on how they make sense of and react to things.

5) Does the person have a more creative way of thinking, or are they more practical? More creative minds often like to play with ideas and talk about possibilities. They might get bored talking about practicalities all the time. On the other hand, more practical minds might not enjoy or even understand where the creative person is coming from when they are playing with ideas and talking about possibilities.

6) Is the person more into facts or stories? Some people love facts while others enjoy stories much more. Fact people tend to read more nonfiction, information books. They often love little details and are often great at remembering facts. Fact people often get bored with stories and sometimes have trouble understanding or relating to them. Story people, on the other hand, tend to read more fiction books and really enjoy getting immersed in stories. They often get bored when conversations dwell too much on details and information, and they are often not as good as the fact people at remembering all the little informational details.

7) Is the person more logical or more emotional? Logical people tend to think more in terms of facts and practicalities and what makes logical sense, while emotional people tend to think more in terms of how things feel and what people's emotional experiences are like.

Example: Mental Styles and Abilities

Let's say that Alexia and Joanna are hanging out. Alexia is really excited about something that happened during her vacation to Hawaii with her family and tells Joanna about it. She tells her that when she was there, she met a cute boy. She blushes a little and says how she was just sitting there on the beach and saw him with his family. She saw him playing with his little sister and being so sweet and kind to her. Then as she was gathering her stuff to take it back to her hotel room, she kept dropping things because it was a lot to carry. The boy came over and introduced himself as Dorian and asked her if he could help her carry her stuff.

Alexia told Joanna how nice it felt having him help her and how they became friends. Later that day they went for a walk on the beach by their hotel together and watched the sunset. He even held her hand. Alexia was getting all gushy telling the story. Alexia said that the next day they both met up again and collected seashells and that he found a bone on the beach. They took the bone to the lifeguard on the beach to see if he knew what kind of bone it was, and the lifeguard loaned them a book with lots of pictures of bones from different animals native to Hawaii so they could see if they could figure out what kind of bone it was. Alexia told Joanna how much fun it was hanging out with Dorian and how they sat side by side for a long time looking at the pictures in the book together.

At the beginning of the story, Joanna seemed bored. But as the story went on, she seemed to get more and more excited. And when Alexia finished Joanna asked in an excited voice "Did you figure out what kind of bone it was?" Alexia said no and Joanna started to ask lots of questions about the bone and the bone book.

As you might imagine, Alexia felt a little bewildered and annoyed. For her, Joanna had missed the main point completely. She was focusing on the bone, while for Alexia the main topic was about the story of how she met a boy and spent time with him. If you did not know something about the way Joanna's mind worked, it would be easy to think that she was not paying attention to Alexia or really interested in her. Joanna seemed bored at first, and after Alexia told her sweet story Joanna did not seem to acknowledge it at all. Then she started talking about something that was not at all central to what Alexia was trying to share.

But if we had a better understanding of Joanna's inside world and her personal context, we would realize that she is much more of a fact person and not so much of a story person. Stories often bore Joanna and she often does not understand important parts of stories. She likes Alexia but often gets bored when Alexia tells her stories.

If Alexia knew this about Joanna, she might not relate to her in the same way. Telling a story about a boy you met and like can be vulnerable. This is the kind of thing you would want others to really understand and show interest in. If you know someone has trouble with stories, you might be cautious about sharing this kind of thing with them and might choose to relate to them in other ways.

Similarly, if Joanna had a better understanding of Alexia's inside world and her personal context, she might be more tuned into her stories and make more of an effort to respond to the story Alexia was telling, because she would know that it is important to her friend.

Intention

Someone's intention can have a huge effect on how we react, respond, and make sense of things. By getting a sense of someone's intention, we can have a much better sense of their context, which can help us to understand and interact with them better.

For example, let's say you were walking down the street drinking a delicious milkshake. Then out of the blue, your friend trips you, making you fall and scrape your knee and spill your whole milkshake on the ground. How do you think you would feel? I imagine you might feel pretty upset with your friend.

But what if you knew he did not intend to trip you? And that he felt really bad about it? You might still be upset but I imagine you would be much less angry with your friend. You would make sense of his actions much differently if you knew his intentions were not bad.

Not considering others' intentions is a pretty common problem, and it can lead to lots of unfortunate misunderstandings. It's always helpful to think about others' intentions before reacting, responding, or making sense of things.

Interpersonal Information

This is information about our relationships with other people. It involves both past as well as present information. Past information is a type of historical information, but it goes into this category because it is historical information that is specifically about our relationships with other people. We can call this *historical interpersonal information* as opposed to *historical personal information*.

Historical interpersonal information is about what our past interactions have been like. It is also about what the overall quality of our relationship with other people has been like up to now. We might experience this kind of historical interpersonal information with our 6th and 7th senses as memories in our body (6th sense) as well as in our mind (7th sense) and as an overall feeling about our relationship (8th sense).

Interpersonal information also involves information about our relationship with other people in the present. We can call this *present interpersonal information.* This would include things such as what kind of information is being exchanged with words and actions. What are the style and quality of our exchanges with others? We have been exploring a lot of these things in our discussion of the prime suspects.

Present interpersonal information also involves our current, in-the-moment sense of the quality of our relationship with the other person, or how we are feeling about our relationship with the other person right then. This in-the-moment feeling is not always the same as our overall feeling about someone. We may have a great overall feeling about our relationship with someone, but have some tension in the present that is making things not so good. Below are some examples of interpersonal information.

Types of Interpersonal Information

How long have we known the person?

Are they someone whom we have just met or we have known for a long time?

Are they familiar to us or not familiar?

This does not always go along with how long we have known someone. We might have met someone new in a class at school but have gotten to know them fast, exchanging lots of information quickly. As a result, they may seem very familiar to us. But there may be other people like the mailman who we have known for years, but because we have not exchanged much information with them, they do not seem familiar.

Is it a formal or informal relationship?

Formal relationships follow more rules, and there is often less of a sense of being at ease and being able to fully be yourself. In formal relationships, we often are more conscious about what is socially appropriate, and we might be more concerned about what the other person thinks about us. These relationships tend to be more serious and we might not always act completely like ourselves. These might be relationships with teachers or doctors or people we work with.

Informal relationships are more casual and often less serious and more playful. We might joke around more in informal relationships and feel more comfortable and at ease being ourselves. These kinds of relationships might be close friends or family members.

Then there are *semi-formal relationships*. These are relationships with people we feel more comfortable being ourselves with. But we still do not feel completely comfortable. This might be people we know but not all that well, such as new friends we are still getting to know or people who are acquaintances as opposed to close friends. Or we might be semi-formal with our parents after we have gotten in trouble or if they are mad at us.

Are we or the other person in a role of authority?

When one person is in a position of authority over another person, we would say that they have a sort of power over them, or perhaps more authority, and thus more power. For example, teachers have authority over students and as a result have more power. Parents have authority over their kids and have more power. Police have a certain kind of authority over people and as a result have more power.

Often, we are more formal with people who have some sort of power over us. But this is not always the case. Parents can have authority over their kids but their relationship can still be very informal. And some teachers are very informal with their students and invite kids to be more playful and informal with them. But even when this is the case, there is often a lack of ease and a feeling we need to act a certain way when with people who have authority over us.

<u>Is the other person the same sex or a different sex?</u>

While in many ways gender differences don't really matter, there are other ways in which they do. Girls and boys often do things differently. And they often react, respond, and make sense of things differently.

For example, boys are often rougher and more physical. They can be more competitive and often joke around by insulting each other in playful ways. Boys also tend to make and enjoy more raunchy types of jokes. Girls are often not like this and tend to be gentler and more supportive as well as cooperative in their play. And they don't tend to play in the same kind of physical way or make insulting jokes in playful ways. Also, not only do girls not make raunchy jokes, but they can also be more easily offended by that kind of joke.

This is really important to understand when interacting with people, because this kind of difference can have a big effect on the way people react, respond, and make sense of things. I often see boys and girls misunderstanding each other in ways that cause big problems because they are not taking into consideration this important kind of interpersonal information about gender differences.

Of course, this is not true for all boys and girls. Some boys tend to react, respond, and make sense of things more like girls traditionally do, and some girls tend to react, respond, and make sense of things more like boys traditionally do. Neither way is better or worse or more masculine or feminine. Both styles are absolutely fine for either gender. But it's very helpful to have an idea of these kinds of potential differences.

Example: Interpersonal Information and First Impressions

You may have heard people talk about how first impressions are important. If you are not sure what that means, let me tell you. A first impression is what we get when we meet someone for the first time. It's the immediate sense we have of someone. It is often said that this first impression sticks with us and affects how we see that person from then on. According to the first impression theory, even if we get other information in our interactions with that person that might challenge our first impression, it won't have a big effect. We will still see them the same way we did in that first encounter.

While this might not be completely true there is something to it. Part of why this has truth to it is because when we are getting a first impression of someone, we have no context of them to help us make sense of their actions. The only information we have is the information they are giving right then. We have no other information to help us understand them and make sense of what they say and do.

First encounters with people often can be a little stressful because even in the best conditions, unfamiliar social situations can be awkward. We don't know the other person. We don't know if they are nice or mean, safe, or unsafe. There is no context and because of this, we might be a little bit on guard, to begin with.

When we first meet someone, we are assessing to see if they are safe, and we depend a lot on our first impressions to determine this. If we are a little uneasy because we don't know the other person, it will be more likely that we will be looking for the negative things in our interactions rather than the positive. Because of this, it is more likely that we will take things that are not clear in a negative way. For example, if someone we don't know scrunches their face up, we might be more likely to take that as irritation or anger than we would with someone we know.

Let's take a look at an example of how first impressions can affect relationships. It was Fred's first day at a new job as a cashier at Starbucks. Normally Fred is a pretty calm guy, and he is usually very polite and professional. In fact, when he interviewed with the person in charge of hiring, he impressed her a lot with his professional attitude, which is part of why he got hired.

His first day of work came. He was very excited and a little nervous, too. On that day there was one other cashier, two people making coffee, and one manager who was in charge of the store. Fred had not met any of them before. Not long after he started working, a lady came up and started complaining about how long she had to wait in line. Fred apologized for the delay and explained that it was his first day. The lady huffed a little bit and ordered her coffee.

After the lady walked away, Fred turned to the manager who was standing beside him and said in a jokey voice, "Wow, that lady should seriously think about switching to decaf." Fred was not trying to be mean. He was just trying to be funny and impress his new manager. But the manager did not seem to think that was funny, and just looked at Fred with an emotionless face, not saying a word. As you might imagine, that made Fred feel bad, so he scrunched up his face and walked away.

Most people who know Fred know he is very respectful and kind. But to someone who does not know him, they will be more likely to see his comment about the lady as a sign of him not being a very nice person and will form an impression of him based on this one piece of information.

Also, when the manager did not respond, Fred scrunched up his face. Again, someone who knew him might just take this as him being stressed because the manager did not respond in a positive way. But remember, when we first meet people we are often looking to see if they are safe. And when we are doing that, we tend to make sense of information like a scrunched face in more negative ways.

As you might imagine, it is more likely that the manager took Fred's facial expression as angry and annoyed rather than stressed and worried that he said the wrong thing. To make things worse, once the manager receives this first impression, it might be hard for him to change it. This first impression gave him information that he will use for future impressions.

Had Fred been more aware of how important interpersonal information is on how others will make sense of things, as well as the importance of first impressions, he might have thought about his interpersonal history with the manager before making that comment. In particular, he might have thought about how long he had known the manager, how familiar he was with him, how formal the relationship was, and if the manager was in a position of authority.

If the manager knew Fred better and was more familiar with him, he might have known that Fred was just joking. But because there was no context for the manager to make sense of Fred's comment, it is more likely that he took his comment as a sign that Fred was not a very nice, respectful, professional person.

Also, the fact that his relationship with his manager was more formal, and that the manager was in a position of authority over Fred, makes it even more likely that a comment like that might be taken as disrespectful. Had Fred made that comment to one of his new co-workers who were not in a position of authority, it still might not have made a great first impression. But it would not be as bad since they were not in a position of authority. Joking with a coworker is not as likely to come across as disrespectful in the same way it might with a manager who you don't really know and who is your boss.

Situational Information

Situational information is information about what is happening in the present that might affect how someone might react, respond, or make sense of things. It's not about what is happening inside the other person or even about your relationship with another person. It is about things around you that might be important to take into consideration. Here are some common situational factors that can have a big effect on the context and on how you and others might react, respond, and make sense of things.

Are you in a formal or informal situation?

Sometimes the formality of a situation does not match how formal or informal we are with someone, and we need to adjust to fit the situation. For example, maybe you are with your friend who you are very informal and playful with. But if you are giving a presentation together in front of the whole school you might need to be much more formal than you usually are with each other because that is what the situation calls for.

Or maybe your work has a team bonding event in which you must organize a talent show and make up silly comedy skits with your boss who you are usually very formal with. This situation will push you to be much less formal with him than you usually are.

In both of these situations, if you are not aware of the situational context and just act based on your past relationship with the person, it will not go over well.

Is there a mood to the situation?

We have talked a lot about mood matching with others. The mood of another person is an important piece of personal information to take into consideration. People's moods contribute a lot to our shared context and if we are tuned in socially it will affect how we react, respond, and make sense of the facts in our exchange with them.

But sometimes there are moods in our surroundings that might also be important to take into consideration. Being at a funeral or in a sad movie or in a meeting where people are talking about something bad that happened would be times in which the mood of the situation would affect how you act. If you act overly happy or playful in these kinds of situations people might think you don't understand or care about what's going on.

There might also be situations like a wedding or birthday party where the mood is very positive. That might not be the best place to be moody or talk about things that are getting you down. You might be at one of those events with someone you feel very comfortable sharing difficult feelings with but the situational context might make it an inappropriate time to express those things.

Are there rules specific to the situation?

Many situations have specific rules dictating how to act. Not following those situational rules can result in negative reactions from others. For example, you are not supposed to talk loud in a library and you are often not supposed to talk at all while you are in class and the teacher is lecturing. On the other hand, it is perfectly ok to talk loud and even scream on the playground.

Is there a time factor?

Not having a lot of time or being in a rush can have a big effect on how we react, respond, and make sense of things. For example, giving very short answers often might make someone feel like you are not interested in them. But if you are in a rush, short answers are appropriate and if the other person realizes there is not much time, they will not take it personally at all. In fact, if there is not a lot of time and you don't give short answers, it might bother others and make them feel you are not very considerate or tuned into the situational context.

<u>Is there a role you or others are serving?</u>

Often, we might need to act differently because of roles that we take on in different situations. For example, an actor might play the role of a villain who is mean and uncaring, while in their real life they are really kind. Or a boxer whose job it is to hit people and try to knock them out might be very gentle in his regular life. Or a rock star who on stage seems really confident and outgoing might be quiet and shy when not performing.

Or maybe it's your best friend who is usually very loyal and takes your side. But if he is in the role of referee in a game and calls you for making a penalty, he may act harshly to you about the penalty you made. If you did not recognize that your friend was just living up to his role you might take his harshness as a personal insult. But when we can recognize that people sometimes have to be in certain roles, it can give us more context, which can aid us in making better sense of things.

<u>Are there other people in your surroundings with whom you have different types of relationships?</u>

In the interpersonal information section, we talked about how there are different characteristics of our relationships with people that affect our interactions with them. But those characteristics are also important to consider even if we are not directly interacting with someone. They are important because they can affect the situational context as well as the interpersonal context.

For example, let's say you are joking around with your friend and telling raunchy jokes. If it is just the two of you, that might be totally fine if it's something you are both ok with. But let's say there is a teacher nearby with whom you have a formal relationship and who is in a position of authority over you. Or maybe there is a group of girls nearby.

You may not be interacting with the teacher or the group of girls directly, so you might think it should not matter. But even though you are not interacting with them directly, their presence within earshot contributes to the situational context and gives you information that you probably should tone down the raunchy joking.

Example: The Mood of the Situation

Let's say you and your friend are hanging out. You are both in pretty good moods and have been laughing and joking around. But then you come home and your dad is there with his friend who just lost his job. His friend is clearly upset. He is teary-eyed and talking in a sad voice. You walk in and say hi and your dad tells you what is going on. Now even though you and your friend have been in a playful jokey mood and are not particularly bothered by your dad's friend losing his job, it still would not be appropriate to keep joking while you are in the same room or even in hearing range of them. The mood of the situation is a sad one. If you joke around in that situation, your dad and friend might take that as you not being very sensitive or caring.

PRIME SUSPECT #19:

CONTEXT MISSING

As you might have gathered from our discussion, context is an incredibly important part of good social relating. Having a good context is one of the most powerful tools in helping to solve social mysteries. When people are having trouble seeing context it can create all kinds of problems in their lives. I call this *Context Missing* and it is one of the most notorious of the prime suspects.

Without a good sense of context, we are likely to misunderstand many social things. And we are likely to act in ways that create problems in our relationships. But the good news is that there are things we can do to have a better understanding of context.

We have actually been talking about many of those things throughout this book. Basically, understanding context has a lot to do with gathering the facts and making sense of the facts. In this case, the facts are contextual information.

Gathering and Making Sense of Contextual Information

Do you remember the key things we talked about at the beginning of the book, the things that a good social detective does to solve social mysteries? They gather the facts and then make sense of them. If you think about it, we have been talking about those two things throughout this whole book.

We use good attention to be aware of the clues around us. We use good verbal and nonverbal listening and relating to help us gather these clues. These tools help us acquire the information we need to create a context so that we can better understand others. Take a look at Appendix X for a summary of all the verbal and nonverbal listening and relating tools we have discussed in the previous chapters.

Once we have all that information, the challenge is making sense of it. To make sense of the facts effectively, it helps to organize the information in a way that is easy to remember and that helps to create a meaningful social picture.

All the pieces of information we gather about others, our interactions with them, and the situations we are a part of, are like individual strokes of a paintbrush. Each stroke holds an important piece of information. But it's only when you look at all the strokes together that you can really start to see the bigger picture.

Context is the way we organize all the individual strokes, all the separate pieces of information. What helps us socially organize those pieces of information are our stories. We create stories of other people, our relationships with them, and the situations we are in, based on the information we gather.

When you read a good book, the author creates stories about the characters. Those stories contain the types of contextual information we discussed. The author paints a picture of the characters and through that, we come to know the characters better. The story helps us relate to them, understand them, and care for them.

We created many stories in this chapter based on information we organized into a meaningful context. And our stories helped us to understand these people and their relationships with others much better. The stories brought us closer to them. Our stories help us to know others better and in doing so to be more intimate and connected with them.

DIY: Creating Meaningful Stories

Being able to create meaningful, accurate stories from the information we gather is a learning process. And the more we practice the better we get. So, let's do a DIY story-making practice.

The first step in creating a contextual story is to identify what we want the story to be about. The three kinds of contextual stories we have been discussing have been about 1) other people; 2) our relationships with other individuals or groups of people; and 3) social situations we might be in. But there are other kinds of contextual stories that can be helpful. For example, we can create stories about different cultures, or eras like medieval times, or different cliques or social groups. It can be really helpful to know how other cultures or eras or cliques respond, react, and make sense of things.

It can also be incredibly helpful to have a good contextual story about ourselves. Being aware of our own personal history, mental style, interpersonal relationships, and situational factors can help us a lot. It can help us understand some of the reasons why we react, respond, and make sense of things the way we do. And this can help us gain a deeper sense of relationship with ourselves as well as help us to relate to others better.

After you decide what you want to create some context around, you want to gather information. You can use the tools we have been talking about in this book to help you gather the facts. Again, you can take a look at Appendix X for a summary of these tools. Then we want to think about what kind of information will be the most important. You can review the different types of contextual information in this book for an idea of some important things you might want to look for.

Once you have a nice amount of information you can start organizing. A great way to do this is to write a little story using the information you have gathered, kind of like we have been doing when talking about the different types of contextual information. Remember when I gave you a whole bunch of seemingly random words, and then I told you the story about the dog taking the fish that used all those words? Kind of like that. But instead of just single words, you want to use the important pieces of contextual information you have gathered.

For an example of this take a look back to the story (page 226) we created about Susan and Donna who both got C's on their report cards. You can also take a look at the story we created from the facts we gathered about Ralph and Peter on page 227.

After you have done all this you can start to make sense of the facts by asking yourself questions. Below is a list of some questions to help you use context to understand others better. For our example, let's say we are creating a contextual story about another person with whom we are interacting.

Questions for making sense of contextual information
- How does this person's context affect how you see them?
- Does their context make you feel closer to or farther away from them?
- Does their context help you understand things they might be sensitive about?
- Does their context help you get a better sense of how they might respond, react, and make sense of things? If so, how?
- Does their context affect how you might respond to, react to, and make sense of things they might say or do? If so, how?

These are just a few questions to get you started. The key is to use this contextual information to think and feel into the inside world of the other person so you can understand them better. We will be talking more about this in the next section on perspective.

Here is a worksheet you can use to organize the information you need to create a contextual story. Give it a try for this DIY. Pick something you would like to have a better contextual story for and use that to fill out this worksheet.

Contextual Story Worksheet

This contextual story is about:

1) Another person

2) Our relationships with another individual or group of people

3) A social situation we might be in

4) Ourselves

5) Something else (specify)

The tools I used to gather contextual information were (see Appendix X) :

The important contextual information I gathered was:

The story I made up to organize the information is:

The questions I asked myself to make sense of the information were:

The conclusions I came to about how they responded, reacted, or made sense of things were:

The way this affects how I might respond, react, or make sense of things that another person says or does is:

Tell me about your day – the importance of contextual current events

There is a specific kind of context missing that I want to talk about a little bit. You can call this a secondary suspect because it is something that can cause us to miss important parts of someone's context. I call it *Current Event Missing*. This is where there is something recent that has happened that affects someone's context in important ways you are unaware of.

There may be times where you have a pretty good context for someone and as a result, have a pretty good understanding of how they respond, react, and make sense of things. But new experiences can affect someone's overall context in significant ways. If we don't have any awareness of these new events, we might respond, react, or make sense of things in ways that are different from what we are used to. And we might make sense of others' actions incorrectly because we don't have the current event information.

Here is an example. Ellen and Jamie are great friends and feel very safe and comfortable with each other. They have both been watching this scary television show called *Stranger Things*. They watch an episode on their own over the weekend and then talk about it at school on Mondays. They like to talk about all the scary things that happen and have a game where they try to scare each other by saying things about the scary characters coming after them in real life. It's been a fun game and they always end up getting each other a little scared and laughing together.

This particular Monday they met up at school and Ellen started talking about the episode. But Jamie seemed a little stiff and did not say much. Ellen kept talking about it and started to play their game of trying to freak each other out. When she did that Jamie got even more tense and furrowed her brow and in an agitated voice said "Can we just stop talking about that!? Can't we talk about something else for a change!" Ellen took Jamie's reaction personally and it hurt her feelings. But she respected her friend's request and changed the subject. But Ellen felt confused and hurt, and the rest of their conversation was very awkward.

There was a reason Jamie was acting so much differently than she usually did. It had to do with a current event that had impacted her. Over the weekend, after watching the episode of *Stranger Things* she decided to see the movie "It," which is about killer clowns. The movie is very scary and it totally freaked her out. She had nightmares after and was still totally freaked out at school on Monday. She could not get the scary images out of her head and would startle a little when she heard loud noises. Jamie had a full-fledged, certifiable freak out, and she was still feeling the aftereffects of it.

So, when Ellen started talking about the scary characters in *Stranger Things*, it was just too much. Jamie usually could handle that kind of conversation. But after seeing the killer clown movie and freaking out, she could not talk about anything scary without it bringing up the fear she had after seeing It. When Ellen started to play the scare-each-other game it was just too much. Jamie got totally stressed and had to stop talking about scary things. If Jamie had not been as scared and stressed, she probably would have asked Ellen to change the subject more smoothly. But she could not contain her stress, so her words came out harshly.

Had Ellen known about this important contextual information, she most likely would have reacted, responded, and made sense of things much differently. First of all, she might have put off talking about *Stranger Things* until Jamie was feeling better. But she would also have made different sense of Jamie's reaction to her.

As it was, without that information, Ellen took Jamie's reaction personally. She took it as her being mad at her and as her being bored with their regular talks about the TV show. But had she known about this current event that took place over the weekend, she would have understood that Jamie's reaction was not at all about her. She would have recognized that it was a result of Jamie being freaked out by the scary movie.

Now the remedy to this kind of current event missing is keeping up on your current events with people. We often do this naturally when we ask people questions like "How was your weekend?" or "What did you do over vacation?" or even the more general questions like "What's been going on in your life lately?" Questions like this invite others to share important things that might have been going on with them, and knowing these important things helps you to have a more complete, accurate context of the other person.

These kinds of questions also show others that you are interested in the other person. And as we have discussed, showing interest can really help build relationships. Asking people that we have not seen in a while about what they have been doing also helps us to reconnect with them. So, catching up on contextual current events can have many benefits.

PRIME SUSPECT #20:

CONTEXT ASSUMING

Another prime suspect which has to do with context is *Context Assuming*. This happens when someone assumes you have the same contextual information about something that they do. Most people have had experiences where someone is context assuming. Usually, this takes the form of someone talking to you about something and making references to things about which you have no clue.

Let me give you an example. Let's say I came up to you and out of the blue, I say "I can't believe him. He just let go and ran away, and I was standing there on the corner with a bunch of barking dogs trying to catch the chicken!" I imagine if I did this you would have no clue what I was talking about. And you might even think I was a little insane. That's because I gave you no context to help you make sense of what I was saying. I *assumed* you had the same contextual information that I did.

Now, what if I gave you some context? Let's say I first told you that I went dog walking with my friend Joe who just started his dog walking business. It was Joe's first day and he was a little nervous, so I told him I would go walk with him and his dogs. He was managing pretty well. He had six pretty big dogs on leashes and was handling them great. But then all of a sudden, a chicken jumped out of a bush. A chicken in the middle of the suburbs! As you can imagine, the dogs went crazy. Joe freaked and dropped the leashes and took off.

Had I said this first, you would have had some context to make sense of this. "I can't believe him. He just let go and ran away, and I was standing there on the corner with a bunch of barking dogs trying to catch the chicken!" But without that important contextual information, you would have no clue what I was talking about.

Context assuming can create a lot of social problems. One thing it does is demonstrate to others that you don't understand them. You don't get their point of view. Because if you did you would realize that they could not make sense of what you were saying without more context. People like to be understood. They like to know that others realize they have a different point of view than them. When we recognize that someone else has a different point of view, we are acknowledging them as a separate, unique person. People like that.

When we don't get others' points of view it can make them feel unseen and like we are not really interested in them as a separate person. Or it might make them think we are not capable of a good friendship because good friends have a sense of each other's point of view.

It might also make others feel not as safe with you because to feel safe we need to believe that the other person will be sensitive and caring about our feelings and needs. But if someone cannot take our point of view it's not likely that they will be able to be sensitive and caring with us, because those things are dependent on seeing things from our perspective.

Now the truth is that we all might have moments of context missing. Sometimes if we are really excited or upset about something, we might rush into saying something and not think about the other person's perspective. But context assuming can be prevented by asking yourself a few simple questions.

The first question is *"What is the other person's perspective?"* Just asking yourself this can help shift your spotlight of attention from your point of view to another person's. The second question is connected to the first one. It's "Do they have the same contextual information that I do about this?" These two questions together can help us tune into others and assess what they know and what they don't, so we don't end up assuming they have important contextual information when they don't.

But if for some reason context assuming gets the best of you, it's ok. If it happens, you can just laugh and say you're sorry and give them more context. Everybody makes mistakes. The trick is to be able to take responsibility for our mistakes and learn from them.

Context and Social Media

The last thing I want to talk about in this section on context is social media. For many of us, the social media world is becoming more and more a part of our relating with other people. It's one of the main ways we exchange information, learn about other people's lives, make plans, and stay connected. It's also how we learn a lot about the world around us, what's cool, what's not, what's trending, what's yesterday, and how others around the world see things. It is amazing and can provide us with so much important information. But despite all it has to offer, when it comes to gathering information about context, social media is often lacking.

We have been talking a lot about how much the information we exchange with others is nonverbal. Facial expressions, body language, body posture and movement, music in the voice--all these things can be fully communicated only when we are face-to-face with others, in real-time. When we text, none of this nonverbal information is exchanged.

Social media is getting better at helping us to exchange more important information with others. You can send pictures and even short videos. You can FaceTime with voice and with video. All these things add more information to be communicated. But even with all those things, you are still only getting a slice of the other person's context.

When you are in the same room with someone and spending time in the same place, you get so much more of their context. You get to experience all of the things that came before and after an exchange. This lets you build a richer context, which lets you see their real reactions rather than just the reactions they want you to see. If you say or do something, people usually have a real, immediate reaction to it. But if there is a delay in the exchange, as there often is in social media, you might not get their real response. You might get a response that is polished up and not as authentic.

So, while relating through social media can be awesome in many ways, it also has its limitations. Let's look at an example. Let's say you are at your friend's house hanging out. If you are there with him in the same space you will get much more of what's going on with him. Let's say his mom is yelling at him from the other room telling him he forgot to take out the trash. Because you are there with him, you hear her yell and you see him tensing when his mom is yelling. After he tenses up, he may relax his face and body and talk to you in a more relaxed way because he wants to be social and positive with you. But you saw his real immediate reaction, which lets you know more of what is really going on inside of him.

Because you experienced what just happened, you know that there is probably some tension in him. And as a result, you might be a little more sensitive with him. For example, you might choose not to playfully criticize him. You might even ask him how he is feeling. Given the information you got from his mom yelling and his tensing, you would be more able to mood match with him.

But let's say you still playfully criticize him even though you have this information. Maybe you want to cheer him up with some playfulness and think joking around might help. If you are in the same place with him you might see a real-time reaction from him that lets you know he is not in a joking mood. He might tense his face and body like he did when his mom yelled at him. Or he may roll his eyes or respond to you in an irritated voice.

This gives you important contextual information that can help you get a better sense of your friend's point of view and how he is reacting to the way you are acting with him. As a result, you might tell him you're sorry and that you were just playing around. And you would probably stop joking after getting that feedback.

What if your interactions with this friend were over social media? Even if you were using something like Snapchat, where you send pictures and short videos, it's still not likely you would have heard his mom yelling or see his face and body tense in response to her. We would have no clue that there was something in his context which might be making him a little more sensitive at the moment. So, you might not respond to him in ways that are sensitive and mood matching. And what if you do sense him being upset but don't know about what happened with his mom? Without the proper context, you might take it personally and think he was upset with you.

To make things more challenging, people often don't want others to see negative things that are going on with them. This is especially true in the world of social media. For example, have you ever noticed that people don't usually post selfies of themselves when they are just getting out of bed or are not looking so good? They tend to post pictures taken from the most flattering angles and when they are looking their best. On social media people often don't share the parts of their story— their context—that is not as positive. They tend to share things that make them look good and make their lives look good. Because of this we are often not really getting all the information. And without all the information our responses might not always be the best.

Knowing some of the important contextual information that might be missing in our more virtual interactions with others can help us be more careful not to say or do things that might be taken the wrong way. I like to have a list in my mind of how much information I am exchanging with others at any given time and have that help me decide how I am going to respond to them.

A good general rule of thumb is to be much more careful with what you say and do when there is less contextual information available. The more information being exchanged, the more likely there will not be misunderstandings. The less information, the more likely there will be misses. And if there is something you think someone might be upset about, try to say it in person or be very careful if you need to say it virtually. Below is a list of some of the common ways we virtually connect with others and what ways they do and do not allow for the exchange of contextual information. This can be helpful in figuring out how careful we need to be.

1) Face to face connecting: This usually provides the most information. You have verbal information as well as all the nonverbal things like facial expressions, eye context, body posture, and movements, and voice music. Here we usually also have lots of situational contextual information, like what happened right before and right after an exchange, as well as everything that is happening in the moment. You are getting information from all five senses, which gives your 6th, 7th, and 8th sense much more information to make sense of things.

In face-to-face interactions it's also harder to withhold information that might not be positive but might be important for us to know when reacting, responding, and making sense of interactions. In addition, you get real-time feedback from one another. You get their spontaneous reactions and they get yours.

Finally, when having face-to-face interactions with others, there is a sense of closeness and connection you can only really have when sharing physical space with someone else. It's something that can be hard to define, but something you can often actually feel in your body if you are tuned into your 6th sense.

2) Video chatting: This provides a lot of information, but there are a few things you might not get with this that you can in face-to-face connecting. If the video camera is only focused on the other person's head, you will miss out on a lot of important body language. You also will not get parts of the situational context, such as what is going on outside of what the camera is seeing. And there is also not that very personal, intimate sense of closeness that you get when you are in the same physical space with someone. But in general, there is still a lot of information being exchanged here.

3) Audio chatting: This would be talking on the phone or online through social media or when gaming online with others. You can still get some real-time feedback from others, as well as verbal communication and nonverbal music in the voice. But there is a lot missing. Apart from voice music, there is no other nonverbal information being exchanged. This eliminates a really big part of the contextual information that is communicated in our exchanges with others. We also miss out on any visual, situational information, such as where the person is and what is going on around them.

And while there is some real-time information available, there is also the possibility of withholding more things when there is no visual connection. For example, it's much easier to mute your microphone and withhold with audio chatting than it is with video chatting. Let's say your friend's mom starts yelling while you are talking to him. He might mute his microphone so you won't hear anything. If you are talking at the time you might not even realize he muted you. He might respond to his mom while you are muted and you won't even realize it. With video, it's much harder to mute someone without them knowing it. And of course, with audio chatting, as with video chatting, you don't get that personal feeling you often do when face-to-face with others.

4) Video clips: A lot of social media offers the ability to send video clips to others. The clips are usually about 6-10 seconds. This can communicate lots of nice nonverbal information as well as verbal information. But these clips can actually be deceptive and give someone the feeling of much more closeness and exchange of contextual information than is really there. That's because some very important things are often missing in these clips. Video clips are missing all the things video chatting is missing. But they also are missing a lot of the situational information and real-time feedback that regular video chatting can offer.

There is another problem that often happens with video clips as well as with straight-up social media. As we have talked about, people often don't want others to see negative things about them. They want to be seen in a good light. Nothing wrong with that. We all want to be seen positively. At times we all manage our image with others. I call this *Image Management.*

The problem can come when our desire to be seen positively leads to us hiding important parts of ourselves from others. This can result in our creating an image that is very different from who we really are, that it communicates very little truth about us to others. I call this *Image Manipulation.* A little image management can be a positive thing. But when it gets to the point where we are manipulating our image so much that others do not know who we really are it can create a lot of problems.

The less information we exchange with others, the easier it is to manipulate our image. When we are face-to-face or video chatting it's hard to hide that much. This is also true with audio chatting. The real-time nature of these kinds of exchanges *keeps it real*, so to speak. But when there is less information being exchanged in real-time, there is the potential to manipulate our image much more. And this can be tempting, especially if people are insecure about themselves or their social abilities to begin with.

With video clips, this kind of image manipulation often takes the form of people redoing their clips several times before sending them. They are trying to create a certain impression to share with others. They might rehearse what they say and make sure they look good. The end result is that they tend to share way less of their real self and instead act in ways they think others will be impressed with, rather than being authentic. This can actually create a sense of being lonely and not really seen by others.

These kinds of image manipulation video clips can also make it hard for others to know how to respond to us. What if your friend's mom just yelled at him and he is really upset, but he sends you a video clip of him doing something funny to impress you? If you were there with him you would be more likely to see his true feelings. And even on video or audio chatting, you might pick up some of his true feelings because it is in real-time, which would make it harder for him to just put on a false image about how he is feeling. But with video clips there is no real-time relating, so he could hide much more. As a result, your responses to him would probably not match his authentic mood. And in the end, he might end up feeling more alone and like he can't be real with other people.

So, while these video clips have some nice aspects and can give much more information than just texting, there is also a lot missing. And keeping this in mind can be helpful when relating to others through video clips.

5) Texting: Texting has become a more popular way of connecting with others. It's a great, efficient way to exchange practical information and stay connected. But just as is the case with all forms of information exchange, we want to be aware of what it can and cannot communicate. Knowing this can help us in how we react, respond, and make sense of information we exchange through texting.

There is no nonverbal information exchanged through texting. No facial expressions or body language. What can make it even more challenging is that there is no voice music either. If you recall, we talked a lot about the power of voice music to help us make sense of things that are communicated. Voice music gives us a lot of important contextual information. Saying something as simple as "Hey man, where are you?" can have multiple meanings based on how we say it. It could be expressing annoyance over the person not being there yet. Or curiosity about where they are. Or even excitement about seeing the person. But in text, there is none of that other information to help us make sense of what is being said. This is the main reason why texts are so often misinterpreted.

Knowing this can help you prevent making texting blunders. As a rule of thumb, you probably do not want to discuss anything that might involve criticism or that could be taken the wrong way over text. And if you need to say something that might be taken the wrong way, make sure to add extra information to provide more context so the other person does not take it the wrong way. For example, if your friend is a little late and you text him "Hey man, where are you?" You might want to add "No rush, I'm just looking forward to seeing you." You can also add emojis to create a sense of nonverbal communication. A simple smiley face emoji at the end of a text can communicate so much and make it clear to others what you are really trying to say.

6) Picture messaging: Another popular way to exchange information with others is the picture message. This might be sending a picture of where you are, which can provide some nice situational context. Or it might be sending a selfie along with your text, which is like a real-life emoji, and can offer a little bit of nonverbal information to add context to what you are texting. I like doing this because it offers more context and can make texting more personal.

7) Social media posts: People post updates about their lives on social media for all their friends and social media connections to see. This can be a great way to get snippets of information about friends that you might not see very often. It can be a wonderful thing. You just want to keep in mind that these kinds of posts can be even less personal. We don't always want to share our more vulnerable things with everyone we know. So, there might be more of a tendency to do heavier *image management* and even *image manipulation* in our more public social media posts.

So, when you read things from friends that are public, it's helpful to keep in mind that there may be much more beneath the surface, and you might be missing a lot of their contextual information even when others are sharing a lot online.

All these ways of communicating can be great. They can bring people much closer and connect us with people we may not have seen in a long time. The key is to keep in mind that the information you get through social media may not be totally accurate or complete. Remembering this can help you to not react, respond, or make sense of things in ways that might cause problems in your friendships with others.

Main Ideas Chapter 11

1. What is context? P - 225
2. How can context help us make sense of the facts? P - 225
3. How can context help us remember things better? P - 226
4. What is contextual information? P - 228
5. What are the three categories of contextual information? P - 228
6. What are the different types of personal information? P - 228
7. What are personality traits? P - 229
8. What are some examples of personality traits? P - 229
9. What is personal history? P - 229
10. What are some important aspects of personal history to consider when trying to understand someone's context? P - 230
11. How can someone's current mood affect context in important ways? P - 231
12. What do we mean by mental styles and abilities? P - 232
13. What are some questions you can ask yourself about others to help get a better sense of how their mind might work? P - 232
14. What is intention? P - 234
15. Why is understanding others' intentions so important in making sense of the facts? P - 234

16. What is interpersonal information? P - 234
17. What is the difference between historical interpersonal information and historical personal information? P - 234
18. What is present interpersonal information? P - 234
19. What are some specific examples of types of interpersonal information? P - 235
20. What is the difference between formal, semi-formal, and informal relationships? P - 235
21. What are first impressions? P - 236
22. Why are first impressions important? P - 237
23. What is situational information? P - 237
24. What are some important kinds of situational information? P - 237
25. What are some of the important ways that context can affect how people respond, react, and make sense of things? P - 238
26. What is context missing? P - 239
27. What are some different things we might want to create contextual stories about? P - 240
28. What are the steps for creating meaningful contextual stories? P - 241
29. What is current event missing? P - 242
30. What is context assuming? P - 243
31. What are some questions you can ask yourself to help prevent context assuming? P - 244
32. What are some of the ways social media can affect the contextual information we get from others?? P - 244
33. What are some of the different types of social media? P - 245
34. How well do the different types of social media communicate contextual information? P - 245
35. What is image management? P - 247
36. What is image manipulation? P - 247
37. What does real-time relating mean? P - 247
38. Why are real-time exchanges better at *keeping it real*?? P - 247

Chapter 12: Perspective Taking

What is a Perspective?

A perspective is a particular point of view or way of seeing something. When someone is making a movie, they can set up the camera to film things from different points of view or perspectives. For example, let's say you want to film someone dancing. You could set up one camera in the front, one behind the person, and one on either side of the person. If you did that you would have four different points of view or perspectives. Because the four different cameras were filming from different angles, they would all get a different picture of the person dancing.

You can imagine that every person is kind of like a camera set up in different ways so that they all get different perspectives of things. Of course, it's much more complicated with people than it is with cameras. With cameras it's mainly the position in which they are set up that affects the difference in perspective. With people, there are tons of things that lead to having different perspectives.

But let's start with how we see things with our eyes. If you and I are sitting facing each other playing cards, we are going to have a different visual perspective. Let's say I'm holding up my cards so you can't see them and you are doing the same. Because of where you're sitting, your eyes will only see the back of my cards while I will be able to see the front of my cards. And I will only be able to see the back of your cards while you will be able to see the front. Because of our different visual perspectives, we will see and experience completely different things.

But people's perspectives have many more layers to them. They don't just involve what we see with our eyes. They also involve what we hear, touch, smell, and taste. In addition, a person's perspective involves what they feel in their bodies and think in their minds. And they also involve what they sense relationally. Human perspectives involve things that happen in all of the eight senses.

Perspectives are the way people "see" things but how we see is not just about what our eyes see. How we "see" things has to do with how we make sense of things. It has to do with the meaning of things. And as we talked about a lot in the section on context, how we make sense of things affects how we respond and react.

If you have two people looking at a beautiful sunset with lots of shades of red and orange, they might "see" it much differently even if they are standing side by side. If one person is color blind, they will see the sunset much differently than the person who is not color blind. They will see it visually differently.

But let's go deeper into perspectives. Say we have two friends, James and Dave. James has been watching the sunset with his girlfriend every Saturday while they cuddle and say sweet sappy romantic things to each other. Dave has also been watching the sunset every Saturday. But he has been watching the sunsets alone, wishing he had someone to share them with.

As we discussed in the section on context, people's unique individual context results in them seeing things differently. It results in them making sense of things differently, which leads to them having different perspectives. All the contextual information that makes up people's individual contexts helps to create their unique perspective in the world.

When it comes to sunsets, James and Dave have very different personal histories. Because of this, they are most likely going to "see" the sunset differently. James' perspective will probably include a warm romantic sense of meaning. Dave's perspective, on the other hand, will more likely be colored with a sense of sadness and loneliness.

Perspective Taking

So, what does it mean to take the perspective of another person? It means being able to imagine how things look, not only through the eyes of another person but also through their minds and hearts. It means being able to imagine what it's like to experience things through all of their eight senses, and being able to imagine how their contextual information affects how they respond, react, and make sense of things.

If we had gathered contextual information on James and Dave, we would know that they have different personal histories with sunsets. Knowing this would give us clues about how they might each make sense of sunsets, which would help us to take their perspectives.

With this contextual information, we might be better able to take James' perspective and imagine that he probably has positive associations with sunsets. He probably has positive sensations in his body which he experiences with his 6th sense. He most likely has positive thoughts in his mind which he experiences with his 7th sense and positive relational feelings which he experiences with his 8th sense. Because of this, we might imagine that when he sees sunsets, his heart feels warm and romantic.

Our contextual information about Dave might lead us to imagine that he might be having negative associations with sunsets. It is more likely that he is having not-so-pleasant sensations in his body and mind and a sense of lacking relationally. We might imagine that he has feelings of loneliness and sadness when he sees sunsets.

Taking the perspective of another is about being able to more accurately imagine how the world looks and feels through their unique camera lens, about how they feel and make sense of things.

Perspective Maps

I like to think of people's personal perspectives as maps. Maps draw a picture of a territory. They give you a perspective. A map of a city draws a picture of all the things in that city and helps us to get around better. Without the perspective of a good map, we might get seriously lost on our travels.

Maps of people help us to understand others and get around the social world better. They are what keep us from getting lost in our social interactions. If you think about it, social mysteries are situations where we are lost on our social travels. And all the tools we have been talking about in this book are things that help us to make better maps of the social terrain so that we can find our way. A good social detective is a social map maker. Mapmakers are called *cartographers,* so in a way, social detectives are social cartographers, making maps of uncharted territories so they can get around better and not get lost on their social travels.

So, what makes a good social map? Good social maps are created from contextual information. The more contextual information you have, the more details you have for your map. And of course, you want the information to be accurate. A map with inaccurate details will only get you lost.

Some maps are accurate but don't have a lot of detail. For example, a general map of Europe might show you where all the European countries are. But it will not be able to tell you how to get from your hotel in Paris to the Eiffel tower if you are on vacation and want to do some sight-seeing. You will need a more detailed map of Paris to make that journey.

So how do you get the information to make accurate, detailed maps? Many of the tools a social detective uses help to make good maps. I like to call these the *social cartography tools*. These are mainly the tools of verbal and nonverbal listening. Being good at listening verbally and nonverbally helps us gather the contextual information we need to create accurate, detailed contexts, which help us make our maps of the social world.

Verbal and nonverbal responding and dancing are ways we use our social maps to get around and interact with others in positive ways, based on the maps we have created. In addition, the way we socially respond and dance help us to gather more helpful information to make our social maps even more detailed. Verbal responding and dancing help in this way because these things make people feel safer, more open, and more desiring of connecting with us which increases the likelihood that they will share more contextual information.

Benefits of Perspective Taking

Being able to take the perspectives of others helps us in many different ways. It can help us to know others better and to understand the way they see the world. When we can perspective take, we become much more skillful at saying and doing things that make our relationships better. And we become better at avoiding saying and doing things that might make them worse. Good perspective taking makes us much better friends to others.

When we understand others' perspectives, we become less likely to take things personally. .Getting others' perspectives helps us to understand that many of the reasons people react and respond the way they do are because of things in their personal context. Not necessarily about us.

A good sense of another person's perspective can also help us feel much more comfortable in our social interactions. When we can take another person's perspective, we have access to their *perspective map*. A good perspective map can help us navigate the terrain of our social inactions with much more ease and certainty and without as much concern about getting lost socially. It's like a *social GPS*. This kind of predictability helps us feel more socially comfortable and confident.

This is a good thing not just for us but for those with whom we are interacting. When we are comfortable and confident, we are likely to enjoy our interactions with others more. In addition, others are going to sense us being at ease, which is going to help them feel safe and at ease with us. And when others feel safe and at ease with us, they are going to like us and enjoy being with us more.

These are all important, practical things that good perspective taking can give us. But there are more valuable benefits to be had as well. Getting other people's perspectives helps us feel closer to them and helps them feel closer to us. We need this as humans. We all want to be understood. It feels so good to be gotten, and it actually feels really good to get others too.

Being understood helps us to not feel alone. The truth is, we are all alone in our own minds. We are inside ourselves thinking things and often even having conversations with ourselves with no one else there but us. But when others understand our perspective it's like they are coming into our minds. It's like they are coming into our inside world and sharing something really special with us.

Understanding each other feeds relationships and makes them stronger and more satisfying. And it's not just having someone understand us that feels good and feeds us. The actual act of understanding someone else helps us feel less alone too. To share something as personal and important as our inside world with others gives something really special to both people, and leaves both people changed in positive ways.

Sharing perspectives also increases a sense of care between people. When we can experience someone else's perspective, we not only get the way their minds make sense of things, we also get the way their heart responds to things. We get a better sense of their emotions.

When we are taking the perspective of another person, we can even feel some of what they are feeling. If they are happy about something, we might feel some happiness ourselves. And if they are sad, we might sense some sadness in our bodies. This is especially true if we have practiced tuning into our own bodies with some of the eight senses DIYs we talked about in the chapter on our senses.

Feelings can be contagious when we are good at taking other people's perspectives. When someone feels some of what we are feeling, we not only feel less alone, but we also feel cared about. And when we are the one feeling someone else's feelings, it helps us to feel more care for them, because the feeling of care comes from really getting and even experiencing a little what others might be feeling and experiencing.

Care is a very powerful thing. It bonds us with others. It helps us be kinder to others. It helps us feel less alone and helps the people we are caring for feel less alone. And it gives us relational nutrients that we experience with our 8th sense.

Did you know that just as we need nutrients to keep our bodies healthy and strong, we also need nutrients to keep our hearts and minds healthy and strong? These *relational nutrients* take the form of things like being understood and cared for and having kindness given to us. And they come from giving these things to others too.

Just as body nutrients come from eating good food, relational nutrients come from good relationships. And when it comes to relational nutrients, care and kindness and being understood are like superfoods. They are the broccoli, carrots, and kale of the relational world. But they taste much better. You might like your healthy veggies but I'll take kindness and care over carrots and kale any day!

PRIME SUSPECT #21:

PERSPECTIVE MISSING

Given the significance of perspective taking you can probably imagine that another important prime suspect is *Perspective Missing*. Perspective taking is such an important ability for people to have. It is probably the number one most important thing we social detectives do when solving social mysteries. Perspective taking is actually what most people do to prevent things in their social world from being mysterious. It is what helps us to build the maps of others' inside worlds. These maps keep us from getting lost on our social travels with people.

So, what happens to people who are not good at taking perspectives when they perspective miss? What happens when they don't have accurate, detailed maps of the inside worlds of the people with whom they are interacting?

As you can probably imagine, they get very lost socially. They have trouble understanding others and because of this are much more likely to say and do things that upset others. As a result, others might not enjoy being around them as much. This can affect people's friendships in big ways and lead to them feeling alone and disliked by people. When you pair not having a good map of others' inside worlds with getting bad responses from others, it can feel really bad. And it can make people feel really stressed and unconfident in social interactions.

This is why perspective missing is one of the most notorious culprits. It causes big problems for many people. I have had so many clients come to me struggling with perspective taking. Many of them feel like they will never be able to really get the hang of making good perspective maps. But there are many things you can do to up your perspective-taking game and keep this prime suspect from messing with you.

In addition to practicing the things we have been talking about in this book, there are some specific exercises you can do to build your perspective-taking skills. It just takes some practice and persistence. And the truth is, even if you are pretty good at taking perspectives, everyone can benefit from getting better. You can never get too good at this. So, let's check out some of the ways to up your perspective taking game.

How to Take Perspectives

As you may have noticed, the basic foundations of perspective taking involve having a good context for someone. Understating context and taking perspective are inseparable. Perspective taking just takes things further in that it involves seeing through the camera lens of the other person in a more detailed way. So, in learning how to take perspective, we need to start by creating good contexts. Let's review the things that help us create good contexts again.

Gathering the facts:

The first thing you need to create the context you need for perspective taking is some good contextual information. The way we get this kind of information is by using one of the basic strategies of a social detective—gathering the facts.

We gather the facts with our 8 senses. The first five senses help us take in information from the outside world. And the 6th, 7th, and 8th senses help us gather information from our own reactions to things.

To gather the facts, we also use good attention, as well as verbal and nonverbal listening, to help us take in information. In addition, our verbal and nonverbal responding and dancing can help us get important information from others. Good responding and dancing skills, such as asking open questions, staying on topic, and not interrupting, can help us in gathering even more context-building information. In addition, if we listen, respond, and dance well in our interactions with others, it will help them feel safer with us and more relaxed. And when people feel relaxed and safe there is a higher chance that they will share more personal, contextual information with us.

Organize the facts:

Human beings can be very complicated. As a result, when we start getting to know others and collecting important contextual information, we often find that there is a lot of it. It can be overwhelming trying to manage all the information we gather about others. But if you recall, we discussed how organizing the information can help us to remember it and manage it better.

You might recall the story of John and his dog, Spot. Remember how when I just gave you a list of words, it was really hard to remember? But when I used the same words in the story of John and his dog, it was much easier to manage and remember all those words. That's because the story organized the words.

Stories can create relationships between separate pieces of information and give them meaning. And these relationships between pieces of information and the meaning the relationships create help make it much easier for us to remember. It's much easier to remember one story and all its connected pieces than to just remember a bunch of random unconnected pieces of information.

For a refresher on strategies for creating contextual stories, take a look at the beginning of the DIY on cre-ating meaningful stories on page 242.

Making sense of the facts.

Once we gather and organize the contextual information, we want to use it to make sense of the facts. But what this really means here is that we use the contextual information to make sense of how others respond, react, and make sense of things. This helps us to understand them better. And this kind of understanding is like a bridge into their inside world, into their perspective. It enables us to begin to see the world through their camera lens, their eyes, mind, and heart. And this kind of seeing is perspective taking. For a refresher on strategies for making sense of contextual facts, take a look at the same DIY on creating meaningful stories mentioned above.

Sometimes we might do a good job of gathering, organizing, remembering, and even making sense of con-textual information, yet still not be able to put ourselves in another person's shoes and fully "see" things as they might. Sometimes we need to do some other things to really bring our contextual understanding to life. I call bringing context to life so we can fully take another's perspective, "embodying." To embody some-thing means to make it your own. When an actor or actress embodies a character they are playing, they take it on so well that they almost become that character. They imagine the character's point of view so vividly that for the time they are acting, they feel like they are that character.

We are not going to become another person. But when we embody the contextual information we gather about someone, it often can almost seem like truly seeing through their eyes, thinking through their mind, and feeling with their heart. This is what I call *fully taking perspective* or *embodying perspective*. So, let's talk about some things you can do to embody contextual understanding so you can fully take the perspectives of others.

Tools for Perspective Taking

Intention and Attention:

The first thing you want to do when trying to take another's perspective in a fully embodied way is to bring your intention and attention to the other person. At the beginning of this book, we talked about the impor-tance of attention in social relating. Attention lets us be aware of the information others are sharing about their inside world. But intention actually helps to guide attention. Intention is a plan to act in a certain way. If you have an intention to study hard for a test, that means you are motivated and planning on studying hard.

An intention is kind of like a commitment you make to do something. When someone has an intention to do something, it is more likely that they will actually do it. When it comes to focusing on things, attention is about what we are actually focusing on. It's about where our spotlight of attention is shining. But intention is about what we *choose* to shine that spotlight on.

We might be really good at paying attention and capable of shining our spotlight of attention on things and bringing those things into awareness. But if we don't have the intention to shine that spotlight on something it will not help us to know that thing any better. For example, someone may be good at shining their spotlight of attention on things but be really bored with math, and as a result not have the intention to shine that spotlight on the teacher when she is teaching math class. Because of this, they will not take in and learn the information the teacher is giving.

Or let's say someone is good at focusing attention but they don't have the intention to pay attention to their friend when they are talking. Let's say that instead, they have the intention of putting their attention on the airplane models they are playing with. If this is the case, they will most likely not take in what their friend is saying. Of course, this will negatively affect their ability to gather important contextual information about their friend, which will make it more difficult for them to fully take their friend's perspective. And this can greatly affect the friendship.

Intention can have a big effect on our social interactions and ability to take others' perspectives. If we are aware of this, we can use intention to help us socially. In the case of perspective taking, we can use intention to help us focus our spotlight of attention on others' inside worlds so that we might come to know them better.

How do we create the intention to bring our attention to others inside worlds? Good self-talk can help a lot. The things we say to ourselves can be very powerful. When we say negative things to ourselves, it can make us feel really bad. When we say positive, kind things to ourselves, it can help us to feel good. And when we tell ourselves to pay attention to others' inside worlds, it creates an intention to help us focus our attention on others.

Here are some things you might want to try to say to yourself to help you create intentions about getting to know people's inside worlds better:

1) I want to know this person better.
2) I want to bring my attention to this person's inside world so I can understand his or her perspective better.
3) I want to pay attention to things that will help me have a better context for this person.
4) I wonder if he or she is seeing things in a way that is similar or different from the way I see things.
5) I wonder how they feel.
6) I wonder what they are thinking.
7) I wonder what they think of me.
8) I wonder how he or she is making sense of things.

You might notice that many of these questions show curiosity about other people. When we have curiosity about others, we will be much more likely to have the intention to know their inside world better. The other thing you can do to create more intention around getting to know other people's perspectives is to practice being curious about people.

Let yourself be curious about how others see and think about things. Let yourself be curious about how they feel about things and why they respond, react, and make sense of things the way they do. This will naturally bring your spotlight of attention to the things that will help you know them better.

Buddy Scan

Once you have made a choice to get to know someone better there are some great things you can do to make this happen. One of my favorite strategies for taking another person's perspective in a more fully embodied way is what I call the *buddy scan.*

We practiced the *body scan* in which we put our spotlight of attention on our own body sensations, so we could have a greater awareness of what we were experiencing inside. Our attention on our body increased awareness of our own body sensations which in turn made our relationship with our body stronger. You could even say that by increasing our awareness of our own inside experience we were able to fully take our own perspective better.

With the buddy scan, we are taking that same spotlight of attention and shining it on another person to become more aware of his or her inside world so that we might be able to more fully take their perspective and have a better relationship with them.

Of course, we are not going to be able to directly know what others are feeling inside their body with the same confidence we would our own body. We can't sense their sensations, thoughts, or feelings in the same way we can sense our own. But the act of putting our attention on them and focusing on what they might be experiencing helps us to be more sensitive and receptive to the clues they might be giving off about their inside world.

There are also things in all of our bodies called *mirror neurons* that can help us to feel in our own bodies what others might be feeling in theirs. Let me tell you about mirror neurons and how they were discovered. There were these scientists who were doing research with monkeys, and part of the research was to measure activity in monkeys' brains.

One day while they were measuring a monkey's brain activity, one of the scientists lifted his cup of coffee to take a sip. When he did, he noticed something amazing. When he lifted his cup, the part of the monkey's brain responsible for moving his arm to lift a cup was activated. The monkey did not have any coffee himself and he did not even move his arm at all. But the part of his brain that is responsible for moving his arm was activated as if he was actually lifting his arm to bring a cup to his mouth. Just seeing the scientist drinking made the monkey's brain act as if he was drinking.

The thing that allowed the monkey's brain to do this is called the mirror neuron system. This discovery with the monkey showed that neurons in one brain can actually mirror and mimic what is going on in another brain. And this is not just the case for simple things like moving your arm. When we are aware of others' experiences, it can turn on similar neurons in our own brain that give us the same experience. This mirroring in our brains can let us directly experience some of what the other person is experiencing.

You might have experienced something like this before. Have you ever seen someone hurt themselves, and you tense your body as if you are experiencing their pain as if you can actually feel a little bit of what they are feeling? The reason you are feeling a twinge of pain may be because your mirror neurons are firing when you watch the person get hurt, and a similar thing is happening in your brain that happened when the monkey saw the scientist drinking his coffee.

Or have you ever seen someone who is sad, and you can't help feel a twinge of sadness in yourself? Or they are really happy about something and you feel happiness too? When this happens, something in your brain and nervous system is getting activated in response to sensing the other person having those feelings. You are mirroring in yourself what they are experiencing.

Can you see how powerful a tool this could be for helping us fully embody the perspective of others? If you are sensing even a little of what someone else is experiencing because your mirror neurons are firing, you can do a body scan on yourself to get important information that helps you better understand their perspective.

For example, if you see a friend get teased by someone, you might guess that he might feel bad about that. But if you actually feel a little of what he might be feeling because your mirror neurons get activated, you are going to be able to understand them much better. You will be able to understand better because you are actually feeling some of what he is feeling. You are embodying his perspective because you are feeling some of it in your own body.

DIY: Buddy Scan

There are many ways you can do a buddy scan. You can do a complete buddy scan or just scan specific parts of the other person. You can also do buddy scans in specific situations which we will talk about in a bit. Let's do a little practice of a full buddy scan and then you can pick and choose different pieces depending on the circumstances.

First, get a partner and face each other. I always like to start a buddy scan by doing a quick body scan on myself first. This helps you get more connected to yourself and the more connected you are to yourself the more you will be able to connect with others. So, turn your spotlight of attention on yourself and quickly scan your eight senses as we did in the body scans we practiced.

Next, make an *intention* to put your *attention* on your partner so you can more fully embody his or her perspective. Then take your spotlight of attention and bring it to your partner. Let yourself review in your mind some of the contextual information you have about them. What do you know about their personal, interpersonal, and situational context? See if you can hold these pieces of contextual information in the back of your mind as you proceed.

The first five senses: Start your buddy scan by trying to put your attention on your partner's first five senses, just as we do with a body scan. Let yourself imagine what they are experiencing with those five senses. If you do this with someone on video, many things will be similar to what you are sensing yourself, which will make it easier.

Your partner is probably hearing and smelling the same things you are. You will probably be feeling the same temperature on your skin unless one of you is wearing a jacket or long sleeves or pants and the other person is not. As for taste, you are probably not going to be eating while you do this, so that will probably be similar. Let yourself imagine what they might be sensing with those senses, and use your own senses to help you imagine.

One thing that will most likely be different will be what they are seeing with their eyes. If you are sitting face to face, your partner will be seeing you while you are seeing them. Let yourself imagine them seeing you. Scan your buddy's visual sensation and let yourself imagine what it looks like to be sitting where they are. Imagine what it's like looking out and seeing you looking back.

The 6th sense: Next, let your spotlight of attention shift to your buddy's sixth sense. Imagine what they might be feeling inside their body. Here is a place where some of the tools we have been learning can help. For example, being tuned into nonverbal communications can give us a lot of clues about what someone might be experiencing in their body.

In tuning into your partner and doing your buddy scan, you might sense that they have a calm face and more flowy, smooth body movements and a posture that seems comfortable and at ease. This information might help you to sense that they feel nice and relaxed inside their body. Or maybe you are sensing tension and discomfort in their face or more robot-type moments and awkward posture.

All these nonverbal communications can activate those mirror neurons we were talking about. Just as the monkey's brain was affected by the scientist raising the cup, our mirror neurons can be activated by all those nonverbal communications. The truth is that those mirror neurons often get activated by nonverbal communications without us even noticing it. We just get a sense of someone and don't know why. But when we are more aware of all those nonverbal communications, we can be even more attuned to others and more able to embody what they might be experiencing.

So, when doing the buddy scan with your partner's sixth sense, let yourself take in those nonverbal clues and imagine yourself as if you were them. Imagine what it might feel like in their body. Use the same kind of poetic descriptions we used in our own body scan.

Do you imagine they are feeling tension or relaxation, warm or cold, heavy or light? Do you imagine they might be feeling tingly sensations? Are there colors, shapes, or textures that go along with the sensations you imagine? Do you imagine their body feels good or bad? Let yourself imagine the details. And don't worry if it's right or not. The goal here is not to perfectly read them. It's to try and tune in and put your attention on them so you can sense them better.

When we think about imagining things, we often think about using our minds. We imagine stories with our minds. We imagine images with our minds. We might even imagine sounds like music with our minds. But we can also imagine with our body.

When doing a good buddy scan around the sixth sense, we want to not just use our minds to imagine. We want to use our bodies too. So, when imagining what your partner might be feeling in their body, try to imagine with your own body. Try to create a little bit of the actual sense that you imagine they are feeling in their body. See if you can not only think about what they are feeling, but also feel a little of what they might be feeling.

The 7th sense: After trying to tune into what your partner might be feeling in their body, let your spotlight of attention move on to their minds. Let yourself imagine what they might be thinking right then and how they might think in general. This is a place where contextual information can offer great clues to help you imagine their perspective with greater accuracy. You can bring to mind important personal, interpersonal, and situation information about your partner and think about how that information might affect the way your partner might make sense of things.

For example, do you have any personal information about them that might give you clues about their self-confidence? If you know they are a very confident person, you might imagine that they are feeling confident about their ability to do a buddy scan with you. You might also imagine that they think you like them. If, on the other hand, you know this person is not so confident, you might imagine they are having self-doubts about their ability to do a good buddy scan, and that they might be thinking you do not like them much.

Once you gather some clues and imagine how your partner might be making sense of things, see if you can take it a step further. Try and embody their perspective and experience in yourself what they might be experiencing. Imagine you are them and you are thinking those thoughts. For example, let's say that based on what you know about their context, you are imagining that they are thinking insecure thoughts. Let's say you imagine they are thinking they are not a good person and that others don't like them. See if you can imagine what it might be like to think that way. And when you do, see if you can imagine how those kinds of thoughts would affect the way your body felt.

If you were personally thinking insecure thoughts like that, would your body feel more awkward and uncomfortable? Would you feel less energy or power in your body? Would your body seem stiffer and robot-like? See if you can feel in your own body a little of what it would be like if you were thinking those thoughts. See if you can embody what your partner might be thinking and feeling as if it were your own self you were sensing. See if you can sense the result of your mirror neurons firing.

The 8th sense: Next you can turn your spotlight of attention to the eighth sense and try to imagine how your partner might be experiencing relationships. You can speculate about how your partner might be sensing other relationships in their life. But a good place to start is to try and sense how they might be experiencing their relationship with you right then and there.

If you recall, the eighth sense relays a lot of information gathered from all the other 7 senses. It takes the information from the first five senses and blends it with how someone is feeling in their bodies and what thoughts they are having in their minds. All these different senses come together to make the bigger relationship cookie.

See if you can take the information you got from tuning into your partner's other senses to get a picture of their sense of relationship with you right then. You can take the information you got from their nonverbal communications and your sense of their comfort level. Combine that with the information you have about their personal history as well as the information you know about your interpersonal relationship with them. All these things will come together to create a sense in you of your partner's sense of the quality of your relationship.

Situational buddy scans:

Once you get the hang of a general buddy scan, you can use it in lots of specific situations to get a better sense of how another person might respond, react, and make sense of specific situations. Here are a couple of examples of more specific buddy scans you can do.

Buddy grub scan:

In case you have not heard the term "grub," it means to eat. An interesting way to practice taking someone else's perspective is to imagine what different foods might taste like to them. This can be especially interesting if you have different tastes than them.

So sometime when you are having food with someone else, imagine you are eating what they are eating. Imagine yourself grubbing on what they are grubbing on. See if you can imagine the flavor of the food they are eating. And let's say it's something you don't like very much but they do. See if you can imagine how something you don't like might taste good to someone else. If you can imagine enjoying something you don't like, you are really doing some good perspective taking.

Buddy music scan:

Another variation is to imagine listening to some music that you might not really like but someone else does. Maybe let your little brother or sister put on some little kid music. Or listen to some of your grandpa's music with him. Now you might not like their music. It might even annoy you. But see if you can take their perspective. Feel into their senses and imagine what it might be like for them to hear that music. Use some of the tools we used in the general buddy scan. You can feel into their nonverbal communications. How does their body respond when they hear this music? What do you notice in their reaction? Let all those good fact-gathering skills help you to better take their perspective.

Another cool one is to put on some music that you really like but that others don't like as much. See if you can feel into the other person and sense what it might be like for them to hear this music they don't like. Again, see if you can feel into their experience and gather facts from the verbal and nonverbal clues that they are giving off about their reaction to the music, to get a sense of how the music might be impacting them.

There are endless situations in which you might find yourself with others, situations in which you might have very different perspectives from them. See if you can try and use a buddy scan in situations like this to get a better perspective of the other person.

Fully Taking Perspective

Once you have tried feeling into the other person's senses and thinking into their context, see if you can take it to the next level. See if you can use this information you have gathered to help you fully take on the other person's perspective as if it were your own, as if you were really them. See if you can imagine you are actually looking through their eyes, feeling through their body and heart, and thinking through their mind.

I often think of fully taking on the perspective of another person as a kind of futuristic virtual reality, first-person perspective video game with a full-on haptic suit. You probably know what virtual reality and first-person perspective video games are, but I will just refresh your memory if you don't.

Virtual reality is a really cool technology where you wear goggles that cover your eyes completely. When you wear them, you are immersed in another world where you can see 360 degrees around you. When you turn your head to the left, the images change to show you what's on the left. Any direction you look, you see just as you do when you are looking around with your eyes in the real world. It's very cool.

A first-person perspective video game is a kind of video game where you are looking through the eyes of the main character, seeing what she or he would be seeing. If you were using virtual reality playing a first-person video game, you could look all around you for the opponents you are trying to play against. Virtual reality immerses you in the game so that you can more fully take the perspective of the main character you are pretending to be. And this gives you a much more realistic experience as if it was really you fighting the bad guys.

Now a *haptic* suit takes this even further. A haptic suit is something you would wear, like a vest or jacket or even a full-body outfit. It has things that vibrate and move on your skin when you are playing virtual reality games. So, if you got hit or shot in a game, the haptic suit would give you sensations to simulate getting hit or shot. Hopefully not too painfully. That would be no fun. But even a little sensation helps to make the experience even more realistic. It helps you to more fully take the perspective of the character so you can have a more embodied experience of the game. By seeing through the characters' eyes, hearing what they might be hearing, and feeling what they might be feeling, you are able to more fully take their perspective.

This is also what we want to do when we take the perspective of others. We want to get a sense of what they are sensing so we can more fully embody their perspective. Of course, it's more challenging to do this in real life than it is in a virtual reality video game. We have no headphones or virtual reality goggles and no haptic suit. So, we have to depend on our own imaginations, mirror neurons, and good social detective skills to do this.

DIY: Virtual Reality Perspective Taking

You might be asking yourself, "How do I create my own fully immersive, 360 degree, haptic suit enhanced experience when doing a buddy scan?" The answer is practice. The more you practice taking perspectives, the better you get. So, let's do an exercise to take our buddy scan to the next level of full-on virtual reality perspective taking.

You can do this DIY practice with your buddy scan partner as well as later on your own. But it's really nice to do it at first with a partner who is also doing a buddy scan with you. It can help to keep you both focused on the practice. It also provides the opportunity to discuss your experience afterward, which can be really helpful in getting better at perspective taking.

Once you have felt into the other person's senses and thought about their context let yourself come back to yourself. Let your spotlight of attention come back fully to your own body, heart, and mind. While paying attention to your own senses, reflect on the things you felt and thought when doing your buddy scan. Reflect on seeing through the other person's eyes, feeling through their body and heart, and thinking from the point of view of their mind.

While staying connected to your own senses, let yourself imagine you are them. Imagine you have put on virtual reality goggles and a full haptic suit and are experiencing the world as if you are them. Let yourself sit with that for a while and really try to experience first-hand what it might be like to be them. When doing this, you are sensing your own body while imagining you are them. This might seem a little tricky at first, but with practice, you will get the hang of it.

You can try to imitate the body postures they might do. Let yourself move your body the way you imagine they might. Make facial expressions they might. You can even say some common phrases they might say with voice music you imagine they would use.

You can let yourself imagine you are walking through a virtual reality landscape as if you were the other person. And let that virtual reality landscape be built out of everything you know about the other person. Imagine going to that person's home and interacting with their family and friends as if you were them. If they have any pets, imagine playing with them. If you have ever been in their room, recall it and imagine your virtual reality perspective-taking goggles transporting you there. Imagine the other person in school and going through all the things they go through day-to-day.

With your eyes closed and your spotlight of attention on your own eight senses, imagine how they might think and feel about things you encounter as you travel through their world with your virtual reality perspective-taking glasses and haptic suit. From what you know or imagine, what might they think and feel when they encounter members of their family? See if you can feel those same feelings and think those same thoughts you imagine in your own body, heart, and mind. Let yourself imagine what their experience would be like doing homework, or eating their favorite foods, or interacting with teachers and kids at school. Let yourself imagine what their experience might be like interacting with you. And let yourself become fully immersed in those things you imagine as if you were to become that person for that moment in time.

At first, some of these things might seem hard. But as with so many things we have been talking about, it's all about practice. The more you practice these things, the better your virtual reality perspective-taking skills will become. It's just like when you play video games. Have you ever played a brand-new video game and at first it just feels like too much information? There are things all over the place shooting at you. You don't know how to use the controls for the game yet. There seems to be way too much going on and it can feel like you will never get the hang of it.

But if you have ever played video games you will know that with practice, things start to make so much more sense. As you persevere and keep trying, all the pieces start to come together. They fit into a more organized whole. The context of the game starts to make more sense and as a result, you are more able to manage all the things happening with much more ease. And before you know it, you're not getting all those "Game Overs," and you are starting to kick some serious video game butt.

It is the same with learning how to fully take perspective. At first, all the pieces of information can seem really overwhelming. But with practice, you become better at organizing all the pieces into a bigger context, just like when learning a new video game. And before you know it, your own personal virtual reality perspective-taking skills are up and running and you are getting other people like a pro.

Perspective Assuming and Perspective Denying

This is a good time to introduce you to two important secondary suspects that can cause problems in social relationships. These suspects are *perspective assuming* and *perspective denying*. I call them secondary suspects rather than prime suspects because they are both types of perspective missing. Let's take a look at each.

Perspective Assuming

Perspective assuming happens when we are overconfident and believe we know for sure what another person's perspective is. It also happens when we just assume everyone sees things the same way we do. When we assume in this way, we are not open to any information that might contradict our point of view. We assume we know and are so confident that we stop questioning and looking for additional facts that might either back up our assumption or contradict it.

There is nothing wrong with not getting someone's perspective. You can look at all the facts and try your best to figure out what someone's point of view is and still miss it. Everyone does that at times. The key is to not assume you know for sure and to check to see if what you think is correct. Know how to recognize when you miss, and to be able to adjust your view of the other person's perspective so that your view can be more accurate.

In Zen, they have the concepts of *expert's mind* and *beginner's mind*. Expert's mind happens when we think we know everything about something. We are so overly confident that we stop learning and looking for new information. On the other hand, beginner's mind looks at something as if they were seeing it for the first time. Beginner's mind does not presume to know everything. And because of this, it is much more open to taking in new information and learning more about things.

In Zen the expert mind thinks to itself, "Why keep learning if I already know everything?" Expert's mind also has trouble seeing when it is wrong because it is very attached to being the expert and being right all the time. Beginner's mind, on the other hand, is very open to new ideas. And someone with beginner's mind is not overly attached to being right all the time which makes it much easier to learn new things and be humble enough to admit when they are wrong.

When we perspective assume, we are using expert's mind. We are assuming we know things we don't and we are not open to learning more about the other person so we can better get their perspective. As you might imagine, this can cause a lot of problems socially.

When it comes to being a social detective, we want to practice beginner's mind in all the things we do socially. We want to always be open to learning new things about people and about our social world. That is how we continue to become more and more socially and emotionally intelligent.

Perspective Denying

Perspective denying happens when we refuse to believe that we might be wrong about our assumptions about someone else's perspective even when the other person is giving us clear messages that we are incorrect. You can probably see how this is related to perspective assuming. But with perspective denying there is a more active refusal to admit we are wrong, even in the face of clear evidence that we are missing the other person's perspective.

What makes perspective denying even more problematic is when we deny someone's perspective to their face. People who are having a lot of trouble with perspective denying will actually tell the other person that they know them better than they know themselves. Someone might say "You don't feel like that" or "You don't really think that or believe that."

As you might imagine, this does not go over very well. People do not like it when others tell them they know them better than they know themselves. It makes people feel very misunderstood, which makes it hard to trust and feel close and comfortable with the person who is denying their perspective.

When someone perspective denies they are caught in expert's mind. They are missing the other person in a very important way. We have talked about mood missing and topic missing and even perspective missing and how problematic these things can be. We have also talked about how we can correct those things and make our relationships better. But if someone is perspective denying there is no room for getting it right. There is no room for taking in new information so we can understand others better. And this gives a clear message that the person has no interest in or ability to really understand us.

Checking Things Out

Gathering verbal and nonverbal facts, getting a better context, and working on our perspective taking can help us to understand others much better. These things give us a lot of information to help us solve our social mysteries, especially the big social mystery we often face of how to understand someone else's perspective.

But the truth is, even with lots of good facts and great social detective skills we can't read people's minds, and sometimes we will not completely get where they are coming from. It's ok if that happens. We don't need to be perfect. Missing someone's perspective does not have to cause big problems in our relationship with them. In fact, dealing with misses in skillful ways can sometimes even make the relationship better.

One of the best things to do when we are unsure if we have gotten someone else's perspective correctly is to check things out with them. Checking things out can be pretty simple. The most direct way to do this is to just ask someone if you are getting them right. Of course, you don't necessarily want to do this with strangers or people you don't know well, and you don't want to do it if it's the wrong situation. You want to use the contextual information you have gathered to determine if checking things out with them is contextually appropriate.

If it is contextually appropriate, you can reflect back to them in a positive way what you imagine their perspective might be. When doing this, be careful not to perspective assume by telling them what they are thinking or feeling. Check things out in a way that is asking rather than telling. This allows room for them to correct you if you are off.

Reflecting back to the other person what you imagine their perspective to be is often referred to as *mirroring*. Mirrors reflect back an image of something. Good mirrors accurately reflect back images. Not-so-good mirrors distort the image and reflect back something that is not true to life. Good friends try their best to accurately reflect back to each other, which makes people feel seen and understood.

In mirroring back someone's perspective you can use phrases like "It sounds like you think ____" or "I am imagining you feel ____." You can say things like "I am wondering____" or "From what you are saying, I get the sense that you think, feel, need, want _____." By phrasing things in these ways, you are checking things out without assuming what the other person's perspective is.

If you are not sure it is contextually appropriate to be directly checking things out with someone, you can ask them what they think. You can say "Hey, is it alright if I check something out with you?" Asking people for their permission to check something out usually makes them more open to hearing what you are saying.

Benefits of checking things out:

There are a number of reasons why checking things out with others can be really helpful. First, checking things out can help you determine if you are on the right track with your attempts to solve the social mystery of "What is the other person's perspective?" If the other person gives you feedback that you are getting them accurately, it can help you be more confident about your understanding of them. Their confirmation can help you build an even better sense of their perspective.

If the other person lets you know you are off in some way, you can use that feedback to adjust how you see them so you can get them better. Feedback that you are not getting their perspective correctly can help you get back on the right path towards a more accurate understanding of them. Without that feedback, you might continue to miss read the other person and get farther and farther away from a good understanding of them, because you are trying to make sense of them using inaccurate information.

Checking things out also helps with perspective assuming and denying. When you check things out with someone like we did above by asking them if your interpretation is correct rather than telling them how they are seeing things, it makes it clear you are not assuming what their perspective is. When you check it out, it lets them know you believe they are a better judge of themselves than you are of them, and that you are not presuming to know them better than they know themselves.

Once you check out your hypothesis and accept it, if they tell you that you are missing their perspective, it makes it clear that you are not perspective-denying. As I mentioned above, when someone is perspective denying, they think they know the other person better than they know themselves. But by accepting the other person's feedback and letting them know you are going to adjust how you see them, you are demonstrating that you honor that they know themselves better than you know them and that you are accepting their point of view instead of denying it. This will help people feel safe and positive about their relationship with you.

One of the other positive things that can come from checking things out is that you are communicating to the other person that you're genuinely interested in understanding their inner world. When we check things out with others, we are saying "I really want to understand you and I want to make sure that my understanding of you is accurate."

By doing this simple thing, people will get the sense that you care about how they see things and that you are interested in their inside world. And as we have discussed, this is a very important thing in friendships. People like it when others are interested in their inside world and how they see things.

DIY: Perspective Taking Games

The more you practice perspective taking, the better you get at it. There are a lot of interesting and often fun ways to practice. Here are a few of my favorite ways to practice getting other's perspectives.

1) Finding Commonalities

It is often easier to take the perspective of people who are similar to us in how they respond, react, and make sense of things. If they are like us or going through things we have gone through, it can take very little effort to understand their perspective because we know it in ourselves. But when people have different experiences than us or have a different way of responding, reacting, and making sense of things, their point of view can seem much more mysterious.

When you look a little deeper, though, the differences we see between us and others are not always as great as they might seem. When we look beneath the surface, we often can see how there are commonalities between what others are experiencing and what we might have experienced at some time in our lives.

For example, let's say you have a new friend, Leroy, who just moved to your town from across the country and does not have many friends. Let's say Leroy is being bullied by someone at school. You may have lots of friends and might not have a bully harassing you, which might make it difficult to relate to Leroy's perspective. But by looking a little deeper, you might be able to find some commonalities between you and Leroy.

The first place you might want to look to find commonalities is into your own past. While you might have lots of friends and no bullies hassling you now, you may have had these kinds of problems in the past. You can ask yourself if you have ever experienced anything like this in the past. Have you ever been bullied? Have you ever had a time in your life where you did not have many friends? If so, reflecting back on these past experiences and what they were like for you can help you to understand your friend better.

But let's say you have always had friends and have never been the target of a bully. Then what? If that is the case, you can look for related things to see if you have had any experiences that are similar in any way. For example, have you ever had your friends absent from school and had to sit alone at lunch? Or have you ever been to a party or event and not known anyone there?

On the days that you didn't have your friends around, you might have felt a little lonely. You might have seen other people being with their friends and felt a little awkward that you were all by yourself. While this is not exactly the same as not having any friends, it can give you a sense of the kind of things Leroy might be feeling.

As for the bullying, maybe you have never been genuinely bullied. But have you ever had someone be mean to you? Again, someone being mean once is not as upsetting as being bullied all the time. But remembering what that felt like can give you a sense of what your friend might be feeling like when he is being bullied.

Once you have found some common experience in your own life, let yourself feel into it. Recall what that was like for you. See if you can go through your eight senses and remember what it was like. What kind of thoughts did you have? What body sensations and emotions did you have? How did those experiences make you respond, react, and make sense of things? Let yourself put on your virtual reality perspective-taking goggles to recall your own past experience with this. Once you do, let your attention go back to the person you are trying to understand better and see if your connecting to your own related experiences helps you to know them better. See if it helps you to fully take their perspective.

2) The Good Friend Inventory

For this one let yourself imagine what you would like in a friend. How would you like them to interact with you? What makes you feel good in friendships? For example, do you like it when friends ask you things about yourself and show interest in you? Do you like it when they call you to see if you want to get together? Do you like it when they are friendly or funny? Does it feel good when they stay on topic, don't interrupt, match your mood, talk calmly, get excited about things?

Think of different qualities you might like in your friends--qualities that make you feel close and safe with them; qualities that make you feel respected and cared for by them; qualities that make you enjoy being with them. Then write these things down on a list of "Things I like in friends."

Next, imagine the things you would not like in a friend--things like being mean or critical, topic, or mood missing, being late, not showing any interest in you, or being bossy; things that might make you feel disrespected, or not comfortable and safe. Write these things down on a list of "things I don't like in friends."

Once you have your two lists, imagine a friend of yours acting in these ways. Imagine what it would feel like if they did things on the first list. Imagine how it might feel in your 6th, 7th, and 8th sense when they were doing these things. Then imagine them doing things on the second list and notice what it might feel in your 6th, 7th, and 8th sense. Really let yourself feel into this.

Next, imagine yourself acting these ways to others and see if you can put on your virtual reality goggles and haptic suit and sense what it might feel like for them if you were doing these things. Can you imagine them feeling a similar way? Of course, people have different ways of responding, reacting, and making sense of things. But this exercise can be a great way of imagining what others' perspectives might be.

3) Argue the Other Person's Opinion

When we have disagreements with others, it can make it difficult to see things from their point of view. This is especially true if there are negative feelings between us and the other person around the thing about which we are disagreeing or if we are really attached to being right.

One of the things that can help in situations like this and can aid us in becoming better perspective takers, is to try and argue the other person's point of view even if we disagree with it. Next time you have an opinion that is different from someone else's, see if you can put on your virtual reality perspective-taking goggles and see things from their point of view.

What would they argue to prove their point? Why do they think they are right and you are wrong? What arguments might they use to justify their position? See if you can argue their case even if deep down you don't agree with it. The goal in this is not to change how you see things. It is just to get a better understanding of why the other person sees things the way they do.

When in a disagreement, we often put so much energy into arguing our point of view that we don't take the time to try and see how the other person is seeing things. But trying to see things from the other person's point of view can be helpful for many reasons.

First, when we are putting all our attention on trying to prove we are right and others are wrong, there is no attention left to try and see things from other points of view. But when we stop trying to prove we are right and try to understand why others are seeing things the way they do, there is the possibility to see things we might have missed.

Second, when we try to see things from the other person's point of view and express to them that we get how they see it, people are often more receptive to hearing our point of view. When people feel heard and understood, they are often able to stop trying to prove their point and are able to try and see ours.

Even if we end up disagreeing with someone, letting them know we can see their perspective makes the disagreement have less of a negative impact on the friendship. Not understanding and not agreeing are two different things. We can disagree and still understand each other. And understanding can make a world of difference because deep down, we all want to be understood. We all want others to understand our perspective.

4) Look for Perspectives in Movies

A great way to practice perspective taking that is also entertaining is to watch movies and try to understand the points of view of the different characters in the movie. For example, if two people are fighting in a movie, try to see why each person is upset. Or if there is a villain who believes in his cause, see if you can understand what in his personal context might have led to him believing what he does.

As we talked about above, it can sometimes be extra hard to take the perspective of someone who sees things differently than us, especially if there are some negative feelings involved. When things are personal, as they often can be with people to whom we are close, it can make it more difficult to step outside of our own perspective to see theirs.

But with a movie, it's not as personal. While there may be very different points of view between the characters, it's still only a movie. We know it's not real. And the characters are not people who affect us in our lives. Because of this, it can be much easier to be objective and look at things from all the different perspectives. So, give it a try. You can even try it with a friend and compare how you see the characters' perspectives. See if you and your friend see things the same way.

I Get It - The Art of Perspective Responding

Three of the most powerful words you can say to build a positive, safe, meaningful, caring connection with someone are "I get it." There is great benefit in letting others know we get them. We all want to be understood. We all want to know others can see our perspective. Of course, there is much more to letting someone know we get them than just saying the words "I get it." In fact, we usually communicate that we get others without ever saying those words. If you think about it, a lot of what we have been talking about in this book have been ways we communicate to others that we get them.

Our verbal responses can let others know we get them. While that might mean saying things that mirror back to them our understanding of their perspective, our verbal responses often let others know this in less direct ways. For example, when we stay on topic it demonstrates that we are with the other person. It helps them know we are understanding the perspective they are communicating and that we recognize what is most important in what they are saying. Similarly, the way we verbally dance with others can also let them know we get them. For example, when we wait for others to finish speaking before we talk, we are letting them know we are with them and getting them.

All of the verbal as well as nonverbal responding and dancing skills we have been talking about help us to communicate that we get others. When we match people's moods in both our verbal and nonverbal responses, it helps others know that we get them. Our body language and posture, our facial expressions, the music in our voices--all of these things can help communicate to others that we get them.

When we are aware of other people's context and our actions reflect that we are sensitive to their context, we are showing them in significant ways that we get them. They may not even know that we are intentionally being sensitive. They may not be thinking "They are acting this way because they get me." But because we are getting them, our actions are more likely to create positivity in our relationships and help them to feel safer and more cared for by us.

For example, if we know that someone is sensitive to criticism and because of that we are careful not to criticize them even as a joke, it will help them feel safer and more cared for by us. Or if we know that they feel reassured about our relationship with them when we make efforts to call them during the week, they will feel the benefits of us getting them even if we are not directly telling them that we understand this important part of their context. If we get that they are sensitive to loud noises and as a result make sure to talk softer to them, it will help them to feel safer and more comfortable with us. We may not be saying directly "I get you," but our actions and the way we are relating to them are saying these things.

The final social mystery in this book comes directly from Johnny Multony's own personal journal. It is his own mystery, the biggest mystery he had faced since he began his journey to become a social detective. It's the mystery he encountered shortly after he graduated from high school. And it seems appropriate to share it with you here, as you are coming to the end of this book and training. Coming this far means you are probably very close to graduating from Social Detective Academy, so it seems only fitting that you get a glimpse into the wonderful world of social mysteries and adventures that awaited Johnny after his graduation. Here is one of Johnny's greatest mysteries, one that made him call upon all his social detective skills and experiences.

Johnny Multony:

When: September 6th, 10:34 AM

Where: Freshman dorms, apartment 328, University of California, Los Angeles

Johnny stood in the living room area of his new college dorm apartment. Slowly he turned in a circle, taking in the space. "This is where I will be living this year," he said to himself. It was a nice space with a couch, tv, and coffee table. It was simple but totally acceptable. Just beyond the living room space was a tiny kitchen that was missing a wall so it seemed almost as if it was part of the living room. Johnny imagined himself cooking up a big batch of mac and cheese in the kitchen while talking to his new roommates sitting on the couch in the living room.

There were also two bedrooms that would be shared by four roommates. Johnny knew a little about the other guys he would be sharing the dorm with, but he had never met them. As he walked around the apartment, he started to feel his body tense up. He noticed his breathing getting shallow and fast, and his heart was thumping a little harder than usual. "I am so excited!" he thought to himself. "But I'm also kinda nervous. I think I need to calm myself a little." For Johnny, one of the ways he regularly calmed himself was to write in his journal, so he took a seat on the couch, pulled out his journal, and started to do a little writing.

Dear Diary: Today I embark on one of the greatest adventures I have ever faced. The adventure of college. Today I meet my new roommates who I will be living with this coming year. I will also meet all the other college students in my dorm in our orientation this afternoon. And next week I get to meet the students in the engineering program I'm in who I will be studying with in the years to come.

I am moving away from my family and longtime friends. Away from a home and town I know so well to a complex new world that is unfamiliar to me. I am so excited about this adventure. But if I am being honest, I'm also scared. How will I gather and make sense of so much new information? So many new facts? So many new people? So many new expectations?

There will be a lot of different perspectives to try and take in order to understand people, make good friends, and get along well with others. And the culture of college and dorm life is so different from high school and living at home. It is completely unfamiliar to me. To be able to take those perspectives well, I will have to gather, organize, and make sense of so many facts. Facts about people's contexts, about how they understand and make sense of things, and about how they react to things. Facts about college life.

It feels a little overwhelming, to be honest. In high school, I got to do these things over many years. Gradually building more detailed contexts for all the people I knew. Gradually understanding each person's context and perspective better. Gradually gathering and making sense of school expectations over time. But now it's all new. And it's coming at me all at once. How will I do it? Where should I start? Even after all these years, it feels overwhelming.

But I am up for this challenge! I am excited about growing up and going off to college. I know I can do it. And even if I make some mistakes along the way I will learn from them and keep with it. I just need a good plan of action so it's not so overwhelming. I know a good plan of action will help me feel less overwhelmed so that the excitement can be stronger than the nervousness.

I am going to turn to you, my trusted diary. I am going to share all my adventures on these pages. I'm going to share with you like I would with my best friends. College will be the next chapter in my ongoing, lifelong diary of a social detective. And today I am going to start by outlining my game plan, outlining the things I am going to do to start building a whole new context of college life. A context that will help me create good perspective maps which will help me to keep from getting lost in this new uncharted territory. Maps that will take me on new adventures with new friends.

To start, I'll do what I suggest to all my students and clients. Start with the facts. I will use all the tools I have to gather detailed, accurate facts. Making sure to pay good attention is the first key. I know that. My intention is to pay attention. Intention of attention. And if I get distracted, I will not be hard on myself. I will just keep bringing my spotlight of attention back to the person or situation I am trying to understand better. Today that will be my new roommates and the other students in my dorm. Next week I will expand that spotlight to help me pay good attention to all the information about the other students in my program. And about my teachers and their expectations of me. And about the school in general.

I will make sure to pay attention to what people communicate verbally. I will pay attention to the main topics and the moods of others. I will pay attention to the likes and dislikes of others. To what makes them feel good and what upsets them. Not only will this help me gather important information, but it will also help me be a good friend.

I also know it's not just what people say that can give important clues, it's also how they say it. I will need to make sure I stay aware of people's verbal dancing. Things like fast talking and verbal crowding communicate a lot. So do things like over and under responding, how people manage the awkward silence, and topic lingering.

Part of what and how people say things comes from their non-verbal communications, as well, so I will need to stay aware of all the other non-verbal things that are communicated-- things like facial expressions, body posture and positioning, body movements, and music in the voice. I know that these things can communicate so much important information that might not be expressed in words, so I will give extra effort to noticing and making note of these things.

"This is a lot to keep track of," Johnny thought to himself. "I'm going to make a list to help me remember." He took his pen back to the journal page and wrote....

Tools for gathering important facts about college life

Attention

Identifying and responding to main topics

Identifying and responding to main moods

Noting peoples likes and dislikes

Noting what makes others feel good

Noting what makes others feel upset

Being aware of how others verbally dance (i.e., fast talking, verbal crowding, over and under responding, managing awkward silences, topic lingering)

Being aware of how others communicate nonverbally (i.e., facial expressions, body posture and positioning, body movements, and music in the voice)

Writing this list helped Johnny relax a little. "Having things on paper always helps," he thought to himself. He took another look around the room, imagining what this next year would bring him. Another wave of tension came. "Ok. Let's get the rest of the plan down on paper." He took a deep breath and brought his attention back to his journal. "What next?"

My responses to others will be really important too. I know that the way I respond to others can have a big impact on the quality of the friendships I build with them. Good responses help to build good friendships. When done right, my responses can let others know I'm paying attention and interested in them. Good responding can help others know that I am understanding them, which can help them to feel safe with me. And if they feel safe, they will be more likely to open up and share important and vulnerable things about themselves with me. My responses can also affect the quality of the facts I gather in my interactions with others. And the better the quality of the facts I gather, the more detailed context I can have, which will help me to make more detailed, accurate perspective maps.

Johnny stared off into space while he thought. "What do I need to focus on around my responses?" he asked himself. After taking a few moments to think about this question, he brought his pen back to the journal page.

I need to make sure I respond on topic and appropriately to the mood of others in my interactions with them. I will also need to pay attention not just to how others are verbally dancing, but to how I am as well. I know that when I get nervous or excited, I can start to talk fast and crowd a conversation. I want to be aware of this so it does not happen too much. When I'm nervous I can also both under- and over-respond at times. Sometimes I under-respond when I'm nervous about what I should say. And sometimes I over-respond when I am not managing awkward silences well. Being aware of how I can do these things will help keep my responding balanced.

I definitely want to be aware of how I might manage any awkward silences that come up. I know that silences are common and that they are not necessarily bad things. Sometimes they can allow for more depth in conversations. But I know that when I'm nervous I can feel a lot more awkward with silences. Sometimes when I don't know people well, I think that the silences mean that they don't like me. And I start to think that it is completely my responsibility to fill the silences. I want to make sure that this reaction on my part doesn't make me do things to fill the silence that create problems in my relational exchanges with others.

Johnny, paused again to think. "I will definitely need to keep an eye on my non-verbal communications," he thought.

I know that when I'm nervous, my nonverbal communications can give it away.

When I'm nervous I can show it by having a furrowed brow or a little frown or just a general tightness on my face. Sometimes my shoulders tense up. Sometimes I slump and cross my arms. When I'm nervous, my body can move in jerky, robot-like ways. And the music in my voice can lack the melody, tone, and phrasing that communicate warmth. When I'm nervous my eye contact is often not the best. I've been known to avoid eye contact when I'm nervous, but when really trying to make eye contact I can laser gaze, which can be intense for people.

Others might not make sense of these non-verbal communications as me feeling anxious or trying to calm myself. If they don't know me, they won't have a good context or perspective map for me. They might not understand why I might respond, react, and make sense of things the ways I do. Most likely others will be trying to figure out if I like them and might take these things as me being offish, cold, or uncaring. Or even worse, they might take it as me being mean. I know that sometimes I have taken others' nervousness as them being mean and not liking me. And it was not until I got to know them better that I realized that it was just their nervousness and had nothing to do with how they felt about me. I need to be extra careful of my non-verbal communications because I don't want others to get the wrong message. That would not be a good way to start new relationships.

One thing that can help me keep my nervousness in check so it does not come out too much in my nonverbal communications is to be aware of how my body is feeling. I can do this by doing regular body scans for my first six senses. I also want to stay aware of how my mind is thinking. Which I can do by scanning my 7th sense with the mind scan. And of course, I want to keep on top of how my relationships are doing, which I can do by staying aware of my 8th sense, my relational sense. I can do this with the buddy scan and by really paying attention to how others respond, react, and make sense of things.

It's all connected! Gathering the facts and making sense of the facts helps us know others better which helps us have better relationships with them. That is a big part of what being a social detective is about. All these pieces come together to help that happen.

"Ok, that's a good start," Johnny thought. "But I need to make sure I do a good job of using all the information I gather to help me see other people's contexts. I know that this is really the key to being able to make good social maps, which will help keep me from getting lost in social situations. But there is going to be so much new information. How do I organize and make sense of all that?" he thought to himself.

Johnny gazed off into space again. "Putting things in categories can help. Using the categories for the different types of contextual information could be good. What types of contextual information will I be collecting? Let me make a list for this, too, so it's easy to remember."

Types of contextual information to gather:

1) *Personal Information:*

   * *personality traits*

   * *personal history*

   * *current mood*

   * *mental styles and abilities*

2) *Interpersonal Information:*

   * *how long have I known the person*

   * *are they familiar to me or not familiar*

   * *is it a formal or informal relationship*

3) *Situational Information:*

   * *is there a mood to the situation*

   * *are there rules specific to the situation*

   * *is there a time factor*

   * *is there a role you or others are serving*

"These categories will definitely help me to organize the facts I gather. What else can I do?" Johnny asked himself. *"I can use my handy contextual story worksheet.* That could also help me organize and categorize all the information I gather, which will help me to not be so overwhelmed with details."

Contextual story worksheet

<u>*This contextual story is about:*</u>

1) Another person

2) My relationships with another individual or group of people

3) A social situation I might be in

4) Myself

5) Something else (specify) _____

- *The tools I used to gather contextual information were:*
- *The important contextual information I gathered was:*
- *The story I made up to organize the information is:*
- *The questions I asked myself to make sense of the information was:*

- *The conclusions I came to about how they respond react or make sense of things were:*
- *The way this affects how I might respond, react, or make sense of things this another person says or does is:*

Writing all these things down helped Johnny to calm. He was feeling much more relaxed after this. "I can do this!" he said out loud as he leaned back on the couch and let his body relax.

The timing was perfect. Just as he put his pen down and closed his journal, the door opened. Standing in the doorway was a tall, well-groomed young man. When the boy saw Johnny, his body tensed up and in a classic robot-like voice he said "Hey." Of course, Johnny's first gut reaction was to think this boy didn't like the looks of him. But then he thought about everything he had just written. He thought about how he himself might react when coming to a new school and meeting new people for the first time. And by thinking about how he might react, Johnny was able to do a little perspective taking right then and there. "I'll bet he is as nervous as I am," Johnny thought.

With that thought, he was able to take a deep breath and relax. "I'm going to help him feel comfortable and safe with me. I'm going to let him know with my attention that I'm interested in getting to know him. And I'm going to start right now in my quest to gather important facts so I can create the best social maps for new friends and college that I can," he thought. Johnny gave a big, warm smile and in an enthusiastic voice said, "Hey! I'm Johnny. Nice to meet you!" The other boy instantly relaxed. They went on to have a great conversation, getting to know each other. This was the perfect start to the first year of college. "This is going to be a great year," Johnny thought to himself. And it was. It was one of the best years of his life.

An Epidemic of Kindness and Care

When we are really able to take others' perspectives, we can't help but have more care and empathy for them. When we see from another person's point of view, our mirror neurons fire and we are more able to feel what they are feeling. As a result, we are naturally going to be kinder and more sensitive to their specific contextual needs.

And do you know what happens when people feel others are being kind to them? They are more likely to be kind themselves. They are more likely to be kind back to us as well as to others in their lives. Kindness and care are contagious. Your kindness and care infect others, helping them to be kinder and more caring.

Can you imagine a world where people were kind and caring to each other all the time? A world where people were skilled at taking each other's perspectives, understanding each other's context, and letting each other know in both words and actions that they care? It could create an epidemic! An epidemic of care! And you know what? You can help to make that happen! It is one of the superpowers of a good social detective: The superpower of perspective taking and understanding others and letting others know you understand them. A superpower that can literally change the world and help to make it a better place.

If you have come this far in this book, you should be really proud of yourself. You have done a lot of good work and learned a lot. We have talked about a lot of things, some that are pretty straight forward and some that are complicated. But remember, practice makes perfect. Practicing the things we have talked about in this book will help you get better at them. And you know what else? Practicing them will help to make the world a better place. And really, that is the biggest goal of any good social detective--to help make the world a better place. So good luck on your journey!

I hope you let me know how your social detecting is going because I am always interested in how my fellow social detectives are doing. Good luck and happy perspective taking!

Main Ideas Chapter 12

1. What is a perspective? P - 251
2. What does it mean to take someone's perspective? P - 252
3. How might we use our eight senses in perspective taking? P - 252
4. What is a perspective map? P - 252
5. What is a social cartographer? P - 253
6. What are some of the benefits of good perspective taking? P - 253
7. How does good perspective taking help us feel cared for? P - 254
8. What are relational nutrients and how do we get them? P - 254
9. What is perspective missing and what kind of problems can it cause? P - 254
10. What are some helpful tools we can use to create good context? P - 255
11. What do we mean by fully taking perspective or embodying perspective? P - 256
12. What is an intention? P - 256
13. How does intention help attention? P - 256
14. How do we create the intention to bring our attention to others' inside worlds? P - 257
15. How can curiosity about others help us gather more contextual information? P - 257
16. What is the buddy scan?? P - 257
17. How do you do a general buddy scan? P - 258
18. What are some specific buddy scans you can do? P - 260
19. What do we mean by virtual reality perspective taking and how can we do it? P - 261
20. What is perspective assuming? P - 263
21. What do we mean by expert's mind and beginner's mind? P - 264
22. What is perspective denying? P - 264
23. What are some things you can ask others to see if you are getting their perspective correctly? - 265
24. What are some benefits of checking things out with others? P - 265
25. What are some perspective-taking games you can play to get better at perspective taking? P - 266
26. What are some ways we show others that we get their perspective? P - 274
27. How does our good perspective taking help us be more kind and caring? P - 274

www.ingramcontent.com/pod-product-compliance
Lightning Source LLC
LaVergne TN
LVHW060152080526
838202LV00052B/4137